RELIGION AND LAW

Discussion of the way in which law engages with religious difference often takes place within the context of a single jurisdiction. *Religion and Law: An Introduction*, presents a comprehensive text for students, drawing on examples from across key Anglophone jurisdictions – the United Kingdom, the United States, Canada, New Zealand, Australia and South Africa, as well as international law, to explore a broad range of issues.

Aimed at a non-legal readership, this book introduces the use of legal sources and focuses on factual situations as much as legal doctrine. Key issues arising from interaction of the religious individual and the State are discussed, as well as the religious organisation or community and the State. The interaction is explored through case studies of areas as diverse as the legal regulation of religious drug use, sacred spaces and sacred places, and claims of clergy misconduct. Taking a broad, non-jurisdictional approach to the key issues, in particular providing insights differing from the dominant US experiences and paradigms, this student-friendly textbook includes a clearly structured bibliography and clear guidance on how to approach relevant legal materials.

D1593535

Ashgate Religion, Culture & Society Series

Series Editors:

Dr Graham Harvey, *The Open University, UK*
Professor Peter W. Edge, *Oxford Brookes University, UK*
Lois Ann Lorentzen, *Professor of Social Ethics, University of San Francisco, USA*

The Ashgate Religion, Culture & Society Series presents a focused cluster of high profile titles exploring the critical issues of contemporary society and culture, and relationships to and within living religions. Each book offers an accessible, stimulating new contribution to key topics. The series explores constructions of religion and religious issues from a range of perspectives, offering accessible texts by scholars based within and outside traditional religious studies who are able to bring immersion in their own disciplines to the study of contemporary religion, culture and society, enriching understanding across all three elements. The series will prove of particular value to higher level undergraduate students for their course studies in the areas of contemporary culture, society, media, law, and religious studies, as well as to academics, graduates and postgraduate readers worldwide.

Religion and Law

An Introduction

PETER W. EDGE
Oxford Brookes University, UK

ASHGATE

© Peter W. Edge 2006

Peter W. Edge has asserted his moral right under the Copyright, Designs and Patents Act, 1988, to be identified as the author of this work.

Published by

Ashgate Publishing Limited
Gower House
Croft Road
Aldershot
Hampshire GU11 3HR
England

Ashgate Publishing Company
Suite 420
101 Cherry Street
Burlington, VT 05401-4405
USA

Ashgate website: http://www.ashgate.com

British Library Cataloguing in Publication Data
Edge, Peter W.
   Religion and law : an introduction
   1. Religion and law
   I. Title
   201.7

Library of Congress Cataloging-in-Publication Data
Edge, Peter W.
   Religion and law : an introduction / by Peter W. Edge.
      p. cm.—(Ashgate religion, culture & society series)
   Includes bibliographical references and index.
   ISBN 0-7546-3047-1 (hardcover : alk. paper)—ISBN 0-7546-3048-X (pbk. : alk. paper) 1. Religion and law. 2. Church and state. I. Title. II. Series.

   K3280.E32 2005
   342.08'52—dc22

2005014477

ISBN-10: 0-7546-3047-1 HBK
ISBN-10: 0-7546-3048-X PBK

Typeset by Express Typesetters Ltd, Farnham, Surrey
Printed and bound in Great Britain by TJ International, Padstow

Contents

Acknowledgements

Insofar as this text is accurate and useful, I am indebted to a large number of individuals and organisations. Particular thanks are due to the library staff of Oxford Brookes University and the Bodleian Law Library; colleagues at the Centre for Legal Research and Policy Studies at Brookes, and in the British Association for the Study of Religion; students on the religious studies, theology, and law degrees at Brookes; Sarah Lloyd of Ashgate Publishing; Dominic Corrywright and Lucy Vickers of Brookes; Sharon Hanson of Birkbeck College, London; and my research students, Peter Griffith and Rajan Mony.

Special thanks are due to Joseph Emilio Giovanni Edge, for an arrival timed to allow this text to be completed.

I have sought to state the law as of 1 September, 2004.

Chapter 1

Thinking About Law Thinking About Religion

Introducing Law and Religion

The publisher of a magazine is found guilty of a crime because they have offended religious sensibilities. An employee gains more flexible working to accommodate prayer times in the wake of a court decision on their rights against the employer. A notice is served on a householder because they host religious meetings involving too many people, involving too much motor traffic at unsociable hours, and disturbing their neighbours. A religious official is allowed to withhold information from the police because of a duty to respect confidentiality, even though that information would benefit the police in locating a serious offender. A child is refused admission to a prestigious local school because they do not belong to the religious community the school was established to serve; another child is admitted to a school but objects to science lessons dealing with the theory of evolution as contrary to their religious beliefs. A religious organisation is characterised as supporting terrorism, and its adherents prevented from recruiting to it, raising money for it, or publicly bearing witness to its tenets; another organisation receives tax breaks which allow it to run a bookshop with lower profit margins than its non-religious competitors. A religious organisation changes its official doctrine on the use of medical products derived from human blood when faced with civil actions by relatives of members who died after refusing blood transfusions; another creates a 'priesthood' in order to gain immigration and taxation benefits, and to make it easier to deal with the makers of official policy. A citizen called to a jury refuses to serve on a capital case as their religious beliefs prohibit execution for any offence; another juror uses a set of Tarot cards to guide their consideration of the correct verdict. A judge prays in private before discharging their court duties; another judge explicitly refers to a religious text when interpreting the law, on the basis that the law was passed to give effect to the religious text.

All of these things have happened, and illustrate the richness and variety of the interaction of law and religion. The purpose of this text is to introduce this area of law to readers with an existing interest in religion. In doing so, I draw upon examples from a number of significant jurisdictions, as discussed below. This text is not, however, intended to be a comparative study of law and religion in Australia, Canada, South Africa, New Zealand, the United Kingdom, and the United States. Neither is it intended to develop a particular thesis on the relationships between law and religion, or to state in detail the laws of particular countries, or particular areas of current interest.

In this chapter, I introduce general ideas relevant throughout the text. If we take law and religion as distinct conceptual categories, why are they important to one another? What do we mean by 'law' and, for that matter, what do we mean by 'religion'? In particular, as I assume no prior legal knowledge, what are the sources used to construct legal doctrines, and how should we approach them? This introductory chapter closes with a very brief overview of the different types of secondary literature to be found on the interaction of law and religion.

In Chapter 2, we consider international and national guarantees of religious interests. A preliminary task here is to provide a working taxonomy of what is meant by 'religious interests'. This done, we move on to consider the nature and significance of international law, and the key international instruments at a global level, and regional instruments such as the European Convention on Human Rights. In particular, we consider the significance of overarching guarantees of religious interests binding upon the State at an international level, or built into the constitutional order of the State itself.

In Chapter 3, we move to consider ways in which the State and the individual can interact. The State has the potential to be a significant threat to religious interests, and it is in that sense that we consider the extent to which religious individuals can resist generally applicable duties to act, or restrain from acting, in a way contrary to their religious convictions. The State also has the potential to act as a powerful protector for the individual, particularly the member of a minority religious community. We consider the extent to which the State will intervene between private individuals to protect the religious interests of the individual.

In Chapter 4 we shift the focus from the individual to the organisation – from the predominantly private exercise of religion by the individual to the lives of religious communities. Here the principal issue is that of entanglement – the extent to which the political organisation of the State can become excessively involved in the religious organisation of the community, and vice versa. On the one hand, we see the potential for suppression of religious communities by control of their organisations; on the other, the possibility of a State dominated by a religious organisation at the expense of members of the State who are not also members of the religious organisation. The State may become involved with a religious organisation not only through its own initiative, but by allowing private individuals to enforce legal actions against religious organisations. Accordingly, this chapter also considers two instances of private actions against religious organisations – claims of employment rights by clergy working for an organisation, and claims by others for misconduct and malfeasance by such clerics.

Chapter 5 briefly concludes the text by re-emphasising some general threads from our discussion of the interaction of law and religion.

Why is Law Important for Religion?

It may be that a useful distinction could be drawn here between the importance of law for the study of religion, and the importance of law for religions within a particular jurisdiction, that is, the area covered by a particular legal system. Although the theoretical structures of law may provide a resource for scholars of religion, it is more likely that their interest will lie in the impact that law can have upon religion. If we regard both law and religion as social phenomena, often coexistent within individual social actors, their interaction seems inevitable. Much of this text is concerned with how law accommodates, restricts, or influences religion. It is useful at this point to summarise the functions that law is often seen as performing in a society of the type discussed in this text, functions which may be carried out in any context, including a religious one (see further Partington, 2000, pp. 11–27).

Firstly, law may be seen as one of many social mechanisms by which social order is maintained. At its simplest, law may help to maintain public order so that other social, and so legal, interactions can occur within the society. Law allows the transition from an endless war of all against all, to a position where self-defence, and the personal defence of property, is not the sole concern of all living within the territory. As part of this creation of the State, law may also serve to define and protect the constitutional and political order. In relation to democratic elections, for instance, we might expect law to define at what age a citizen is entitled to vote, how the legislature is to be composed and the like – although in the jurisdictions discussed here law has a strictly limited role in determining how those votes are to be translated into political power. Law may also have a role in the ordering of difference within a society, including economic difference. For instance, criminal law has an important role in protecting private property; while employment law has an important role in providing non-discrimination guarantees for members of groups who have suffered historic discrimination and exclusion from opportunity in the workplace. Finally, law may be seen as having a specific role in relation to the moral order of a society. Most legal rules have some moral content – the law of murder for instance appears to contain a moral judgement that it is 'wrong' to kill another person except in very narrow circumstances such as self-defence. More contentious is the situation where the law provides support for a moral proposition which is not so broadly accepted within society, for instance that a permanent relationship between a man and a woman is the appropriate foundation for human reproduction and child-rearing.

An example may briefly illustrate this function. In *Edward Books and Art Ltd v R* (1986) 35 DLR (4th) 1 (Can.), the Supreme Court of Canada considered a law which required some retail businesses to be closed on particular days, including Sunday. Some retailers were exempt from this limit if they closed on Saturday instead. The Court found that the purpose of the legislation was a secular one, rather than simply enshrining a religious prohibition on trade on that day, although it did have an adverse impact on particular religious groups such as Jews and Seventh Day Adventists. In terms of the preceding paragraph we could see Sunday trading laws as being aimed at keeping public order (particularly if trading on a Sunday might result in inter-communal violence and disorder); economic order (in ensuring that shopworkers have one day in which they cannot be required to work each week, and that this day is common to many different retail concerns); or moral order (supporters of Sunday trading laws sometimes refer to the importance of one day each week being available for families to be together).

Secondly, law may be seen as a mechanism for the resolution of disputes between individuals without endangering public order. This can occur at a variety of levels, from constitutional litigation between organisations with different views on the legitimacy of abortion for non-medical reasons, to a dispute over a bad debt. In practice, using the full panoply of the law to resolve a dispute is often a clumsy way of dealing with it, and litigation, by which a court gives an authoritative judgement on the legal merits of the dispute, is often viewed as the last resort even by legal advisers. Instead, parties may negotiate in the shadow of the law, with the legal position of the parties being one factor, albeit often a very significant factor, in determining a mutually acceptable resolution to the dispute. In the religious context, Bradney and Cownie have noted the dangers of placing too much emphasis on law as a mechanism for resolving dispute, even in this expanded sense (Bradney and Cownie, 2000). The sources of law drawn upon in this text tend to arise from disputes, or as responses to social problems, and so over-represent dispute resolution. Nonetheless, this is clearly a function that law is capable of performing. In England, for instance, the law has been used to resolve disputes between members of religious organisations (see Hill, 2001).

Thirdly, law may be seen as a mechanism by which policy makers can respond to social problems. This may lead to an increase in the sheer volume of law within a particular jurisdiction, as successive social problems are dealt with by law, and so turned into specifically legal problems. It may also result in policy makers taking an action within their power – the exercise of their law-making powers to change legal rules – rather than engage with the social problem itself. In particular, we may acknowledge a particular social problem could usefully be engaged with, without accepting that law is the best social mechanism for doing so. Consider intolerance between members of religious groups – although it would be possible to react to this problem by legislation making it a crime to promote, or even perhaps to manifest, such intolerance, it may be more useful to address the root causes of this intolerance through other initiatives. A good example of law seeking to deal with a social problem within a religious context is the United States prohibition on religious discrimination in the workplace (see Jamar, 1996; Engle, 1997).

Fourthly, law may be seen as a set of rules regulating relationships between individuals. In the personal context, for example, there are rules concerning what sexual relationships are acceptable within a particular jurisdiction, for instance in relation to homosexual activity; while in the commercial sphere particular rules may govern the formation of agreements between companies, or special formalities attach to transactions such as the leasing of real estate. If the laws are sufficiently certain, an individual will be able to arrange their affairs in such a way as to be law-abiding, and relatively assured of the support of the legal system should a dispute arise later. So we might see the law of blasphemy, which in England prohibits some expressions of some religious concepts, as an indication of the outer limits of incivility in some religious discussions. In *Ramsay and Foote* (1883) 15 Cox C.C. 231 (UK), Lord Coleridge CJ approved a passage suggesting that the law of blasphemy 'visits not the honest errors but the malice of mankind. A wilful intention to pervert, insult and mislead others, by means of licentious and contumelious abuse applied to sacred subjects, or by wilful mispresentation or wilful sophistry'.

Fifthly, law may be seen as an important mechanism for controlling State power, and in particular in securing the rights and freedoms of the individual. This is a particular theme in relation to religious rights, which are discussed at length in the next chapter.

Finally, law may provide a mechanism for empowering individuals and organisations. At its most straightforward, most organs of the State derive their power from some legal statement – for instance the powers of a prison service to detain a convicted prisoner, or the powers of an aviation regulator to inspect and restrict air travel. Law can also provide individuals with the power to arrange their affairs in a way which gives them more power – for instance by pooling their resources as an organisation for the advancement of their religion, an organisation which may enjoy a taxation status different from its members, and which may be capable of continuing after the death of its founders.

The potential impact of these different legal functions upon individuals because of their religious beliefs, identity, or practices is clear. It may also be that legal values can be a strong influence on religious values. Consider for instance, the practice of polygamy. In *Reynolds v United States* 98 US 145 (1878) (US), the Supreme Court had to consider whether a law criminalising polygamy, the practice of which was endorsed by the Church of Jesus Christ of the Latter Day Saints at that time, restricted free exercise when applied to a Mormon man. The Supreme Court ruled that the religious liberty guarantees under the First Amendment prohibited any law against mere opinion, but did not protect 'actions which were in violation of social duties or subversive of good order' (ibid., at 164). In a later polygamy case, the Supreme Court reiterated the exclusion of polygamous acts from the First Amendment (*Davis v Beason*, 133 US 333 (1890) (US)). The religious practices of the mainstream Church, and perhaps even the development of its doctrines, may have been directly influenced by this finding. Even where the law does not act to prohibit a religious belief or activity, structural expectations may also be influential on the development of the religious community (consider Reid, 2000).

To recap. Law can be used to keep order; resolve disputes; respond to social problems; regulate broader social relationships; control State power; or empower individuals. Law matters to religion because of the extent to which this can impinge on individuals, communities, and organisations.

Why is Religion Important for Law?

Religion can be important for law in the same sense as, for instance, political belief or sexual practice. In all these cases, a proper appreciation of the context of a particular legal situation can enrich the application and development of the law. For instance, when law enforcement agencies consider how to deal with an armed group, properly understanding their religious beliefs may provide a key to evaluating whether immediate response, with the risk of injury, is needed (Tabor and Gallagher, 1995). When assessing whether a prison should be required to provide a particular choice of menu for an inmate, a religious conviction that some foods are forbidden might indicate the inmate would suffer an especially heavy burden should this not be accommodated (Creighton and King, 1996, 9.43).

In the light of this, we may treat the religious interests of an individual as no more than an explanation for their activities or special needs, rather than a distinctive interest of that individual. For instance, decision makers need to give weight to the right to individual autonomy, which may arise because an individual wishes to reject medical treatment that would be contrary to their religious beliefs. The interest to be borne in mind is not some special religious interest but the general interest everyone has in controlling their own bodies (see Eisgruber and Sager, 2000). It is not uncommon to find religious interests compacted into some other category in this way. One example of this is the classification of at least some religious activity as a hobby or leisure pursuit. The leisure theorist Chris Rojek gives 'traditional rituals, festivals or processions which occur on holidays and festival-days' as examples of leisure activity. By the same route, he sees the conflict over access to Stonehenge, including access by individuals who view it as a pivotal sacred site, as raising 'important questions of citizenship rights and the state's management of leisure resources' (Rojek, 1995).

Treating religion as simply part of the context in which law operates is defensible if religion has no special characteristics requiring separate analysis, perhaps leading to different outcomes. Courts, legislatures, and jurists frequently assert, however, that religion does have special characteristics. These are outlined below, but it should be noted that all of them are based on assumptions whose truth can be questioned. In particular, except for the positivist argument taken from legal structures themselves, all are based on assumptions about what actually happens in the lives of individuals, and society more generally. Legal decision makers seem, on the whole, comfortable with these sorts of general assumption.

A positivist approach to the special status of religion would argue for a special place in analysis because religion receives special treatment in both international law, and the domestic law of most jurisdictions (cp. Sisk, 1998). For instance, one clause of the International Covenant on Civil and Political Rights, a globally applicable treaty legally binding upon those States who have accepted it, begins 'Everyone shall have the right to freedom of thought, conscience and religion' (ICCPR art.18). This is stated even though the ICCPR contains extensive guarantees of the right to freedom from torture, freedom of expression, privacy and the like (see further Harris and Joseph, 1995). Similarly, the Canadian Charter of Rights and Freedoms lists the fundamental freedoms as: '(a) freedom of conscience and religion; (b) freedom of thought, belief, opinion and expression, including freedom of the press and other means of communication; (c) freedom of peaceful assembly and (d) freedom of association' (Constitution Act 1982 s.2 (Can.)). The difficulty with this approach is that it only moves the fundamental problem a step away – we give religion a special place because the law does, but why does the law do so? Is it right for it to do so? These questions are better resolved by reference to values outside of law.

One such resolution would be to argue that, as religious interests are more profound than other interests, they are entitled to separate recognition. If we make this assumption, it may be considered as disrespectful to class one individual's religious interests with another's leisure interests, or a third's commercial interests. Recognition as a religion can seem important to many communities of religious adherents. There may well be a sense in which religious communities in a plural society, particularly minority or unpopular communities, need recognition as religious communities. Classifying all religious activities and organisations as, for instance, part of the leisure sector may well be perceived as disrespectful, trivialising, or indeed an example of State hostility to religious activities (Carter, 1987). One serious problem with this argument is that it requires very broad assumptions about the way in which religious beliefs and practices interact with other beliefs and practices within the same individual. Within a cultural framework that distinguishes between the sacred and the secular, and between religious activities and leisure activities, this may be a fair assumption. It becomes less clear when an individual's framework does not draw these distinctions.

A slightly different argument from that of profundity is based on the importance of religious beliefs, identity, and practices to the individual concerned. We may be entitled to assume that for many religious adherents their religious beliefs, practices, and identity occupy a position of special importance in their life. This assumption can form the basis for a variety of different arguments giving the religious interest weight. The most significant is the argument from self-identification: '[r]eligious beliefs ... form a central part of a person's belief structure, his inner self. They define a person's very being – his sense of who he is, why he exists, and how he should relate to the world around him. A person's religious beliefs cannot meaningfully be separated from the person himself: they are who he is' (Conkle, 1988, pp. 1164–5). It may also follow from this assumption that the religious adherent, when placed in a position where their beliefs and practices conflict with the law, suffers a special harm when compared with an individual in conflict with the law for some other reason (see Garvey, 1986). For instance, a member of a pacifist religious community who is required to pay taxes subsidising the armed forces may be considered to suffer some harm over and above that suffered by the individual in the same situation who would prefer to spend their tax money on home repairs or entertainment.

This argument focuses on the religious individual and their interests, but it is also possible to argue that the significance of religion to communities justifies its special consideration. In other words, the assumed link between religious interests and cultural and other collective interests requires explicit recognition of the religious interest. The link between religion and ethnicity, especially in legal terms, is a complex one. Nonetheless, in many instances an individual's religion forms part of a broader social context. This collective approach raises a utilitarian argument for respecting the religious interest – bluntly, if religion is a matter of communities rather than of individuals, failure to respect a religion might result in public order problems (*Kokkinakis v Greece* (1994) 17 EHRR 397 (ECHR) per Valticos J). It can also be argued that where religion has a community aspect, especially for a minority community, respecting that religion is an important step in ensuring that members feel a full part of a plural society. The European Court of Human Rights has described freedom of thought, conscience and religion as 'a precious asset for atheists, agnostics, sceptics and the unconcerned. The pluralism indissociable from a democratic society, which has been dearly won over the centuries, depends upon it' (ibid., at para.31). Finally, if the religious interest can form part of a community identity, it may form part of the basis for unjustified discrimination against an individual who is a member of that community. Certainly, numerous examples of discrimination and persecution on the grounds of religion can be found (Brownstein, 1990; Adams, 2000). In this case, respecting the religious interest might be seen as a reaction to the broader social problem of unjust discrimination.

A final practical ground for the special consideration of religion is based upon the interests of society as a whole, including those who are not members of the religious community being considered. There is a theme in many areas of law that religious adherents and religious organisations can be assumed to benefit society as a whole by virtue of those characteristics, and so their protection as such produces social benefits. One commentator has noted that 'religious groups are of special value to a democracy, and the state should nurture them rather than reject them' (Carter, 1993). Others have argued that religious beliefs constitute a force for social cohesion (Tregilgas-Davey, 1991). It may also be that consideration of religious interests can be seen as a test of the rights culture of a particular society more generally. As Adams argues:

> religious liberty and the provision of fundamental human rights are ultimately inseparable ... the international community will never ensure free association without permitting religious minorities to meet, free speech without allowing religious speech, non-discrimination and due process without granting religious minorities equal substantive and procedural rights under the law, democracy without allowing religious minorities to vote and run for office, indigenous rights without protecting indigenous religions, the rights of parents and children without protecting their right to sectarian education, and women's rights without ensuring their freedom to follow or reject religious teachings and customs. (Adams, 2000, p. 64)

As well as these significant practical reasons why religion is of interest to lawyers, there are important theoretical problems posed to law by religion. McConnell argues that 'liberalism was born as a solution to the problem of religious pluralism' (McConnell, 2000 at 1265). A liberal legal order is faced with a particular set of problems in relation to religion, caused by renunciation of authority over religious issues, coupled with a need to retain authority more generally. This is a point that may usefully be expanded on here.

In a context where it is seen as legitimate for the State to determine religious truths, no special problem is posed to State authority. Religious issues can be resolved, in principle at least, as easily as any other issue coming before the court. In early English charity law, for instance, the State developed the superstitious use, a trust that supported false religious purposes, and therefore was to be held void (Jones, 1969 at 11,15). Many of the older cases were decided in a context where it was considered legitimate to distinguish between the State religion and 'the schisms of nonconformity, the errors of Rome, or the infidelity of Judaism or heathenism' (Newark, 1946 at 235). This was possible because the State had identified religion with a particular discipline. When religion is equated with a particular religious faith, whose doctrines can be expounded by an authoritative organisation, or derived from an authoritative textual source, the courts can determine religious issues by making use of the discipline of that single religion (cp. Weiss, 1964). This may not only involve disputes concerning that religion, but also the proper way to deal with other religious systems, as is the case for instance with dhimma in Islamic law (An-Naim, 1988; Hofmann, 1998).

The legal systems discussed here have, however, moved from this position (see more broadly Heim, 1990). Continuing with the example of English charity law, it has become established that charitable religious purposes are no longer limited to those of the Church of England. Non-Anglican denominations of Christianity, including very small denominations, have been accepted (*Thornton v Howe* (1862) 31 Beav. 14 (UK); *Re Watson* [1973] 3 All ER 678 (UK); *Re Schoales* [1930] 2 Ch. 75 (UK)), as have Judaism (*Re Michel's Trust* (1860) 28 Beav. 39 (UK)), Buddhism (*Re South Place Ethical Society* [1980] 1 WLR 1565 (UK)), and less formally, Islam, Hinduism, and a range of other religious movements relatively new to the jurisdiction (see Edge and Loughrey, 2001). This recognition of a variety of religions has been combined with a formal insistence by the courts that they no longer have any jurisdiction to pronounce on the truth or otherwise of a particular religious belief (Mumford, 1998).

In recognising that multiple religion systems can exist within the jurisdiction, and that it is inappropriate for the legal order to choose between their competing views of reality, that legal order is faced with a particular problem. What are the courts to do when faced with a religious claim whose truth must be determined as part of the resolution of the dispute before them? Examples of this drawn from family law and criminal law illustrate the two facets of the problem.

In relation to the care and custody of children, the courts may be required to intervene in child rearing when there has been a breakdown in the relationship between the parents who are unable to agree on how the child should be treated. This can involve the courts in resolving issues normally regarded as purely the concern of the parents. In *T v T* [1974] FL 190 (UK), for instance, the court became involved in a dispute between a Jehovah's Witness parent, and a non-Witness. Stamp LJ discussed at some length the impact of the child being raised by the Jehovah's Witness parent, but added that 'if the father and mother were both Jehovah's Witnesses nobody, certainly no court, could possibly say, or would think of beginning to say, that the children should not be brought up as Jehovah's

Witnesses' (ibid., at 191). In resolving such disputes the courts will have regard to the best interests of the child – indeed in the UK, as opposed to some extent to the US, this is the paramount interest (see Hamilton, 1995). Across a range of jurisdictions, the common, although not universal, approach is to avoid making a finding about the intrinsic merits or demerits of the religion (Ahdar, 1996). Instead, the truth or otherwise of the religions tenets are set aside, in favour of a focus on the impact upon the secular interests of the child. In determining these interests, values and practices derived from religion will be considered, and cannot be reserved from evaluation simply because they are religious (Schneider, 1992). Thus, the courts seek to separate the values of the parents from their religious context in order to avoid making a ruling on the merits of the religion itself.

To some extent, however, it is unavoidable that a judicial criticism of the impact of a religion on the child can be read as a criticism of that religion, for instance a finding that a religion makes it more likely the child will become a liar or murderer in later life. This can be exacerbated by the style of the judgement. A good, if extreme, example is *Re B and G* [1985] FLR 493 (UK), where the English Court of Appeal considered a decision to grant custody to the non-Scientologist parent, although this would involve taking the children away from their current home. The trial judge, Latey J, had appeared to take the view that granting custody to the Scientologist parent would result in the children being raised as Scientologists, and that this would not be in their best interests. Perhaps in part because of the injudicious intemperance of the language used, Latey J appeared to work on the basis that Scientology itself was undesirable, rather than determining the characteristics of the life the child would lead, and then feeding those characteristics into the best interests balance. He described Scientology as 'both immoral and socially obnoxious ... corrupt, sinister, and dangerous' (ibid., at 157), and commented on the character of the founder of the religion very strongly. The Court of Appeal found that the statements of the judge:

> added colour to the suggestion that what the judge primarily had in mind was the exposure of [S]cientology rather than the interests of the children which was in fact and in law all he was concerned with. However, towards the end of the judgment the judge did relate the practices of [S]cientology to the circumstances of these particular children. He did carry out the balancing exercise. Although he plainly felt strongly that these children were at risk from exposure to [S]cientology, I find no reason to suppose that in carrying out that essential balancing exercise he did not do so judicially. (ibid., at 502–3 per Dunn LJ)

Thus, profound issues are raised when religious values seek to engage with a secular legal order (Bradney, 2000b). An even more profound example of the problem of renouncing metaphysical authority while retaining the authority necessary for the functioning of a legal system can be found in criminal law. What if a defendant wishes to deny part of the crime with which they are charged by an explanation which can only be accepted if the court also accepts a religious claim by the defendant – for instance that they were not falsely calling upon spirits, because the spirits truly answered the call? In English law, the courts have accepted that such claims can be resolved by the criminal courts, and that the defendant is not entitled to an acquittal simply because contentious issues concerning religion are involved (*Lawrence* (1876) 36 LTR 404 (UK)). In a famous case concerning mediumship, Viscount Caldecote CJ in the English Court of Appeal declared that:

> the only matter for the jury was whether there was a pretence or not. The prosecution did not seek to prove that spirits of deceased persons could not be called forth or materialised or embodied in a particular form. Their task was much more limited and prosaic. It was to prove, if they could, that the appellants had been guilty of conspiring to pretend that they could do these things, and, therefore, of conspiring to pretend that they could exercise a kind of conjuration to do these things. (*Duncan* [1944] 1 KB 773 at 778 (UK))

Even more than with a clash of secular and religious values, when the courts become involved in a similar dispute about facts, keeping legal authority while renouncing metaphysical authority is a difficult juggling act.

To recap. Religion matters to law, (a) because of its role as providing part of the context to a legal discussion; (b) because of the distinct place to be given to religious interests in legal analysis, whether because of the taxonomy of rights in international and constitutional law, the profundity of religious interests, their centrality to the rights of the individual believer, their importance to broader cultural and communal life, or their role in society as a whole; (c) because of the special problems posed to any liberal legal discourse which seeks to develop a legal pluralism in response to a growth in religious plurality.

What is Law?

So far, I have suggested that law and religion matter to one another without having made it clear what it meant by either term. In this section I introduce some key ideas relating to the composition of law. As most non-lawyers' first contact with law will be through secondary sources, a useful way to approach the issue might be to focus initially on legal discourse.

It is potentially misleading to refer to legal discourse, if that is taken to mean a single form of discourse. Legal scholarship is a diverse and increasingly difficult to define field of academic work. To draw from a recent collection of published papers on law and religion, it can comfortably encompass discussion of the moral identity of persons (Ducharme, 2001); the correct approach to the interpretation of legal texts (Andries, 2001); the decided cases of the European Court of Human Rights (Martinez-Torron, 2001); the approach of English law to the Jewish *get*, or bill of divorcement (Freeman, 2001); and the relationship of politics and sociology to the academic study of law and religion (Bradney, 2001).

Within this broad category, it may be useful to separate discussions about law from legal discussions, as Bradney does when describing his text on law and religion as a book about law, rather than a law book (Bradney, 1993). Discussion about law can draw upon a wide variety of methodological and theoretical perspectives – as would be the case in a critique of a particular legal provision by a Christian theologian writing from theology; or a discussion of use of legally registered places of worship by a geographer using conventional tools of quantitative social research. Legal discussions, on the other hand, are more likely to constitute either explorations of what the content of law is, or evaluations of that law against values internal to the legal system itself. For instance, a paper exploring the legal meaning of a particular piece of legislation, or considering how far existing cases leave an unacceptable area of uncertainty, would be a legal discussion.

In either case there is something being discussed called 'law', and in the latter category not only is law the subject of the discussion, but the methodology used for the discussion is a distinctively legal one. Some forms of both discussion take place at a level of abstraction where broad legal principles (such as the idea of human autonomy) are the subject for discussion. In many other cases, however, where particular laws are relevant to the discussion, it is necessary to identify, at least to some extent, the content of these laws before discussion can follow. In the case of legal discussion, this identification may constitute the sole aim of the discussion, but more commonly there is an ulterior motive: in the case of the commentator to move onto some form of critical evaluation of the law, in the case of the legal advisor to move onto concrete advice for their client. This section outlines the sources of law which form the core of legal discussion, and which are often necessary to understand the law forming the subject matter of a discussion about law.

The Constitution

The constitution is the fundamental law of the State, which contains the legal rules constituting State institutions and delineating their authority. These institutions are often divided into three branches – the legislature, which enacts new laws in the form of legislation; the judiciary, which applies laws to resolve particular disputes and may in the process develop them in new ways; and the executive, which is responsible for enforcing the law, and carrying on the normal business of government. This separation of State powers underpins the United States Constitution, for instance, with the legislature (Congress) defined in Article I; the executive (the Presidency) defined in Article II; and the judiciary (the Supreme Court and other federal courts) defined in Article III (United States Constitution 1787 (US)).

As well as providing for the exercise of State power within the legal system, the constitution may explicitly limit this power, particularly in relation to the individual. This is most obvious where the constitution contains a set of fundamental individual rights that the State is obliged to respect. The Canadian Charter of Rights and Freedoms, for instance, contains an extensive list of individual rights that the courts are empowered to protect (Constitution Act 1982 s.24 (Can.)). We return to these constitutional rights in relation to religious rights in Chapter 2. The constitution may also assert fundamental values that should pervade the exercise of State power. This can be seen most explicitly in the most recently drafted of the constitutional documents considered in this text, the Constitution of South Africa. Early in the text the foundational values of the new South Africa are expressed as human dignity, the achievement of equality and the advancement of human rights and freedoms; non-racialism and non-sexism; supremacy of the constitution and the rule of law; and democratic government (South African Constitution 1996 s.1 (SA)).

As this fundamental law gives power to the legal system, it is not possible for the constitution to gain its authority from that legal system. Instead, recourse must be had to some other source of authority. Practically speaking, all the States discussed in this text base their legitimacy upon a democratic mandate, but there are significant formal distinctions between the countries. Neither the South African nor United States constitutions are based upon the legitimacy of the former regime. Instead, both have recourse to broader political and philosophical values for their legitimacy. The US Constitution begins by establishing the source of its authority: 'We, the People of the United States ... do ordain and establish this Constitution for the United States of America' (United States Constitution 1787 preamble (US)). Similarly, the South African Constitution begins: 'We, the people of South Africa ... through our freely elected representatives, adopt this Constitution as the supreme law of the Republic' (South African Constitution 1996 preamble (SA); van Wyck, 1994). In the case of Canada, Australia, and New Zealand, on the other hand, the former regime retained sufficient legitimacy and authority, at the time of the enactment of their primary constitutional documents, to underpin the constitution. Thus, the Canadian constitution is based upon an Act of the United Kingdom Parliament (the Constitution Act 1867 (UK)), that of Australia likewise (Commonwealth of Australia Constitution Act 1900 (UK)), and of New Zealand upon legislative and judicial authority derived from the former place of New Zealand in the British Empire (Mulholland, 1995 at 22–31). The formal source of authority for the United Kingdom constitution itself is more difficult to locate.

At this point it is useful to separate the idea of a constitution from that of a written constitution, and particularly a constitution written as a single document. This conflation may be in part due to the significance and influence of the US Constitution. A routine library search will quickly reveal a document called just that, dated to 1787. Surely this must be the US Constitution? Unfortunately not. If you wished to be able to state the content of the US Constitution you would also need to be aware of the 27 Amendments to the 1787 document, made between 1791 and 1992 and including an Amendment (the 18th) which was itself removed by a further Amendment (the 21st). This would not suffice to understand the law, as these documents have been extensively, and authoritatively, interpreted by the United States Supreme Court. Even this would not be sufficient, however, as there may exist constitutional understandings by key constitutional actors as to how they should behave. Before the 22nd Amendment of 1952, for instance, there was no legal rule that a President could not serve more than two terms, although this was an understanding, or convention, that had been followed by Presidents prior to Roosevelt. Thus, even the US Constitution is not to be found in a single written source.

Nonetheless, there is some strength in the idea that the US Constitution is based on, if not contained within, a single documentary source. Although the details of the constitution are more distributed, the fundamental structures of the constitution are contained in a single document that prevails over any inconsistent law or practice. This document is concise, intended to be understood on one level by the non-specialist, and of special civic and educational value. In this sense, the United States, South Africa, and Australia all have a single constitutional document. Similarly, although the key constitutional documents of Canada are separate measures, they are to be cited as the Constitution Acts, 1867 to 1982 (Constitution Act 1982 s.60,61 (Can.)), and are little harder to parse as a single document than the US Constitution and its Amendments.

The situation is more complex in New Zealand and the United Kingdom. The United Kingdom lacks a constitutional document of the type envisaged in this section, so that the UK constitution emerges from the normal sources of law discussed below – that is legislation, judgements of the normal courts, academic commentary, and practice. In the absence of a formal constitutional document these sources are of primary, rather than secondary, importance in the constitution. There is no agreed mechanism for changing the de facto constitution, nor necessarily agreement about what it actually contains. The New Zealand position is fundamentally the same, but in 1986 a number of constitutional rules were brought together in a single document, which also made significant constitutional reforms (Constitution Act 1986 (NZ)).

As we will see in Chapter 2, religious rights form an important part of the constitutional fabric of all six jurisdictions. The discussion above raises an important preliminary point which may be dealt with here. What is the status of these constitutional rights? In the United States, Canada, South Africa, and Australia they form part of the definition of State power. In Australia, for instance, the central government, the Commonwealth, has no power to make a law establishing religion, imposing religious observance, prohibiting the free exercise of religion, or imposing a religious test for office with the Commonwealth (Commonwealth of Australia Act 1901 s.116 (Aust.)). As such they will prevail over any legal source except a constitutional amendment which may be politically or, as in the United States, legally difficult. In New Zealand and the United Kingdom, however, they are normal laws with, at most, the status of legislation, and accordingly can be overridden by a normal act of the legislature. Thus, although of considerable practical and constitutional significance the New Zealand Bill of Rights 1990 and the United Kingdom Human Rights Act 1998 should not be regarded as having a similar potency to, say, the First Amendment to the United States Constitution with its religious liberty guarantees.

As a final point in relation to constitutions, so far I have discussed 'the' constitution of each of the States discussed. In some cases, however, the country is not a single entity with all State power placed with central government, or delegated from central government. Instead, it is a federal system with the national constitution giving authority over some matters to the central government, while empowering (or leaving empowered) regional or local government structures to exercise equal authority over other matters. Once again, New Zealand and the United Kingdom are unusual in this respect, with local authorities in both countries receiving all their powers from central government, which accordingly has the competence to remove them. This is the case even for the devolved government structures of the United Kingdom, which exercise authority delegated by the United Kingdom Parliament, rather than authority of their own derived from a federal constitution.

Legislation

If a written constitution is a formal piece of legal text that lays down the values and rules that should govern the entire legal order within the State, a piece of legislation is a similar piece of text dealing with a specific issue, but laying down a legal rule that is intended to be binding upon everyone who finds themselves in the situation covered by the rule in future. Although legislation may be enacted to clarify the existing law, for instance by bringing together provisions from different pieces of existing legislation and ensuring greater consistency of language, it may also explicitly change existing law, or create new legal doctrines. This act of, potentially radical, legal change clearly has significant political implications. In all six countries, the national legislature is dominated by democratically elected representatives. In the United Kingdom, for instance, the legislature is Parliament, which is dominated by the House of Commons, composed of democratically elected Members of Parliament. In New Zealand, the House of Representatives exercise legislative power in conjunction with the Sovereign, who is required to assent to any measure which has received the support of the House.

The national legislatures all possess considerable competence, and are subject only to any limits imposed by the national constitution. In the United States, Canada, Australia, and South Africa, this in effect means that a piece of legislation can be declared 'unconstitutional', and thus invalid because of its clash with the constitution (see Mason, 1986). Because of the absence of a higher form of constitutional law in New Zealand and the United Kingdom, however, the national legislatures may make or unmake any law whatsoever. Even here, the legal order may require that if the national legislature wishes to violate constitutional norms – for instance by allowing summary execution without trial – it expresses itself with the utmost clarity, anything less resulting in the legislation being interpreted in accord with these norms.

The competence of the national legislatures, combined with their role in the political life of the country, mean that there is considerable pressure on their time. In particular, measures may only be able to progress through the legislative process swiftly enough to become law if they command a degree of support from the government of the day or, failing that, clear support from the individual legislators. Even with this support, limits on legislative time make it impractical to consider in great detail every possible aspect of a given legislative situation. Consider, for instance, a measure aimed at dealing with the humane slaughter of animals for human consumption. Some matters of general principle are best dealt with by the legislature, for instance what the aim of the legislation should be, whether there should be an exception for kosher or halal slaughter, what powers should be given to the executive to enforce the law, and what punishments the courts should be empowered to give for failure to meet the standards of the measure. But should the national legislature debate and determine how much space a particular sort of animal should have while awaiting slaughter, or the details of hygiene procedures to prevent the spread of contamination, or the layout of forms applying for permits under the measure?

The jurisdictions under consideration generally see legislation as being a form of law that needs to be set down with some detail, although drafting tastes have experienced considerable change, and are not uniform even within the common law world. This is not necessarily a function that needs to be carried out solely by the national legislature, however, as it is possible to delegate the details of legislation to other bodies, or officials. Legislation produced in this way is an important legal source. In the United Kingdom, for instance, there are more than twenty-five pieces of delegated, or secondary, legislation for every piece of primary legislation passed by Parliament. Although similar in appearance to legislation proper, this secondary legislation has two significant differences. Firstly, drafting and enactment may well be detached from an open political process entirely, constituting more the administrative work of the government department responsible. Secondly, because the legislation is made under authority delegated from the national legislature, if the legislation is an abuse of that authority it may be declared invalid as falling outside the powers which had been delegated, which will often depend upon the exact terms of the grant of authority. This is the case even for New Zealand and the United Kingdom, which as I have said do not question the authority of primary legislation.

Because of the apparently self-contained nature of much legislation, it is easy to conclude enquiry into an area of law with the text of a statute or, at a slightly more sophisticated level, of the statute and any statutory instruments issued under it. This neglects a concept central to the understanding of legislation, that of statutory interpretation.

Let us take as an example a, now repealed, piece of English law dealing with membership of the House of Commons. The House of Commons (Clergy Disqualification) Act 1801 (UK) had been passed in response to the election of the Reverend Horne Tooke, an ordained priest of the Church of England and well-known radical. There was doubt as to whether it was appropriate for clergy of the Church of England to sit in the Commons, given their separate representation in Convocation and their spiritual role (Gay, 2001). Section one of the Act stated that: 'No person having been ordained to the office of priest or deacon or being a minister of the Church of Scotland is or shall be capable of being elected to serve in Parliament ...'. If we leave the law concerning clerical membership of the House of Commons with this text, the law may appear straightforward. But although legislation is written in the general, it is applied in the particular, and seeking to apply such legislation to individual cases reveals the need to find extended meaning even in seemingly patent provisions.

In *In re MacManaway and In re the House of Commons (Clergy Disqualification) Act 1801* [1951] AC 161, PC (UK) a superior United Kingdom court, the Privy Council, was required to interpret this provision. In the case before them MacManaway had been ordained as a priest in the Church of Ireland, but had chosen to relinquish his rights as a priest in that Church. He was elected to the House of Commons. Could he take his seat? He was not a cleric of the Church of England, which was after all the particular problem that had inspired the legislation, but he had been ordained a priest. Moreover, he had undergone episcopal ordination. The Privy Council held that he was barred from the House of Commons by the Act, as it extended beyond priests of the Church of England to encompass all persons who had undergone episcopal ordination.

This is an important explanation of the provision, which would not have been obvious from looking at text of the Act. But it still leaves areas of uncertainty (see Edge, 2001). For instance, at the time of the 1801 Act the Church of Ireland had been part of the United Church of England and Ireland, and at the time of the decision in *MacManaway* it followed the Church of England in practice and doctrine. Might the provision only apply to clergy within a member of the Anglican Communion and ministers within the Church of Scotland? If it applies to every episcopal ordination, does it apply to every body with officials named as bishops, priests and deacons, or is it limited only to ordinations that would be recognised as such by the Church of England? If so, would a deacon of the Church of Jesus Christ of the Latter Day Saints be excluded from the House of Commons? Or does it apply to individuals who, in a sense moving beyond particular religious traditions, have been 'ordained' to a 'priesthood'? In that case, would it cover an Imam? If we throw in the fact that a special provision barred those who had taken holy orders in the Roman Catholic Church (Roman Catholic Relief Act 1829 s.9 (UK)), would that affect our interpretation of the section?

My example began with a judgement of an important court of the jurisdiction in question, and it is clear that the courts' pronouncements on the application of legislation to particular factual situations is of considerable importance. Although *MacManaway* did not resolve every point of interpretation of the 1801 provision, it does allow us to state with a high degree of confidence that the measure extended to priests of the Church of Ireland. Failure to make use of judicial glosses upon legislation is a common flaw in work by those from other disciplines seeking to make use of legal materials. It is easy, however, to give too much weight to the judicial context, and regard interpretation of statutes as a special judicial function, as the sole preserve of the courts.

Statutory interpretation is, rather, a fundamental and automatic function of every reader of a piece of legislation. A student or scholar seeking to understand the area must come to an interpretation of the legislation in their area of interest. A legal advisor seeking to guide their client so as to arrange their affairs in compliance with the law must interpret. An advocate in court seeking to defend their client in a criminal charge must interpret, and convince others of the validity of their interpretation. It is not possible to approach this source of law without at least a few ground rules on how to read statutes in the common law tradition.

It is easy to reach a very high degree of detail in the rules of statutory interpretation, so that it can appear a mechanistic process requiring only knowledge of the canons, presumptions, and the like of statutory interpretation and the application of the appropriate ones to the problem before the reader. Unfortunately, the principles enunciated by the courts as useful when interpreting legislation can be inconsistent – to take a proverbial analogy, he who hesitates is lost, but you should look before you leap. Do proverbs favour swift action or not? At the other extreme, it is easy to take the view that judges in particular are goal orientated, and will select whatever tools of interpretation are convenient to securing the result they favour in the case before them. Gall neatly resolves the two tensions in a way applicable to all the legal systems under discussion: '[t]he interpretation of statutory provisions is a somewhat subjective process. A judge may select a particular rule of statutory interpretation or use a particular aid to interpretation and decide not to be receptive to an alternative rule or aid in interpretation. Nonetheless, that subjective exercise must be conducted in the context of an objective search for legislative intention' (Gall, 1995 at 385).

Statutory interpretation by the student, scholar, or legal advisor may thus be considered as a two-stage process. To accurately state the law, we need to accurately state how a judge would interpret the statute. To accurately interpret the statute, the judge must determine the legislative intention of the maker of the provision. This is not the same as determining the actual intention of an individual drafter of the legislation, or (more difficult still) the collective intent of the legislative body who gave the provision legal effect. The judge should not make use of some special, or idiosyncratic, insight into what the legislature would really have wanted to have happened in the case before them, if only because this would render it very difficult for citizens to conform their behaviour to the law, as they would have no tolerably reliable way of predicting the way a judge would interpret the provision. Rather, it is the meaning which the legislature must have intended the words used in the measure as enacted to bear.

In determining the meaning of a provision, the judge is likely to feed the available information into one of three main models. Firstly, they may decide to give the words of the provision their 'literal meaning', which if plain and unambiguous should be taken to be their legal meaning, even if this results in manifest injustice. Although the idea of a literal meaning has come under increasing attack, it remains popular with some judicial interpreters of legislation. Secondly, applying the 'golden rule', they may follow this approach until it leads to a manifest absurdity or inconsistency, at which point they may modify the grammatical and ordinary sense of the words as necessary to avoid the absurdity. Thirdly, they may focus on the legislation as a measure intended to effect needed legal change, and consider what 'mischief' the legislation was meant to address. In doing so, they would consider the law before the provision, the mischief and defect which this law did not provide for, the remedy which the legislature resolved upon, and the true reason for the remedy. The judge should interpret the legislation to advance the policy of the provision by suppressing the mischief. A concrete example of these different approaches at work may be useful.

In *R v White* [2001] EWCA Crim 216, 1 WLR 1352, CA (UK) the defendant had called the victim 'an African bitch' during commission of a criminal offence, and was convicted of a racially aggravated form of that offence. The defendant was a black man, born in the West Indies, and he argued firstly that he could not be found guilty of the offence, as he was of the same racial group as the victim, and secondly that 'African' was not a racial term. The key provision talked of demonstrating towards the victim racial hostility based on the victim's membership of a racial group, and defined racial group as a group of persons defined by reference to race, colour, nationality (including citizenship) or ethnic or national origins (Crime and Disorder Act 1998 s.28 (UK)). How is the provision to be applied to this case?

On the first point, taking the literal rule we might conclude that nothing in the provision specifies that the defendant and the victim need to be of different racial groups, so that if the hostility is based on the victim's racial group, the defendant's racial group is immaterial. If we regarded this as an absurd result, we might apply the golden rule to interpret 'hostility based on the victim's membership' to exclude hostility shown by a member of that same group, whose animus must have arisen from some other characteristic, or from the conduct of the victim. If we preferred to take an approach based on the mischief the provision was intended to deal with we might reflect upon the string of racist crimes of violence which had inspired the legislation, and see it as aimed at racist crime directed against members of ethnic minority groups, rather than intra-communal violence and abuse.

On the second point, taking the literal rule we might be hard pushed to find African applied to any single group defined by common race, colour, nationality, ethnicity, or national origin, being more of a blanket term encompassing a broad range of all these characteristics. If we regarded this as an absurd result, we might prefer to interpret the term as referring to skin colour, and so bring it within the provisions. If we were concerned with the mischief of the provisions, which were aimed at racially motivated crime without necessarily endorsing a vision of different 'races', let alone a clear way of differentiating between them, we might also find African fell within the term.

The Court of Appeal took two different approaches to resolving these issues. On the first, that of intra-communal offending, Pill LJ very briefly dismissed the defendant's argument, seemingly on the basis that there was nothing in the literal meaning of the Act which excluded such hostility. On the second point, however, he took an approach much closer to the golden rule, or even the mischief based approach. In particular, he noted that 'given the statutory intention to be comprehensive, it would be surprising if describing a woman as a 'black bitch' would qualify on the grounds of colour, and 'Sierra Leonean bitch' on the grounds of nationality but to call her an 'African bitch' would fall outside the section' (ibid., at 1357-8).

As can be seen from this case, a variety of interpretative approaches may be taken even by the same judge. As may be expected, the emphasis on these three approaches differs both within national judiciaries, and between the six jurisdictions. Australia, for instance, has given a statutory preference to a mischief based approach (Acts Interpretation Act 1901 s.15AA as amended by the Statute

Law Revision Act 1981 s.115 (Aust.)). Whichever approach the judge takes to interpretation, they may have recourse to a considerable range of information in coming to their conclusion. In particular, it is important that the judge interprets the provision in question within its proper legal context, both extrinsically and intrinsically, by which I mean the context beyond the statute itself, and within the statute.

On the extrinsic context, some rules of interpretation are generally applicable within a jurisdiction, and will be relevant to interpreting any statute. For instance New Zealand legislation gives a set of default interpretations of common terms, and lays out general rules of construction such as the appropriateness of using the preamble to an Act to assist in explaining its purport and object (Acts Interpretation Act 1924 s.4, 5(2) (NZ)). Similarly, there may be judge crafted presumptions as to the meaning of legislation, which particular provisions would need to be displaced by strong implication or perhaps even explicit terms. For instance, in Australia there is a presumption that legislation does not intend to allow a person to take advantage of his or her own wrong (*Holden v Nuttall* [1945] VR 171 (Aust.)); and in the United Kingdom a presumption against giving statutes retroactive effect (*Re Athlumney* [1898] 2 QB 547 (UK)). Additionally, the judge will take account of the body of law the statute engages with, including existing statutes and judicial decisions. Clearly, this is very important where the statute use technical terms that already bear a particular legal meaning, but it is also significant to show the mischief being addressed by the measure. The courts may also take some account of the debates of the legislature that created the measure, although this is not without dangers, and is not always considered appropriate within our jurisdictions. On the intrinsic context, a key point is that the statute should be interpreted as a whole, and that every part of the statutory text bears some meaning. Thus, the court may have regard to the preamble of the Act, and its structure and use of headings, as well as the interaction of a proposed interpretation with the rest of the provision.

Decisions of the Superior Courts

It will be clear from the discussion above that judges have considerable power to determine the content of the law. In most of the jurisdictions to be discussed, the judges have the power to interpret the constitution in a way that makes particular legislation unconstitutional, and so ineffectual. Additionally, with their power to interpret and apply legislation to the case before them, the judges have considerable power to fine tune, perhaps even to alter, the impact of legislation. This raises an important issue – how is this judicial power to be restrained?

Here, legal systems are faced with two competing pressures. On the one hand, as I mentioned above, citizens have an interest in consistent application of a body of law, so that uncertainty in the law is itself an evil against public policy (*Barnett v Harrison* [1976] 2 SCR 531 (Can.)). As one of the oldest sources of law in the Isle of Man states, it is important 'that one Doome or judgement be not given at one time, and another Tyme contrary' (Customary Laws 1422 s.32-33 (Isle of Man)). This would draw legal systems towards a position where, once a judge had interpreted the Constitution, or a statute, that interpretation would be binding upon all other judges considering the same point. This would, however, place considerable lawmaking power in the hands of 'a small group of men who temporarily occupy high office' (*Florida Department of Health v Florida Nursing Home*, 450 US 147 (1981) (US)). It could also lead to a loss of flexibility, with weak interpretations of the law, or interpretations which failed to consider properly particularly factual situations, becoming fixed.

The solution adopted in our jurisdictions is to allow at least some judges some power to make authoritative rulings on the Constitution and legislation, but to temper this by the power of later judges to refine, or even reject, the interpretation. This combination allows 'a blending of the value systems of both past and present judges, leaving room for both continuity and change' (Maltz, 1989). An example might be useful.

With the development of rights, and benefits, related to employment in the English jurisdiction the courts have on a number of occasions addressed the question of whether a cleric or minister was an employee of their church or other religious organisation (see Edge, 2000). The first case where this arose concerned the position of a curate of the Church of England (*In re National Insurance Act 1911, On Employment of Church of England Curates* [1912] 2 Ch. 563 (UK)). This was only a decision of a single judge sitting in the lowest of the English superior courts, but as the first decision on the point it was clearly of general importance. The judge, Parker J, found that Church of England curates were holders of ecclesiastical office, who were not controlled by their vicar, and who had no contract with anyone, let alone a contract of employment. Accordingly, for the purposes of the social security legislation under consideration, the curate was not an employee.

Immediately after the decision, we could imagine it being used in a number of ways – its use retrospectively determining its meaning. If a later court read the case as turning on the emphasis on ecclesiastical office then, because of the special status of the Church of England in English law, we would not expect to see it applied to any other religious community. If the court read the case as turning on the absence of contract, however, we might expect to see it applied to members of other religious communities where their position was analogous to that of a Church of England curate. In the absence of other cases surrounding the precedent in which we are interested it is difficult to indicate its meaning. A good analogy might be a word in a sentence – there are more meanings to 'right' in the abstract than in the sentence 'Turn right at the traffic lights'. As cases develop, however, the meaning of the earlier cases in the sequence becomes refined – although this is not to say that the judge in the earlier case intended, or would be in agreement with, the meaning their words are found to bear.

In our example, the courts were later required to consider whether an officer in the Salvation Army was an employee (*Rogers v Booth* [1937] 2 All ER 751 (UK)). The case reached the Court of Appeal, a court responsible for reviewing and if necessary correcting decisions of first instance. As we will see, such courts have especial significance in the generation of binding precedents. The officer wished to show that she was classed as an employee of the Salvation Army in order to claim benefits for an injury sustained during her work for them, and argued that, unlike the *Curate's Case*, her relationship with the Salvation Army was governed by contract, so that she was an employee. In other words, she sought to limit *Curate's Case* to ecclesiastical officers only. She enjoyed only limited success, with the Court of Appeal finding that her agreement with the Salvation Army was not intended to be legally binding, because of its details. Again, *Rogers v Booth* is capable of being read in at least two different ways – narrowly, by indicating that on the particular facts before the Court of Appeal the relationship was not one which the parties intended to be legally binding, or broadly, by indicating that relationships between ministers and churches (both terms being very broadly defined) were rarely, or even never, intended to be legally binding because of their nature.

Rogers v Booth was interpreted by a judicial body below the level of the superior courts as turning on the spiritual nature of the relationship (*Barthorpe v Exeter Diocesan Board of Finance* [1979] ICR 900 (UK)), but later cases show that the better reading is that each case must be judged on its own facts (*President of the Methodist Conference v Parfitt* [1983] 3 All ER 747 (UK)), although there may be a presumption that in this sort of spiritual relationship the parties did not intend to create a legally binding contract (*Satokh Singh v Guru Nanak Gurdwara* [1990] ICR 309 (UK)). Thus, later cases collapsed the range of possible later meanings.

Although the above illustrates the way in which precedent works over time to define the law, it is a more difficult task to explain the exact mechanisms by which this process functions. As with statutory interpretation, neither the extremes of absolute judicial discretion, nor that of mechanistic application of clear rules, explain the process by which judges consider themselves bound by earlier precedents. Additionally, and again as with statutory interpretation, the jurisdictions in this study vary considerably as to the weight they give to earlier judicial decisions. Nonetheless, a few rules of thumb will be useful.

Firstly, the position of the court which decided the case in the national hierarchy is crucial. Below a certain level, courts are not capable of binding any later judge. In England, for example, although there are judicial officers below the High Court, for instance stipendiary magistrates who have a varied jurisdiction including minor criminal offences, their decisions do not create binding precedents. Lower courts are required to follow the decisions of the courts above them. This may be because the higher courts are assumed to give more accurate judgements because of the greater experience and expertise of the appellate judiciary, or because higher courts can reverse the judgements of lower courts but not vice versa. In the English jurisdiction, for instance, the House of Lords is the final court, and so is at the top of the hierarchy. Below the House of Lords is the Court of Appeal, below that court is the High Court. This raises a question of principle. If courts are required to follow decisions made by courts above them, and courts below them are required to follow their decisions, what of decisions made at the same level? This is particularly pressing in the highest court of each jurisdiction, because if that court is always bound by its previous decisions it may lead to excessive rigidity in the law, while if it regards itself as totally free to depart from these earlier precedents it may lead to excessive uncertainty (see Murphy and Rueter, 1981). In the jurisdictions under discussion, the highest courts are increasingly willing to depart from prior decisions where necessary (Practice Direction 1966 (UK); *Harris v Minister of the Interior*, 1952 (2) SA 471 (SA); Gall, 1995 at 350–3).

Secondly, it is the authority of the court, not the individual judge, which gives a precedent its binding power. This is particularly important when it is considered that appellate courts tend to consist of multiple judges, while courts of first instance have only a single judge. The extra consideration of the case may lead to better results, but it can also lead to differing judgements. At its most obvious, a court with three judges may divide with one judge finding for the appellant, and the other two judges finding for the respondent. A statement of law based on the findings of the minority rather than the majority cannot refer to binding precedent for its authority. More subtly, judges can reach the same decisions by very different routes. Consider again the finding in *Rogers v Booth*, which, it will be recalled, was in the Court of Appeal. What if of the three judges one had found that there was an employment relationship on the grounds that there existed a contract; one found that there was no employment relationship because spiritual offices were intrinsically incapable of constituting employment; and the third judge found that there was no employment relationship because there existed no contract? The authority of the court would be behind the outcome in the case before them, finding that there was no employment relationship (2:1, judges 2 and 3 against judge 1). It would also be behind the proposition that the existence of a contract was determinative of the employment relationship even for spiritual officers (2:1, but this time with judges 1 and 3 against judge 2). If later decisions focus on the more general principle, there may still be a difference of emphasis between judge 1 and judge 3, making the choice of which judge to quote when referring to the majority of the court crucial.

Thirdly, not every part of a court's judgement acts to bind later courts, even those below it in the hierarchy. Here there is an important distinction between ratio decidendi and obiter dicta. Although commonly referred to as ratio, ratio decidendi is not to be confused with the 2:1 majority discussed above. Rather, it constitutes the elements of the decision which had to be resolved in order for the court to make the ruling that it did. Everything else the judges may say in the process of giving their judgement is obiter dicta, and is not capable of binding any other court. This is clearly a significant distinction, and unfortunately not one which is always easy to identify in particular cases. Consider *MacManaway*, discussed above in relation to statutory interpretation. The ratio decidendi of that case may be found in the propositions that (a) the 1801 Act applies to all who have received Episcopal ordination; (b) priests in the Church of Ireland receive Episcopal ordination; therefore, (c) the 1801 Act applied to MacManaway, who had been made a priest in the Church of Ireland. But is this not a broader finding than the judges had to make in order to reach their decision? Could we not reformulate it more narrowly as (a) the 1801 Act applies to all who have received Episcopal ordination recognised by the Church of England; (b) ordination of priests in the Church of

Ireland is recognised by the Church of England; therefore (c) the 1801 Act applied to Macmanaway? Or even as (a) the 1801 Act applies to ordinations within the Anglican Communion; (b) the Church of Ireland is within the Anglican Communion; therefore (c) the Act applied to MacManaway? All three formulations produce the same result in the case before the court, but have different implications for the statement of law upon which future courts may wish to draw.

The distinction between ratio and obiter has considerable play in it, and is one way in which judges can escape from previous precedents they regard as undesirable. The narrower a ratio a decision is later given, the narrower its reach as a binding precedent. We can see this in the process of distinguishing, which is sufficiently important to merit separate discussion in a moment. Nonetheless, it seems fundamentally sound. Judges do not, on the whole, concern themselves with a sweeping philosophical discussion of every point that may be of interest in a general area raised by a particular dispute. Rather, legal professionals have deployed their arguments in order to win the case currently before the court, and these are the arguments the court is required to resolve. We would expect the time and attention the courts give to these arguments to be very much greater than an issue which does not arise in the case before them, and in which counsel for neither side, nor even the judge, has any interest in.

Fourthly, earlier decisions are only binding in so far as they are applicable to the facts in the current case. A decision that Christianity was a religion is not, necessarily, decisive of the question as to whether Islam is a religion. A judge who wished to avoid the impact of the earlier decision might find that the material facts in the earlier case included that the belief system in question was based on the Old and New Testament; a judge who wished to make use of it might prefer to find that the material facts included monotheism involving worship of a Supreme being. The first judge would distinguish the earlier decision from the case before them, while the second judge would not. Although this is also a reading of the ratio decidendi of the case (with the first judge reading it narrowly, the second more broadly) it is such a common way for judges to deal with earlier precedents that it may usefully be regarded as a separate factor to take into account in considering a precedent.

So far, for simplicity, we have talked about judicial lawmaking purely in terms of their interpreting other sources of law. Additionally, however, there exists a body of customary law which is to be found exclusively in the decisions of the courts, and which does not rely upon the interpretation of particular statutes for its authority. This customary law, or common law, has a very different texture from legislation, and is worth discussing briefly. In particular, as the common law it has a form derived mainly from traditions in English law, although it has come to be understood and developed in different ways in the United States, Australia, New Zealand, and Canada. South Africa also partakes of a different legal tradition, the civilian tradition of continental Europe, making the development of precedent used in South Africa more complex than the other jurisdictions (see further Hahlo and Kahn, 1968 at 237–60; Zimmerman and Visser, 1996b; du Plessis and Kok, 1989 at 6–26).

The common law developed in England very gradually, over a very long period. Common law legal rules derive their authority, not from legislation, but from statements of principle in earlier court cases. Before the Norman Conquest, it could scarcely be said that there was such a thing as English law. The population was small, settlements widely scattered, and travel difficult. Administration of justice tended to be local. Each local community would have its own court in which, for the most part, local customs would be applied. These customs, the beginnings of legal rules, varied considerably from one area to another. The Norman Conquest had little immediate impact. William I promised that the English should keep their rights and their law, which meant their customary law. At the same time, however, the Normans developed a strong central government and over the following 200 years greatly increased control over the administration of the law. This was a gradual process, bringing with it the decline of local courts. Central courts, sitting permanently at Westminster, developed with jurisdiction over legal disputes. At the same time, the practice grew up of sending royal judges to visit most parts of the country so as to establish closer royal control of the administration of justice.

These new institutions, particularly the travelling judges, brought with them an important change in the law itself, by unifying local customs. As they went around the country on circuit, the judges tended to select and apply certain customary rules in all cases, rather than enquire into local customs in every case. This process was assisted by the King who sometimes created new legal rules that were to apply nationally, and by the central courts which had nationwide jurisdiction. The different local customs were therefore replaced gradually by a body of rules that applied throughout the whole country, and were known therefore as the common law. This process was substantially completed by the end of the thirteenth century. The formation of the common law took place when there were few statutes or other forms of written law. The judges accordingly looked to previous decisions in order to maintain consistency. This was the beginning of the emergence of the doctrine of precedent in the common law courts, as discussed above.

With the expansion of the English state into other territories, the common law too was exported. Thus, it can be found in most Canadian jurisdictions; most jurisdictions of the United States; New Zealand; and Australia. All of these jurisdictions had a particular, colonial, inheritance from the English legal system. In South Africa, although parts of the territory shared this inheritance, others had an established legal system based on Romano-Dutch law, rather than this common law tradition. With the incorporation of the territories into the British Empire, and eventually the Union of South Africa, the legal system as a whole became a mixed one, with strong elements of the common law tradition (Zimmerman and Visser, 1996a).

Academic Commentary and Other Secondary Sources

So far we have discussed the primary sources of law, by which I mean texts which are themselves legal texts, and have the authority of State power to enforce them.

In this section I will briefly consider the role that secondary sources, including academic commentary, have to play in developing the law.

There are an enormous variety of secondary materials on law, written with very different readerships and for very different purposes. Consider, for instance, the question of employment of clergy by churches, touched on in the section above. We might expect to see a discussion of the issue in a bulletin of current developments intended for human resource managers; updates to a loose-leaf encyclopedia for practicing employment lawyers; undergraduate textbooks introducing law students to employment law; monographs dealing at length with a particular theoretical perspective on employment law or Church/State relations; collections of cases and materials on employment law (such cases and materials collections function as readers in other disciplines); and articles in general academic journals, or in specialist journals dealing with employment law or law and religion.

In sharp contrast to the sources discussed above, secondary sources can only ever be of persuasive value, and this value will depend upon the source in question. As Farnsworth puts it in relation to the United States: 'the effect of secondary authority depends more upon its intrinsic worth and upon the court's esteem for the particular writer than upon any veneration of scholars in general' (Farnsworth, 1996 at 83). As may be anticipated, the courts give relatively little weight to secondary sources whose primary purpose is pedagogical or summative, particularly where the intended readership are not legal professionals or academics.

Although the common law systems have not given as much weight to academic commentary as continental systems, more advanced commentary may sometimes be made use of by the courts, with or without acknowledgement, in discharging their duties as outlined in the preceding sections (see Bennion, 1997 at 17–22). In the United States, for instance, a series of academic commentaries intended to systematically restate the legal rules and principles in a number of areas, the American Law Institute Restatements, are regularly cited by the courts (see Clarke and Ansay, 1992 at 45). Some treatises have developed a considerable de facto authority, both as summaries of the established law and statements of the likely content of the law in areas of uncertainty. In English criminal law, for instance, the treatise on criminal law originally authored by Smith and Hogan is frequently cited by the higher courts for both purposes. More specific or speculative areas, or very recent developments, may be addressed through journal articles in specialist legal journals, which are apt to be more tightly focused and argumentative than full texts.

Soft Law and Law in Practice

As well as these sources of law, there is much to be learned from documents which are taken as a strong source of institutional policy, or have been used by the courts to clarify terms used by a formal source of law. For instance, in the English jurisdiction the courts will have recourse to the Highway Code, a code of practice for road users, in deciding whether a criminal offence such as careless driving has been committed. The Highway Code is not a legal document, but rather a source of 'soft law', which can be given de facto, but not de jure, power by a real source of law. In an example more directly relevant to our discussion, in England many charities formed for religious purposes are registered as charities for the advancement of religion. There are many ambiguities in this category of charity. The statutory body responsible for registration, the Charity Commission, issues guidance to prospective charities, and sometimes reports the way it has interpreted the legislation and cases in the area (see Edge and Loughrey, 2001).

As well as these sources of soft law, considerable attention has also been focused by legal scholars on how rules of law are actually used in practice. At its simplest, there may be such a significant difference between what the sources of law say, and how legal actors actually operate, as to render a statement based simply on the sources impoverished. A useful example may be drawn from a case before the European Court of Human Rights.

In *Manoussakis and Others v* Greece (1996) 23 EHRR 397 (ECHR) the applicants had been prosecuted for establishing and operating a place of worship without first registering it. The court came to the conclusion that the registration requirement per se was not a contravention, but that the way in which it was applied was. In particular, the legislation made it possible to delay without actually rejecting an application, and the Greek authorities had 'tended to use the possibilities afforded by the above-mentioned provisions to impose rigid, or indeed prohibitive, conditions on practice of religious beliefs by certain non-orthodox movements, in particular Jehovah's Witnesses' (ibid., at para. 48).

To address the question which heads this section, a legal argument is an argument based upon the use of sources of law according to the legal methodologies outlined above. These can be ranked in a hierarchy from constitutions, through primary and secondary legislation and decisions of the superior courts to soft law and academic commentary.

What is Religion?

In the previous section, because of the intended readership of this text, it was necessary to go into the definition of law at some length. Again based on the intended readership, a general overview of the different ways in which religion can be defined will be omitted. Instead, in this section I wish to consider legal definitions of religion, and the working definition of religion upon which this text is based.

As will emerge from the body of this text, to refer to 'the' legal definition of religion can be misleading. Not only have different jurisdictions in this text developed different definitions, albeit influenced by common traditions and at times making use of definitions developed elsewhere, but even within a single legal system 'religion' may bear a variety of meanings. In the case of the US, Canada, South Africa, and to a lesser extent Australia, there are provisions in the national constitutions that require a meaning to be given to 'religion'. Given the overarching impact of constitutional rules, it is unsurprising to find that these have been immensely influential within their jurisdiction. But consider the position of New Zealand and the UK, neither of which have much experience of such an overarching religious rights guarantee. Where do we find 'the' English law definition of religion? In fact, there is no such single definition – rather a body of related definitions which depend upon the context in which they occur. Given the rules of interpretation discussed above there is no reason why a statute intended to protect individuals from being victimised because of their membership of a religious group should be interpreted in exactly the same sense as a statute intended to provide for fiscal benefits from the State for bodies doing socially useful work.

Although the details of each jurisdiction may usefully be dealt with in the next chapter, common problems that any such definition must cope with can be identified here. Additionally, as this is a text on religion and law, it is important that we come to some working definition of religion. As Johnson observed, 'How can we say anything about religion if we do not know what it is?' (Johnson, 1984 at 839). Even if we take the view that law, and legal discussion, should not say anything about religion, it still has much to say about the interaction of law and religion. For this discussion to occur, it is necessary to establish the characteristics of the social phenomena under discussion before we can examine their implications. In particular, problems could arise if we did not have an explicit definition of religion underpinning this text – not least that we may inadvertently be considering different issues, through differing but unarticulated conceptions of the term. Thus, a working provisional definition of religion is necessary for this text.

For those involved in the making of law, however, there may be notable advantages in not defining religion. In the legislative process, which it will be recalled may explicitly accommodate political debate, silence on definition of religious and spiritual matters may lead to what appears to be a consensus. A participant in the drafting of the Education Act 1944 (UK) noted that: '[t]he churches were in such a state at the time [that] we thought if we used the word "spiritual" they might agree to that because they didn't know what it was. They all had very clear ideas about what religion was, and they all knew that they didn't agree with anyone else's definition of it' (in Hay and Nye, 1998 at 5).

More broadly, a number of commentators have argued against a legal definition of religion (for example, Berg, 1997; Freeman, 1983). Cumper has argued that the absence of a definition of religion, at least at an international level, has three main advantages. Firstly, it avoids the technically very difficult task of drafting a definition which is flexible enough to satisfy a broad cross-section of world religions while precise enough for practical application to specific cases. Secondly, the absence of a definition means that those bound by a guarantee of religious rights cannot give a restrictive definition to religion, a particular danger for minority religions whose characteristics may not match any general definition. Thirdly, the variety of conscientious, religious, and spiritual beliefs would present problems to a definition based on traditional, Western, views of religion:

[t]he twentieth century has witnessed the establishment of a plethora of new beliefs. These range from new religious groups (often called cults) to humanistic philosophies that stress Man's innate potential and believe that human spirit is eternal. The recent emergence of the New Age movement with its subtle blend of ancient mysticism and religious faith further blurs the distinction between religion and philosophy ... humanist and secular philosophies are as often sacred to their adherents as religious belief in the traditional sense (Cumper, 1995 at 359)

It is undeniable that the task of defining religion for legal purposes is extremely difficult. Numerous court systems have found creating such a definition problematic, even for overarching religious liberty guarantees. Neither the organs of the European Convention on Human Rights (Evans, 1999), nor the International Covenant on Civil and Political Rights (Cumper, 1995) have developed a detailed definition. The issue has been left open by the Supreme Court of Canada (Horwitz, 1996). The well developed, but chaotic, cases and commentary on the First Amendment to the United States Constitution provide a wide variety of definitions, and anti-definitions, none of which have achieved dominance (see further McConnell, 1990; Frame, 1992; Ricks, 1993a).

There are difficulties in defining religion which are common to any consideration of the term which is not, itself, based in the discipline of an exclusive religion (see Park, 1994 at 32–9). A legal definition exists primarily to achieve one or more of the functions of law discussed above, in other words for use by actors in the legal system to achieve their particular goals. This explicitly utilitarian role for a legal definition of religion has a number of important implications.

Firstly, the definition must be clear enough to allow the resolution of disputes when they occur, and preferably to allow citizens to plan their conduct in the knowledge of whether or not their activities will be classed as religious ones.

Secondly, if we focus on legal definitions as tools by which actors achieve their aims, there is a danger either that a particular definition might be abused by those seeking a goal, or that the public might perceive that such abuse is occurring (Hall, 1996 at 9). This is particularly the case where there are fears that insincere claims to religious status are being made in order to secure a secular benefit that would be desirable independent of any religious context. Numerous examples of such benefits could be given. One commentator on the United States experiment with the prohibition of recreational alcohol, for example, recounts an anecdote concerning Jewish communities who had been granted a special exemption for their religious observances: 'At the outset of prohibition, for example, the congregation of Los Angeles' Talmud Torah Synagogue numbered 180. Within fourteen months almost 1000 new members had joined, many of them impelled, it would seem, by a desire less than spiritual. In the spring of 1921 the majority voted to oust their Rabbi Gardner, not, according to him, 'for any violation of [Prohibition], but quite the reverse' (Kobler, 1974 at 250–1).

Although in the abstract individuals not entitled to such an exemption from generally applicable legal rules might feel resentment, this may be exacerbated if the non-exempt individual suffers a loss thereby. In the context of the workplace, for instance, in one case Lord Denning MR expressed concern that: 'If it should happen that, in the name of religious freedom, [a worker] were given special privileges or advantages, it would provoke discontent, and even resentment among those with whom they work. As indeed it has done in this case' (*Ahmed v ILEA* [1977] ICR 491 (UK)). In relation to custody disputes Mumford has warned that 'by putting too much emphasis on freedom of religion, the parent who makes child-rearing decisions motivated by reasons of faith ... may be seen to have an advantage in cases of dispute over the parent who makes different decisions for secular reasons' (Mumford, 1998 at 135). Consideration of religious interests may also lead to individuals or groups being given a role in public policy, and thus concerns that religious claims are being used insincerely to gain such a voice. In South Australia, the federal Minister responsible for aboriginal affairs had halted construction of a bridge, on the basis that it compromised the 'secret women's business' of members of the Ngarrindjeri nation. A Royal Commission was required to determine whether this was a sincere claim or a fabrication on the part of those who claimed the existence of the secret religious practice (*ALRM v South Australia* [1995] EOC 92-759 (Aust.)).

The point here is not that religious interests should be ignored because of concerns that any special consideration will be abused, or because the majority population might conclude that they are being abused. Most legal rules are capable of some level of abuse, or of portrayal as being abused, especially when we factor in the possibility of a court coming to a factually incorrect decision. Rather, it is important to acknowledge that in many instances the recognition of something as religious may involve some social cost, or cost incurred by another individual (Lipson, 2000). A proper definition of religion provides the basis for justification, or criticism, of the incurring of these costs.

If the nature of law poses especial problems for defining religion, changes in the religious make up of the jurisdictions discussed in this text sharpen the difficulties. Some spiritualities pose especial challenges to traditional views of what constitutes a religion, particularly those which, in French's taxonomy, are postmodern as opposed to traditional or modern religions (French, 1999). Horwitz suggests that there is a 'possibility that individual judges will craft biased definitions of religion that reflect a majoritarian scepticism about the claims of religious adherents whose beliefs and practices do not resemble the tenets of mainstream religions' (Horwitz, 1996). We do not need to accept that judges and other decision makers would do this maliciously, or even consciously, to recognise the possibilities for this sort of outcome where they are asked to protect religious rights without a definition which leads them to reflect on the variety of religious experience.

In relation to 'religion' as a term in legal discourse, its different definitions will be explored where relevant in the text, beginning in the next chapter. These specific definitions aside, I would suggest that, in order for the discussion in this text to proceed, there needs to be some working definition of 'religion' and related terms. Such a working definition is not being put forward as applicable to every legal source that uses the word 'religious'.

A variety of strategies have been adopted by writers and courts seeking to define religion. The range of possible approaches may usefully be illustrated by considering the decision of the High Court of Australia in *The Church of the New Faith v The Commissioner of Payroll Tax* [1982–3] 154 CLR 120 (Aust.). In that case, the High Court had to consider whether Scientology was a religion for the purposes of the Victorian taxation legislation. As the highest appellate court in Australia, cases before the High Court are decided by a number of judges. In this case, two different approaches to the definition of religion were developed by two pairs of judges. Mason ACJ and Brennan J favoured a definition based on belief in a supernatural being, thing, or principle coupled with acceptance of canons of conduct in order to give effect to that belief. They accepted that there were different intensities of belief or of acceptance of canons of conduct among religions, but found that such differing emphases were not relevant to the question of whether the system was a religion. Wilson and Deane JJ, on the other hand, found that there was no single characteristic which could be used as a legal touchstone for inclusion or exclusion in the definition of religion. Instead, they preferred to consider the most important of the factors which could go to answering the question, factors which 'must, in the view we take, be derived by empirical observation of accepted religions' (ibid., at 173). In this case, they considered particularly important indicia were belief in the supernatural, ideas relating to man's nature and place in the universe and his relation to things supernatural, standards and practices of supernatural significance, and the existence of an identifiable group which sees themselves as a religious one.

Both judgements reject endorsing the metaphysical truth of some systems, and lack of truth of others, as a definitional strategy. This approach would cause serious problems for a pluralist legal system such as Australia (see further Stark, 1999). Similarly, both judgements retain the authority of the court to determine whether a particular system is religious, rather than rely upon self-identification. To allow pure self-definition, as opposed to recognising the importance of self-conceptualisation in a test, would fail to sufficiently protect the interests of those not seeking such an identification (see Edge, 1996). They differ, however, in the way in which the court is to make this determination across multiple religious systems.

Wilson and Deane JJ draw a fundamentally unreasoned analogy with systems already recognised as religious. They do this, not by direct reference to such religions, but by the reliance they would place upon characteristics derived from the observation of accepted religions. Although this would bring in a proper consideration of the scope and variety of religious experiences and practices, assuming 'accepted' was interpreted sufficiently broadly, it does require the judges to draw an analogy without any understanding of why the analogy is to be drawn. If we say that X is like Y, we implicitly define the commonality. For instance, a statement that a cat is 'like' a dog will have one meaning to a speaker discussing the admirable qualities of companion animals, and quite a different one for a wide ranging omnivore discussing the tastes of different meat animals. Similarly, for a judge to rule that Scientology is like Catholicism, that judge must have determined the legally relevant characteristics that the two systems have in common.

Determining which characteristic is legally relevant is not a matter of observation, but of analysis.

In exploring reasons why religion matters to law, above, I discussed a number of characteristics. Many of these are shared with other types of interest. For instance, if religion is important because of its impact on minority groups in a particular society, so is literature, music and song. Thus, a high level of impact on minority groups could only be a determining characteristic of religion if we wished to include these other activities. The problem of authority, however, is not generally applicable, and will be used here to develop a working definition of religion.

The core concept of freedom of religion, and thus of a goal-orientated definition of religion, seems to me to arise not from substantive issues such as individual autonomy, public order and non-discrimination, but from the special procedural problem posed by statements concerning metaphysical reality (for a similar conclusion reached by a different route, see Macklem, 2000). I have already suggested that defining religion is difficult because of the pluralist nature of the legal orders under discussion. This pluralist nature also provides the key to producing a definition. The difficulty the legal system has with defining religion is that the modern legal order renounces the capacity to adjudicate statements about metaphysical reality, while it retains jurisdiction over other statements about reality. If this renunciation is the central concept of religious freedom, then freedom of religion is intended primarily to protect statements about metaphysical reality, and beliefs and practices flowing from such statements, because such statements cannot be properly evaluated by the legal order – particularly where the statements are non-rational (see Hall, 1996 at 11; Feofanov, 1994). In effect, the legal order implements a Kantian ideal in seeking to act justly where all individual positions are unknown, although it may be argued that a 'theory that is totally "fair" to everyone of any worldview remains a mirage' (Ahdar, 2000 at 9).

A definition of religion based on metaphysical claims must be defended against a number of important criticisms. Firstly, it may be argued that it reinforces a particular worldview, where it is meaningful to distinguish between metaphysical and non-metaphysical reality. In doing so, we import a tenet of particular belief systems into a statement intended to be of general application across belief systems. There is considerable strength in this criticism. From the perspective of a believer in particular phenomena, characterising them as distinct from other phenomena may be inappropriate. The issue is, however, not whether the individual believes the statement is on a par with statements concerning, for instance, the freshness of a pint of milk, but whether the court denies the statement such a character, in order to renounce jurisdiction. This emphasis on the role of the courts, rather than on the ability of science to address particular concerns, avoids some of the difficulties posed by distinguishing between scientific statements, social science statements, value judgements and religious beliefs (see Clements, 1989).

Secondly, it may be argued the stance excludes atheists and agnostics from the protection of freedom of religion. This is to mistake my position – a statement about metaphysical reality is different from a statement predicated upon the existence of that metaphysical reality. An atheist who argues that there is no non-material reality makes as firm a statement about a characteristic of metaphysical reality as does an individual who argues that metaphysical reality emanates from a single divine being. The definition does, however, exclude religious individuals and communities whose basis is orthopraxy, rather than orthodoxy. Because of the central place given to 'belief' in the international and domestic definitions of religion for legal purposes discussed in the next chapter, this seems a necessary compromise for ease of exposition. It is, however, a limitation worth making explicit here.

Thirdly, it may be argued that this very broad criterion will allow any claim to be presented as a religious claim. The point here is that the statement must be concerning metaphysical reality, rather than occur in a context where such statements have been made. For instance, a statement that giving a child a life saving blood transfusion will result in their eternal damnation is a statement about metaphysical reality; a statement that such a transfusion will cause an allergic reaction and the death of the child is not, even if it forms a tenet of a broader system within which metaphysical statements arise. As Frame notes:

> [consider a situation where] someone today claimed to believe that beings from Mars, with greater intelligence and power than us, are living, say on Mount Saint Helens. If she claimed that such beings have 'supernatural' powers, then such powers are beyond the physical laws investigatable by the material sciences and the belief would be religious. If, instead, the beings are alleged to be merely more highly developed material creatures, they would be within the range of investigation by the material sciences and beliefs about them would be entitled to no special preference over other scientifically accessible beliefs. (Frame, 1992 at 850)

Fifthly, this working definition does not seek to explain why the court renounces jurisdiction in these areas, yet it retains it in others. The ability of the court to determine any issue involving values, or indeed any issue at all, has become contentious (for example, Sapir, 1999), but the courts remain willing to act in these areas. Consider, for instance, the determination of the best interests of the child, discussed above.

A final point to make in developing this definition is that a particular level of development, comprehensiveness, antiquity, or distribution is not required. In particular, a statement about metaphysical reality remains such whatever view one may take of its intellectual merits and whether it occurs as part of a wider, consistent belief system, or in isolation, or in seeming conflict with other such statements the individual may assert. It might be argued that by rejecting these elements the focus of this text is not, in fact, upon religion at all. Certainly, this approach is far removed from that of, for instance, Durkheim, who defined religion as: 'a unified system of beliefs and practices relative to sacred things, that is to say things set apart and forbidden, beliefs and practices which unite into one single moral community, called a Church, all those who adhere to them' (Durkheim, 1915 at 47). It might be argued that by rejecting these elements the focus of this text is spirituality rather than religion. If this is a valid distinction, I would argue that the individualistic structure of international human rights guarantees, including those of religion, emphasises spirituality, but within the terminology of religion.

Approaching the Literature

In this text, compared with a purely legal one, I make extensive use of the secondary literature on law and religion. In part this is because of the territorial scope of some of the discussion that follows, and the limitations of my own expertise. Perhaps more cogently, secondary materials tend to be more easily accessible, and less problematic, for readers from other disciplines. The discussion of primary sources earlier in this chapter was necessary to establish an understanding of the primary sources of law – essential to understanding any legal discussion – but in practice most readers with a focused interest in the law will go initially to the secondary literature and only later, if at all, to the primary materials. In this section, I will introduce some of the different categories of literature relevant to the study of law and religion. Bearing these in mind may make use of the literature a little easier. In particular, the reader new to legal literature may wish to consciously identify their reading by reference to methodology, territory, topic, and readership in evaluating its usefulness for their purposes.

Methodology

Earlier in this chapter I suggested that there was a distinction between a discussion about law, and a legal discussion. This suggests one methodological distinction, based on how far the writer accepts and works within a legal argument, and how far they look to other discourses to inform, or even drive, their discussion. At one extreme, we might find a purely technical reflection on the proper understanding of a particular legal provision. For instance, Barber's discussion of outrageous behaviour in Anglican places of worship is concerned almost exclusively with the correct interpretation of the relevant statutory provisions, with his evaluation of the provisions drawing exclusively upon legal sources and legal values (Barber, 1996). Further along, we might find a predominantly technical discussion of what the law is combined with an analysis of whether that is appropriate based on some broader value such as dignity or equality, or justice. For instance, Lupu in his study of exempting religious organisations from non-discrimination effectively evaluates the law against 'norms of religious liberty and associational freedom' (Lupu, 1987 at 395). At perhaps the furthest extreme, we might find a discussion which briefly, and uncritically, gives a simple statement of the law before moving on to the centre of the discussion based on some other approach. For instance, Unsworth's discussion of blasphemy in English law deals relatively concisely with what the law is, in favour of a much more broadly based concern with the blasphemy controversy as 'a commentary on the relationship between law and culture in Britain at the end of the twentieth century, and as symptomatic of some of the pivotal conflicts which are characteristic of late modern societies' (Unsworth, 1995 at 658).

A further useful distinction may be based on the source of any non-legal discourses – in the context of a multidisciplinary work, which disciplines are being combined with legal argument? Multidisciplinary approaches to law are increasingly common, and in his recent review of United Kingdom scholarship Bradney argues for such an approach, particularly in relation to scholarship from political and religious studies (Bradney, 2001). Within law and religion we can find perspectives drawn from sociology, politics, religious studies, theology, and philosophy. In some cases, the combination of disciplines has become so well established within legal scholarship as to constitute a subdiscipline in itself – so approaching law from a philosophical stance is a substantial part of jurisprudential analysis; while taking a stance based on the empirical traditions of the social sciences is a substantial part of sociolegal scholarship.

Territorial Scope

Perhaps a more pragmatic categorization is by territorial scope. Some legal scholarship is explicitly unconcerned with particular territories. For instance, Macklem discusses justifications of securing freedom of religion without siting that freedom in any particular territory (Macklem, 2000). Undoubtedly his discussion is most applicable to discourses based on particular assumptions, and emerges from a broadly Western/United States frame, but there is nothing in his arguments which seeks to impose territorial limits to the conclusion. This may seem a commonplace, until it is recalled that law can, and frequently does, differ from country to country. Any assertion I may care to make about the content of law should probably be read as being limited to the law applicable to a particular territorial area – a particular jurisdiction. So to that extent, legal scholarship which claims, either explicitly or implicity, no territorial limits is comparative unusual.

In terms of scope, below this limitless category we find commentary concerned with international law. In the next chapter I will discuss the principal international legal guarantees of freedom of religion, and briefly explore some of the key ideas of international law. For the moment, it is worth noting that international law, in its own terms, transcends national boundaries and will evaluate its own claims as superior to those of any particular nation state. It may be thought that a discussion of international law must be global in terms of its territorial scope. Even the most widely accepted international laws have a territorial limit, however, in that they cannot necessarily claim enforcement by the organs in control of a particular territory. So a discussion of the United Nations guarantees of freedom of religion, such as Scheinin's discussion of the Universal Declaration of Human Rights (Scheinin, 1992), is limited in territorial scope. I return to the distinction between international and domestic law in the next chapter. Additionally, as we will see in the next chapter, international law is not always applicable to all countries. Countries may join together, by use of treaties, and agree to be bound by international legal rules which do not bind states who have not entered into that agreement. Thus, particular international legal rules, and hence commentary upon them, may be limited to only a small number of territories. A good example for our purposes is the European Convention on Human Rights, a regional human rights instrument binding upon a geographically distinct group of countries. We can thus see commentary upon the ECHR, such as the discussion of the religious liberty guarantees by Dunne, as limited by territorial scope (Dunne, 1999).

The most obvious limitations, however, are by jurisdiction – that is, by reference to a particular set of laws within a particular legal territory. Very often a commentary discussing the law in one jurisdiction will be valuable in considering the law in other jurisdictions, and may explicitly deploy generally applicable arguments intended to influence developments elsewhere. It would be a serious mistake, however, to take a commentary on (say) freedom of religion in the United States and assume it is an accurate legal description of the situation in Australia. As we will see in the following chapter, even a very superficial consideration of the fundamental laws of the two countries reveals serious differences in approach. Much of the secondary literature discussed in this text is, either implicitly or explicitly, limited to a particular jurisdiction, and it is important not to lose sight of this when making use of it.

As a final note on territorial scope, I have already suggested that some writers will discuss one particular jurisdiction, but with a clear eye to their analysis and arguments being taken up in relation to other jurisdictions. Increasingly, scholars are engaging in evaluations, and comparisons, of multiple jurisdictions in particular areas. For instance, in her analysis of religion and family law in the English jurisdiction, Hamilton made explicit use of United States materials, and her key conclusions include reflections of the similarities and differences between US and English approaches (Hamilton, 1995). Similarly, Efaw aims to improve the analysis of US treatment of religious difference in the armed forces by reflecting on the way similar issues are dealt with by the British Army (Efaw, 1996).

Topic

As the remainder of this text will illustrate, the range of topics which can be covered by work on law and religion is vast. Discussion in this text is structured around clusters of factual situations. There are, however, alternative ways to break down the topics, which will help understanding the structures in the debates.

Firstly, and particularly common in the literature with a relatively small multidisciplinary input, a topic may be defined by reference to a legal category. The work of Barber, discussed above, could sensibly be categorised as falling within the category of criminal law. Also within this category we could place discussion of religion and intent in determining criminal liability (Hilbert, 1987), of blasphemy (Kearns, 2000), or of the role of clergy in criminal juries (Pattenden, 1999). The strength of work based on this sort of classification is that it matches with common classifications within legal scholarship. A specialism which covered both criminal law and employment, on the other hand, would be seen as encompassing two distinct bodies of law, and two sets of expertise. Additionally, just as a writer in law and religion may be able to deploy particular expertise within a legal category, scholars who define their specialism more closely in line with these legal categories will be able to make a substantial contribution to discussion within that category – without necessarily having a significantly broader interest in the interaction of law and religion.

Secondly, a topic may be defined by factual situation. This often matches the expectations of a non-legal audience, but poses significant problems in terms of expertise across all the legal categories which may need to be considered to address the topic (Edge, 1998). A recently completed project of my own may usefully illustrate this (Edge, 2002). In order to explore the legal treatment of sacred places it was necessary to consider not just the law controlling use of geographical space generally (planning law), and the process by which particular places can be marked as religious places (registration of places of worship), but also, as it turned out, special rules governing unseemly conduct in such places (criminal law), and provisions for dealing with those seeking to worship at the ancient monument at Stonehenge (public order law).

Thirdly, a topic may be defined by the religious community involved. There is a comparatively small body of general work in this area, requiring as it does both an intimate knowledge of the religious community in question, plus a preparedness to engage in a comprehensive study of those areas of law which have proven problematic for its members. Examples include a study of Sikhs in the United Kingdom (Juss, 1995), an edited collection on Islam in Europe (Ferrari and Bradney, 2000), and a discussion of the treatment of Scientologists in Germany (Browne, 1998). More common is a focus on both a particular religious community, and a subset of relevant legal issues. For instance, Winslow's discussion of Native American sacred places (Winslow, 1996), or Muramoto's analysis of the refusal of blood products by Jehovah's Witnesses (Muramoto, 1998a; Muramoto, 1998b).

Readership

A final categorisation could be by the target readership. The most accessible to non-lawyers are pieces aimed at those with little or no legal knowledge. Although the importance of sources of law is often not discussed at length in these pieces, knowledge of broader legal doctrines is not assumed. So, a piece dealing with the employment status of clergy may briefly explain what a contract of employment is, the broader doctrine of contract being essential to proper understanding of the topic. The next most accessible are those aimed at students new to law, but whose programme of study involves a considerable breadth of legal knowledge. An obvious example would be a text aimed specifically at an undergraduate legal market, in those countries where law is an undergraduate degree. Although some broad familiarity with law is assumed, the writer recognises that the readers will not have very much experience in legal arguments. The third type of output aimed at an academic audience is addressed primarily at other legal scholars. As might be expected, these can involve a relatively high level of background knowledge and practice in legal argument. Against this, the piece may involve a multidisciplinary approach making use of perspectives familiar to the reader.

Along with this body of academic literature, however, is work aimed explicitly at supporting the legal profession. Even substantial, comprehensive, texts aimed at the legal profession differ considerably from undergraduate textbooks dealing with the same subject. In particular, they are often focused more on the practical application of the law, and assume an advanced level of general legal knowledge. Additionally, many short pieces, especially those appearing in journals with a professional emphasis, will be aimed at providing the readers with an update on new developments in an area of existing expertise. These notes of new cases and forthcoming legislation are particularly inappropriate for a reader who does not understand the context in which these new developments are occurring.

Chapter 2

Religious Interests in International and Domestic Laws

The Idea of Religious Interests

In the previous chapter I suggested that, as a useful working definition, 'religion' consists of statements about metaphysical reality, and beliefs and practices flowing from such statements. Although this is useful as a way of gauging whether a particular system is 'religious', in practical terms the concept of religious interests is more significant. By religious interests I mean claims for consideration by the legal system arising from the claimant's religion.

One advantage of focusing on religious interests, rather than religion, is that it then becomes possible to compare these interests with interests arising from non-religious contexts. This is important because, as we will see, the overarching religious liberty guarantees dealt with in this chapter constitute part of a broader scheme of protecting human and civil rights. These rights can arise from a religious context, but not solely from such a context. Consider, for instance, a landlord who for religious reasons is not willing to let the property to a couple in a sexual relationship who are not married (thereby excluding unmarried heterosexual couples and homosexual couples). Unless we can base an excluded couples status in their religion, rather than say their sexuality, it is impossible to compare their 'religion'. It is rather easier to compare their interests, however, that of the landlord being a religious interest, that of the couple being based in privacy and non-discrimination (see Markey, 1995). In a given legal situation, it is unlikely that only a single set of claims from one religious context will be put forward as relevant to the outcome. Rather, such claims will constitute one element which must be given proper consideration in the decision making process. The legal decision maker will be required to balance competing interests in order to achieve an appropriate outcome. An overemphasis on the religious aspect in a scenario can lead to a failure to appreciate fully the different interests at stake, and thus fail to strike an appropriate balance between them.

A further advantage of stressing religious interests, rather than religion, is to emphasise the human-centred nature of the legal systems discussed in this text. Arguments based on the protection of a particular religion are not given weight by legal decision makers because of the interests of that particular religion. Rather, the religion is used as a form of shorthand for the individual interests of the adherents of that religion. Similarly, when we look at discussions of religious organisations, they are considered as representatives of their (human) members. So, in the context of this text, it is more useful to discuss the protection of, for instance, Catholics, rather than of Catholicism – although protection of Catholicism may occur as a way of protecting Catholics.

Additionally, the religious interest can be involved when neither a religion nor religious organisation is directly involved. In the United Kingdom, for instance, there have been moves to require Freemasons to declare their membership of that organisation when taking up certain posts in public life (Home Affairs Committee, 1997). An international body, the Human Rights Committee, has indicated that the State cannot compel an individual to reveal their religion (Human Rights Committee, 1993). It is relatively clear that, for most Freemasons, Freemasonry does not constitute a religion (cf. Hannah, 1954). Nor are the Grand Lodge and other Masonic organisations religious ones, at least in terms of English law (*United Grand Lodge of Ancient, Free and Accepted Masons of England v Holborn B.C.* [1957] 1 W.L.R. 1080 (UK)). By requiring Freemasons to publicly register their membership, however, the State would require them to publicly register their monotheism, monotheism being a prerequisite of Masonic membership. In turn, monotheism is not a single religion, although it is undoubtedly a characteristic of many religions. It would seem clumsy to describe registration rules as affecting the religion of Freemasons, but it undoubtedly would involve their religious interests, and this would need to be taken into account in constructing a registration scheme.

The final advantage of using religious interests to refer to the legally significant issues raised by religion is that it introduces the idea of a plurality of religious interests – a cluster of related interests and claims which, although having much in common, have their own distinctive characteristics. A similar conclusion may also be drawn from considering the legal documents discussed in this chapter – for instance, the way in which the New Zealand Bill of Rights Act 1990 deals with freedom of belief, freedom of religious practice, and freedom to form a religious community under separate sections. Before moving on to discuss religious interests in international law, it may be useful to briefly describe one taxonomy of these interests.

A Taxonomy of Religious Interests

In developing a taxonomy of religious interests, it is worth stressing that, however we categorise them, there is often a close interrelationship between them. For instance, Hervier-Leger has observed that '[a] central element in the formation of religious identities, whether for individuals or groups, is the process by which the individual or group is notionally incorporated into a line of believers' (Hervier-Leger, 1994 at 124). In terms of the taxonomy in this section, this is a close relationship between organisational and identification interests, so that a legal measure which restricts organisational and community life might be seen as impacting directly on the formation of the individual's religious identification.

I have already suggested that the legal systems discussed in this text privilege religious belief as the foundation for religion as legally recognised. We will see this in the definitions of religion discussed below. One form of religious interest, therefore, might be categorised as religious belief. The individual has an interest in being able to form and maintain their own religious beliefs, even in the absence of their seeking to express these beliefs in any way detectable by an outside observer. At the most extreme, this interest may be infringed when the individual is subjected to coercive measures which change their beliefs in a way which constitutes an unacceptable infringement of their autonomy. So, if there exists a phenomena such as brainwashing, use of such techniques against an individual to change their religious beliefs would involve this form of religious interest. Under the ECHR, for instance, it has been found that protection of belief prevents the State from indoctrinating individuals on religious matters (*Angelini v Sweden* (1988) 10 EHRR 123 (ECHR)), and may also require the State to protect the individual from improper influence to change their beliefs (*Kokkinakis v Greece* (1994) 17 EHRR 397 (ECHR)). It does not, however, prevent the State from conveying information on religious communities in an objective but critical manner, so long as such information does not 'pursue aims of agitation or indoctrination endangering the freedom of religion' (*Universelles Leben e.V. v Germany* (1996) HUDOC 27 November (ECHR)).

A connected but separate interest is the interest in a religious identity. It seems to me that there is a distinction between belief – which may be purely internal – and identity, which carries with it an element of externality. The difference may be drawn out by the discussion of brainwashing in *Kokkinakis v Greece*. The majority of the European Court of Human Rights were prepared to accept that improper proselytism could amount to an attack on another's freedom of belief. Judge Marten was much less convinced that coercion could ever cause an individual to change their beliefs. He recast the coercion problem: '[c]oercion in the present context does not refer to conversion by coercion, for people who truly believe do not change their beliefs as a result of coercion; what we are really contemplating is coercion in order to make somebody join a denomination and its counterpart, coercion to prevent somebody from leaving a denomination' (*Kokkinakis v Greece, op.cit.*). Being required to assert that one is a member of a particular community, to me, raises the interest in a religious identity, even if no more is required of the individual. It is fair to add, however, that many taxonomies of religious interest compact the issues raised here into religious belief, or religious practice, a further category discussed below.

Less controversial, however, are the interests raised by membership of a religious community. In *Ahmed v United Kingdom* (1981) 4 EHRR 165 (ECHR), for example, an Islamic applicant had resigned from his full-time post after he was refused permission to attend a mosque during working hours. The Commission rejected the application on the basis that the interference with his religious interests was justified, but noted that: 'the right to manifest ones religion "in community with others" has always been regarded as an essential part of the freedom of religion' (ibid., at para.5). The possible importance of communal religious interests is clear. Particular communal activities might be mandated by the individual's beliefs, for instance group prayer in company with coreligionists, or particular religious activities requiring a number of participants. Members of unpopular or persecuted religious groups may consider organisation important to secure their rights, or to provide 'networks and brotherhood, and thus emotional and often financial support' (Wilson, 1991 at 18). Additionally, there is a less easily identifiable cultural element to the formation of religious organisations. A religious adherent may see sharing time and experiences with co-religionists, apart from time spent in manifesting their religion, as part of their religious identity. This may be of especial importance where the religious community is a small, heterodox, one. In a discussion of world religions associated with minority ethnic groups, Knott observed that: 'the traditions have centres or places of worship which are used not only for religious purposes but also for social and cultural occasions. Communal worship has become important not only for its spiritual value but also as an opportunity for meeting at a social level; this would not have been necessary for many groups in their place of origin' (Knott, 1998 at 148).

A more specific sub-section of these communal interests is that raised by religious organisations. In *Hasan and Chaush v Bulgaria* (2000) HUDOC 26 October (ECHR), the Grand Chamber considered that: 'religious communities traditionally and universally exist in the form of organized structures. They abide by rules which are often seen by followers as being of divine origin. Religious ceremonies have their meaning and sacred value for the believers if they have been conducted by ministers empowered for that purpose in compliance with those rules. The personality of the religious ministers is undoubtedly of importance to any member of the community. Participation in the life of the community is thus a manifestation of one's religion, protected by Article 9' (ibid., para. 62). Lekhel has gone so far as to suggest that 'legal entity status for religious communities is a prerequisite to genuine freedom of conscience', meaning communities structured as organisations (Lekhel, 1999). Within the United Kingdom, the fears of representatives of religious organisations that the new human rights guarantees would be used against religion were addressed by a requirement that courts must have 'particular regard' to the importance of religious rights where dealing with questions which 'might affect the exercise by a religious organisation (itself or its members collectively) of the Convention right' (Human Rights Act 1998 s.13 (UK); see Cumper, 2000a).

Although it may be useful to structure religious interests by reference to belief, identity, and community, these are primarily matters of status, and only rarely the source of conflict within the legal systems discussed in this text. On the whole, the right of the individual to hold a belief; to identify as an adherent of a particular religion; or to identify as a member of a particular religious community, are all uncontentious – although some issues are raised by adhering to a particular religious organisation where that organisation has been identified by the state as involved in terrorism (see Edge, 1999). Problems much more commonly arise where the individual seeks to act upon one or more of these statuses. An example for each will help to illustrate the point.

The most significant category here is acting upon, or to adopt ECHR language, manifesting, religious belief. For instance, an individual may believe that divine law mandates a particular method for the preparation of meat for human consumption. The individual may then seek to act upon that belief by only consuming meat prepared in that way. This would constitute a manifestation of that religious belief, as for instance in *The Jewish Liturgical Association Che'are Shalom ve Tsedek* (2000) HUDOC 27 June (ECHR). In that case, the Court noted that it was uncontested 'that ritual slaughter … whose purpose is to provide Jews with meat from animals slaughtered in accordance with religious prescriptions … is an essential aspect of practice of the Jewish religion' (para.73), before going on to find that the slaughter was therefore a manifestation of religious belief. Although, as is discussed below, the ECHR does not treat every act motivated by religious belief as a manifestation of that belief, for the purposes of that taxonomy we will make just that assumption.

An individual can also manifest their religious identity. To some extent, this may be seen as a manifestation of a belief that a particular expression of identity is required or desired by religion; but identity can be expressed independently of belief. A comparison between two cases from employment law may illustrate this point. In the United States case of *Wilson v US West Communications*, 58 F.38 1337 (US), the plaintiff was a Roman Catholic who had taken a religious vow to wear a badge with a colour photograph of an aborted foetus, and a slogan opposing abortion. A number of her co-workers were offended, and two claimed harassment. The employer attempted to accommodate this by, inter alia, suggesting she keep the badge covered. She refused, and was dismissed, her dismissal being justified by the Court as in the interests of her co-workers. In *Boychuk v H.J. Symons Holdings Ltd* [1977] IRLR (UK), an Employment Appeals Tribunal upheld the dismissal of a woman who insisted on wearing badges proclaiming her (homo-) sexual orientation, on the basis that 'a reasonable employer … can be allowed to decide what upon reflection and mature consideration, can be offensive to the customers and the fellow employees'. In *Wilson*, the employee was manifesting their belief; in *Boychuk*, their identity.

Finally, an individual may manifest their membership of a religious community or organisation, both through involvement in the life of that organisation as a member, and by exercising a leadership role within it, as in *Serif v Greece* (1999) HUDOC 14 December (ECHR). As a consequence of the complex relations between Greece and Turkey, the religious and judicial posts of the two Grand Muftis were regulated by the State. Although a 1920 law allowed for promulgation of detailed rules governing the election of these officers by the Muslim community, no such rules were ever promulgated, and the officials had been appointed by the State. In 1990, Muslims made arrangements to elect Grand Muftis, the President amended the law to match existing practice, and the election went ahead. The applicant was elected to one of the posts, but not appointed by the State, and was later charged with usurping the functions of a minister of a known religion and wearing the uniform of an official without the right to do so. The Court took an extremely strong stance on State interference with disputes between religious communities, finding that criminalising a leadership role in a religious community could not be justified.

In conclusion, when approaching religious interests it may be valuable to have some idea of how religious interests may be classified. The structure suggested in this section may be summarised as:

	Status	Manifestation
Belief	e.g. belief in X (a deity)	e.g. worshipping X
Identity	e.g. identifying as a follower of X	e.g. wearing holy symbols of X
Community	e.g. identifying with other followers of X	e.g. being a priest of The Temple of X

Religious Interests in International Law

International Law

This section introduces those provisions of international law bearing most directly on religious interests. Before doing so, it is important to briefly describe the development of international law, and in particular its interaction with national (or domestic) law. In most cases national law is sovereign within the territory that the State controls. By sovereign we mean that nothing can prevail against national law, and that national law can itself do anything. As we discussed in the previous chapter, national constitutions may put limits on the exercise of this sovereignty, but these limits are themselves derived from the sovereign power of domestic law. So, the United States Constitution imposes limits upon the powers of Congress to legislate for the federal jurisdiction, but these limits are themselves legal ones.

Although some States may purport to exercise a jurisdiction over territory outside their control, as a practical matter the legal authority is limited by political geography. The United Kingdom Parliament may be able to enact legislation restricting the activities of French nationals in France, but it is unlikely that this legislation would be given any status by the officials in control of France. Thus, we have a model of the legal world as a composite of many different legal systems, each of which is controlled by a sovereign State. But individual States have relationships with organisations and individuals beyond their territorial limits: '[b]ecause the state, while internally supreme, wishes to maintain its sovereignty externally and needs to cultivate other states in an increasingly interdependent world, so it must acknowledge the rights of others. This acceptance of rights possessed by all states, something unavoidable in a world where none can stand alone, leads inevitably on to a system to regulate and define such rights and, of course, obligations' (Shaw, 1997 at 37). This system is known as international law.

As I discuss below, during the early stages of its development, the primary legal focus of international law was the relationship between States, with coverage of individuals being incidental to this primary focus. Even here, however, international law had some application to religious interests. During the twentieth century, particularly after the Second World War, international law became increasingly involved in the definition and protection of fundamental human rights, including religious rights. Although we can now point to an increasingly well-developed body of international law concerning individual rights, we cannot at the same time point to universal protection of these rights within particular States. In some cases, the violations of international law will arise from the actions of, for instance, State officials who at the same time violate their own domestic law. But what of the situation where a provision of domestic law is itself contrary to international law?

From the perspective of international law, we may be justified in saying that the provision is unlawful; but from the standpoint of domestic law, the provision is itself law. The distinction arises because, while domestic law is enforced by the mechanisms of the domestic legal system, international law has its own, less immediate, enforcement mechanisms. In some cases these mechanisms are extremely nebulous – indeed, one ground commonly used to attack the status of international law as law is that in the absence of an adequate enforcement mechanism it is a set of moral and political norms rather than a legal system (see Shaw, op.cit., 2–12).

If international law lacks an enforcement mechanism as straightforward as the police and courts of a domestic system, the sources of international law are similarly more complicated. In the previous chapter we saw the sources of domestic law – primarily constitutions, legislation, and decisions of superior courts. At the international level, however, there is no single body capable of creating new rules, and no single court system capable of authoritatively interpreting existing rules. Instead, the sources of international law include: '(a) international conventions, whether general or particular, establishing rules expressly recognised by the contesting states; (b) international custom, as evidence of a general practice accepted as law; (c) the general principles of law recognised by civilised nations; (d) ... judicial decisions and the teachings of the most highly qualified publicists of the various nations, as subsidiary means for the determination of rules of law' (Statute of the International Court of Justice, article 38(1)).

Of these sources the simplest, and for our purposes the practically most significant, are international conventions, also known as treaties. These are international agreements 'concluded between states in written form and governed by international law, whether embodied in a single instrument or in two or more related instruments and whatever [their] particular designation' (Vienna Convention on the Law of Treaties 1969, article 2(1)). These agreements can range from a treaty between two States binding them to agreed terms on a matter of common concern (for instance, the provision of professional clergy for minority religious communities in the two States); through agreements by a number of States in a particular region (for instance, an agreement by all States with coastal territory on a particular sea to observe certain pollution standards);

to agreements between most or even all States around the world. Although something of an oversimplification, for our purposes we can work on the basis that these treaties only bind the States which have entered into them (cp. Shaw, op.cit., 74–7).

The Work of the United Nations

The primary focus of international law during the nineteenth and early twentieth century was upon State interests, although this might impact upon particular individuals. States had an interest in the fate of their diplomats and other nationals when abroad; and were sometimes linked by religion or ethnicity to citizens of another State. In the latter case, the two States might agree a treaty promising protection or special treatment to the minority groups in their territory. This was a particular concern of the League of Nations, founded in 1919, which supported treaties to respect the rights of specific minorities, including religious minorities, within particular countries. There remained, however, an element of extra-territoriality – the treatment of the individual raised issues between two States. Henkin explains even the minority rights treaties in this way: '[p]owerful States promoted minorities treaties because mistreatment of minorities with which other States identified threatened international peace. Those treaties were imposed selectively, principally on nations defeated in war and on newly created or enlarged States; they did not establish general norms requiring respect for minorities by the big and the powerful as well; they did not require respect for individuals who were not members of identified minorities, or who were members of the majority' (Henkin, 1989 at 208). The development of human rights regimes since the formation of the United Nations in 1945 marks, therefore, a watershed in international law.

The principal function of the UN was to secure and maintain peace, and there are only a few references to human rights in the founding document of the UN, the United Nations Charter. One purpose of the UN was the promotion and encouragement of respect for human rights and fundamental freedoms for all without distinction as to race, sex, language or religion (UN Charter, art.1), and the General Assembly, a key organ of the UN, was expected to make recommendations regarding the realisation of human rights for all (UN Charter, art.13). Although there were no enforcement mechanisms within the Charter, and the content of human rights was not described, it did provide for the establishment of a Commission to promote human rights (UN Charter, art.68).

The Commission, the UNCHR, was formed in 1946. Its early tasks included the drafting of an international Bill of Rights (Alston, 1992). Initially, the UNCHR put forward a document intended as a common standard of achievement for all nations, rather than a legal document – the Universal Declaration of Human Rights (the UDHR). The UDHR emerged from a context, according to its own preamble, where: 'disregard and contempt for human rights have resulted in barbarous acts which have outraged the conscience of mankind, and the advent of a world in which human beings shall enjoy freedom of speech and belief and freedom from fear and want had been proclaimed as the highest aspiration of the common people' (UDHR, preamble).

The UDHR contained an extensive range of rights, such as liberty and security of the person (UDHR, art.3); due process (UDHR, art.9,10); freedom of expression (UDHR, art.19); and social and economic rights such as the right to social security (UDHR, art.25), and to an education (UDHR, art.26). The UDHR included a provision dealing specifically with religious rights (Scheinin, 1999). Article 18 provides: 'Everyone has the right to freedom of thought, conscience and religion; this right includes freedom to change his religion or belief, and freedom, either alone or in community with others and in public or private, to manifest his religion or belief in teaching, practice, worship and observance'. Although the UDHR was not legally enforceable, its influence was considerable, especially as treaties intended to implement it did not come into force until 1976 (Steiner and Alson, 1996 at 120).

It was intended that the UDHR should be followed by more detailed and comprehensive provisions in a form that would be ratified by, and binding upon, the member States of the United Nations. This process was more complicated and protracted than originally envisaged. In 1952 it was decided that the UDHR should be given effect, not by a single Convention, but by two documents – the International Covenant on Civil and Political Rights (ICCPR), and the International Covenant on Economic, Social and Cultural Rights (ICESCR). Both Conventions came into force in 1976.

The ICCPR differs in a number of ways from the UDHR (see Cumper, 1995). Firstly, while the UDHR recommends the values that States should observe, the ICCPR binds those States to observe its guarantees. In particular, the States agree to ensure to all within their jurisdiction the rights guaranteed, if necessary taking legislative or other action to do so (ICCPR, art.2). Secondly, the ICCPR establishes an institution to support its values. The Human Rights Committee (HRC) has a number of roles, including consideration of periodic reports from member States (see Evans, 2000). Thirdly, in part as a consequence of the legally binding nature of the ICCPR, the rights declared are more detailed. This includes an explicit recognition of when it is appropriate for the State to violate a prima facie right.

The non-discrimination guarantee under the ICCPR covers discrimination on the grounds of religion (ICCPR, art.2(1)). The most relevant guarantee in the ICCPR is contained in Article 18. Article 18(1) guarantees everyone the freedom of thought, conscience and religion, which includes 'freedom to have or to adopt a religion or belief of his choice, and freedom, either individually or in community with others and in public or in private, to manifest his religion or belief in worship, observance, practice and teaching'. Article 18(3) provides that manifesting religion or belief 'may be subject only to such limitations as are prescribed by law and are necessary to protect public safety, order, health or morals or the fundamental rights and freedoms of others'. Article 18(2) deals with a more specific point, forbidding coercion which would impair an individual's freedom to have or adopt a religion or belief of their choice. Article 18(4) also deals with a specific issue, the obligation of the State to 'have respect for the liberty of parents and, when applicable, legal guardians to ensure the religious and moral education of their children in conformity with their own convictions'.

As with many international and constitutional guarantees in this area, the interest guaranteed goes beyond religion alone. Rather, freedom of thought and conscience are entitled to equal protection under the Article (Human Rights Committee, General Comment 22, para.1). As Cumper notes, 'Article 18 is not restricted to the protection of long established religions. Instead it covers theistic, non-theistic, and atheistic beliefs, as well as the right not to profess any religion or belief' (Cumper, 1995 at 358). Although the Human Rights Committee has indicated that religion and belief should be widely construed (Human Rights Committee, General Comment 22, para.2), it has not provided a clear definition of either term.

The right outlined in Article 18(1) includes not only the right to have a religion or belief but, more concretely, the right to manifest that religion or belief in 'worship, observance, practice and teaching'. Worship has been interpreted to include 'ritual and ceremonial acts giving direct expression to belief as well as various practices integral to such acts' (Human Rights Committee, General Comment 22, para.4), and so is capable of being extended to the construction of places of worship and observance of religious holidays. Observance and practice constitute wider terms, capable of covering much conduct directly related to a religious conviction, including dress, grooming customs such as the cutting of hair or the growing of beards, and special diets. Teaching is not limited to formal religious education for adherents of the same faith, but can also encompass proselytism, including the distribution of religious texts and publications (Stahnke, 1999).

This manifestation of religion or belief is subject to the restrictions outlined in Article 18(3), although it is important to note that these do not apply to the right to have or adopt a particular religion or belief, which is an absolute right. For the State to justify a restriction of the Article 18(1) rights, it must demonstrate that the restriction is 'directly related and proportionate to' one of the listed aims of protecting public safety, order, health or morals or the fundamental rights and freedoms of others (Human Rights Committee, General Comment 22, para.8.).

Of more specific focus than the general guarantee in Article 18(1), Article 18(2) repeats part of that Article, but in a way that emphasises the importance of having or adopting a religion or belief free of coercion. Although the text does not refer to changing of religion or belief explicitly, it would seem implicit in the reference to adopting a religion or belief – potentially controversial for religions which do not incorporate a broad freedom for members to dissociate themselves from it (see Arzt, 1996). Thus, coercion may not be used to impair the freedom of the individual to retain their current beliefs, or adopt new ones. Coercion clearly covers physical force or threats, as well as the use or threat of criminal sanctions (see Cumper, op.cit., at 370–1). The HRC has suggested that restriction of access to benefits such as education, medical care and employment can also constitute coercion. The position of extreme emotional or psychological pressure is less clear.

The influence of these guarantees is difficult to gauge (McGoldrick, 1991). In particular, it should be noted that the ICCPR lacks strong enforcement mechanisms

(Ghandi, 1998). State Parties are required to report on the measures they have taken to give effect to their obligations under the ICCPR, which may be reported on by the HRC (ICCPR, art.40). State parties generally submit such a report every five years, but reports are often submitted late, and may be put in abstract, formalised terms that reduce their value as an accurate statement of the situation within the jurisdiction. Strengthening this mechanism, States may choose to accept an additional part of the ICCPR, which authorises the HRC to consider complaints from individuals claiming to be the victims of ICCPR violations, and for the Committee to forward its views about these communications (First Optional Protocol to the ICCPR). Any views the HRC forms on a complaint 'are not to be understood as strictly binding in law and cannot be enforced' (Opsahl, 1992).

Both the UDHR and the ICCPR deal with religious rights as part of a parcel of fundamental human rights. The UN is responsible for more specific international agreements, however, which can have clear application to religious interests (Tahzbib, 1996). A number are of particular interest. The Convention on the Prevention and Punishment of Genocide defines genocide as prohibited conduct committed 'with intent to destroy, in whole or in part, a national, ethnical, racial or religious group as such'. Prohibited conducts include killing members of the group, causing serious physical or mental harm to them, deliberately inflicting conditions on the group calculated to bring about its physical destruction, imposing measures intended to prevent births within the group, and forcibly transferring children of the group to another group. The International Convention on the Elimination of All Forms of Racial Discrimination 1965 has some application to religious discrimination, as the Convention includes discrimination based on ethnic origin, which can include a religious element. The protection of minority rights can, in a similar way, involve an indirect protection of the religious interest (Dinstein, 1992).

The most specific additional instrument, however, is the Declaration on the Elimination of All Forms of Intolerance and of Discrimination Based on Religion or Belief (on which see Sullivan, 1988). This directly addresses discrimination based on the grounds of religion or belief, including theistic, non-theistic and atheistic beliefs. The Declaration lacks the status of an international agreement, and strong enforcement mechanisms, but does lay down norms of conduct and has been supported by special rapporteurs examining compliance. Article 1 provides a religious freedom guarantee very similar to ICCPR art.18, but this is supplemented by an article dealing purely with non-discrimination. Article 2 states: '(1) No one shall be subject to discrimination by any State, institution, group of persons, or person on grounds of religion or other beliefs. (2) For the purposes of the present Declaration, the expression "intolerance and discrimination based on religion or belief" means any distinction, exclusion, restriction or preference based on religion or belief and having as its purpose or effect nullification or impairment of the recognition, enjoyment or exercise of human rights and fundamental freedoms on an equal basis'.

The non-discrimination guarantee prohibits intentional and non-intentional discrimination by both the State and private individuals and bodies. Additionally, the State is required to take positive measures against religious discrimination (Declaration, art.4). The State is also required to take appropriate measures to combat intolerance, which Sullivan sees as 'the emotional, psychological, philosophical and religious attitudes that may prompt acts of discrimination or violations of religious freedom' (op.cit.).

The UN guarantees lack strong mechanisms by which violations by States may be investigated, the rights of individual victims clearly and authoritatively stated, and provision made for remedial action. In part, the relative weakness of the enforcement mechanisms under the UN guarantees may be a practical consequence of its global application. In relation to the ICCPR, for instance, for the HRC to take on a more forceful role in enforcement it would need to develop an organisation capable of holding hearings and determining facts in relation to violations across the world. The range of languages which the HRC would need to be able to deal with, and the sheer volume of possible investigations, could be enormous. Instead, as we will see in following sections, a number of regional human rights schemes have been developed. Adopting human rights guarantees modeled on the ICCPR, these regional schemes address similar concerns in a narrower range of countries, which offers logistical, diplomatic, and cultural advantages.

Regional Human Rights Documents: The ECHR

The States dealt with in this text are, between them, members of a number of important regional human rights mechanisms. For instance, the United States have ratified the American Convention on Human Rights, while not accepting the jurisdiction of the associated Court; and South Africa has ratified the African Charter on Human and Peoples' Rights. In this section I will discuss what is perhaps the best developed and most influential of these regional mechanisms, the European Convention on Human Rights (see generally Evans, 1996; Evans, 1999; Evans, 2001). The United Kingdom is a signatory to the ECHR and, as we will see, has recently taken steps to give it more direct effect in domestic law.

The ECHR represents both a regional manifestation of international concern with fundamental human rights, and part of a broader agenda of closer European union. In the Statute of the Council of Europe 1949, the member States reaffirmed a common heritage, and stated that one of its aims was 'to achieve a greater union between its Members', in part through 'the maintenance and further realisation of human rights and fundamental freedoms'. This movement for European union manifested itself through a range of different bodies, which it is important to keep distinct. In particular, it is important not to conflate the European Union (EU) with the ECHR. The laws of the EU are capable of direct application to the legal systems of the relatively small membership of the EU, while Convention rights are rules of international law, governing at that level a much larger group of nations. Additionally: '[t]he kind of issues dealt with by the EC/EU ... do not primarily relate to the religious liberty of the individual, but touch upon more collective and structural matters. EC activity stretches, for example, to: labour law (including legislation on working hours), privacy legislation, mass media law, taxation and the law relating to legal persons. Here, indirect burdens on religious exercise are considered. One example is taxation, where religious purposes and organizations are mentioned in the conditional exception, along with charitable and social institutions. Other instances are more symbolic in nature. The Council Directive relating to trade marks, for example, allows refusal of registrations should offence be given to religion' (van Bijsterveld, 2000 at 174).

If the ECHR is not as immediately applicable to domestic law as the laws of the EU, it is still fair to say that the mechanisms by which it is enforced represented a major advance on the international guarantees discussed above. There are two strong enforcement provisions under the Convention. The less frequently used is the inter-state case, by which a member State alleges that another State has failed to meet its obligations under the Convention (ECHR, art.33). More significant is the individual application, which was intended to 'provide an international remedy for an individual whose rights had been infringed by a sovereign State. A person would, in his or her individual capacity, have direct recourse to an international organ ... and ... a State could be brought before the Court if a case was taken up' (Robertson and Merills, 1993 at 8–9). Applications could be considered by State organs, initially the European Commission and Court of Human Rights but now the Court acting alone (see Bratza and O'Boyle, 1997). The member States are bound by the finding, and, although in some member States, this judgement does not directly alter domestic law, the relatively close-knit nature of the States signatory to the Convention makes direct, explicit, disobedience to such a ruling unlikely in most cases. It is possible, however, for a State to make the minimum change possible to the law, awaiting further judgements against it before it amends the law further; or to delay for some considerable period making any changes required.

From its inception, the Convention was intended to provide relatively strong protection for a relatively narrow range of fundamental rights and freedoms. Many of the rights found in the UDHR were not included in the Convention, which focuses on 'those rights and essential freedoms which are practised after long usage and experience in all the democratic countries. While they are the first triumph of democratic regimes, they are also the necessary conditions under which they operate' (Consultative Assembly of the Council of Europe, Official Report, 7 September 1949 at 127). Amongst these rights are several dealing explicitly with religious interests. Before moving on to discuss the relevant provisions, however, it is worth reiterating a warning from the previous chapter. In the discussion of legislation, I pointed out the significance of understanding judicial rulings on particular instruments, and not simply looking to the bare text of legislation in order to state the law. This also applies to international law. In relation to the ECHR, the instrument should be seen as a living instrument, whose meaning and application has been substantially developed by the European organs set up under the Convention. As an example, when the Convention was drafted in 1950, and indeed for some decades thereafter, some member States had an explicit, clear, and well-understood prohibition on some forms of sexual activity between men. The Convention does not contain any express guarantee against discrimination on the grounds of sexual orientation, or a right to commit homosexual acts, or for that matter heterosexual acts. Developments in the right to privacy, however, have made it clear that the State cannot prohibit male homosexual activity simpliciter (*Dudgeon v United Kingdom* (1981) 4 EHRR 139 (ECHR)). Thus, the meaning of the Convention, and so the obligations upon the member States, has been developed by the Convention organs. In doing so, they seek to realise the objectives and purposes of the ECHR (*Wemhoff v Germany* (1979–80) 1 EHRR 55 (ECHR)), and are not bound by the beliefs, practices, and laws present during the drafting of the Convention (*Tyrer v United Kingdom* (1981) 2 EHRR 1 (ECHR)). Thus, in the discussion that follows it is necessary to refer to the findings of the Commission and Court.

For our purposes the most important guarantees under the ECHR are found in Article 9. Article 9 does not stand alone, however, but is simply one component of a broader scheme. This can reduce its scope. As a general principle, the organs of the ECHR deal with claims in relation to the most specific guarantee. In *Johnston v Ireland* (1986) 8 EHRR 214 (ECHR), for instance the Commission chose not to deal with a claimed right to divorce under Article 9, but rather under the more specific provisions dealing with the right to marry (ECHR art.12) and the right to respect for a private life (ECHR art.8). This rule, coupled with a reluctance by the ECHR organs to deal with freedom of religion unless absolutely unavoidable, resulted in a relative shortage of Article 9 jurisprudence until recently (see Gunn, 1996; Stavros, 1997). Article 9 can also be enlarged by its place within the ECHR. Although non-discrimination now has a distinctive place within the Convention regime (see Moon, 2000), in the original system it was dealt with by Article 14 (see Livingstone, 1997). This Article provided that the rights elsewhere in the Convention were to be 'secured without discrimination on any ground such as sex, race, colour, language, religion, political or other opinion, national or social origin, association with a national minority, property, birth or other status'. Because of Article 14: 'a measure which in itself is in conformity with the requirements of the Article enshrining the right or freedom in question may, however, infringe this Article when read in conjunction with Article 14 for the reason that is of a discriminatory nature' (*Belgian Linguistics Case* (1968) 1 EHRR 252 (ECHR)). Not every instance of differential treatment is discrimination, however, as the State may seek to justify its differential treatment. This will fail if the distinction has no objective and reasonable justification, or there is no reasonable relationship of proportionality between the means employed and the aim sought to be realised (ibid.).

The application of Article 14 to religious interests has tended to be patchy and cautious (contrast for instance *Wingrove v United Kingdom* (1997) 24 EHRR 1 (ECHR) with *Tsirlis v Greece* (1996) 21 EHRR CD30 (ECHR). This may be changing. In *Thlimmenos v Greece* (2000) HUDOC 6 April (ECHR), a Jehovah's Witness had been convicted of felony for refusing to serve in the armed forces, and served a prison sentence. Fifteen years later he passed examinations in chartered accountancy, but was refused entry into that profession as a felon. The Government defended this application of the law as neutral, and unconcerned with the religious beliefs of the applicant. The Court disagreed, finding that '[t]he right not to be discriminated against in the enjoyment of the rights guaranteed under the Convention is also violated when States without an objective and reasonable justification fail to treat differently persons whose situations are significantly different' (ibid., para. 4.4). If this approach finds favour, the State may be required to take account of the different impacts of its actions upon members of different religious communities.

Article 9 consists of an absolute right to freedom of thought, conscience and religion, including the right to change religion; a right to manifest such a belief; and a number of qualifications to the right to manifest, which allow the State to impose limits on manifestation. The article provides: '(1). Everyone has the right to freedom of thought, conscience and religion; this right includes freedom to change his religion or belief and freedom, either alone or in community with others and in private or public, to manifest his religion or belief, in worship, teaching, practice and observance. (2). Freedom to manifest one's religion or beliefs shall be subject only to such limitations as are prescribed by law and are necessary in a democratic society in the interests of public safety, for the protection of public order, health or morals, or for the protection of the rights and freedoms of others'.

As with the ICCPR, the right protected by the ECHR extends beyond religion simpliciter, to encompass thought, conscience, and religion. The definition of religion under the ECHR is a matter for the Convention organs, rather than self-identification by the claimant (*M'Feeley v United Kingdom* (1980) EHRR 161 (ECHR). There is relatively little guidance on how the ambit of Article 9 is to be interpreted.

In terms of the content of the belief system, the ECHR has accepted Islam (*Ahmad v United Kingdom* (1982) 4 EHRR 126 (ECHR)), Krishna Consciousness (*ISKCON v United Kingdom* (1994) 76A DR 90 (ECHR)), Jehovah's Witnesses (*Kokkinakis v Greece* (1994) 17 EHRR 397 (ECHR)), the Divine Light Zentrum (*Omkarananda and the Divine Light Zentrum v Sweden* (1981) 25 DR 105 (ECHR)), and the Church of Scientology (*X and Church of Scientology v Sweden* (1976) 16 DR 68 (ECHR)). A metaphysical element is not required, however, as ethical or philosophical convictions such as opposition to abortion (*Knudsen v Norway* (1986) 8 EHRR 45 (ECHR)), pacifism (*Arrowsmith v United Kingdom* (1978) 3 EHRR 218 (ECHR)), or veganism (*H v United Kingdom* (1993) 16 EHRR CD44 (ECHR)) are also protected.

Although the beliefs protected are not to be categorised by their content, there is a suggestion in the jurisprudence that the beliefs must be distinguishable from mere opinion or idealism (*Vereniging Rechtswinkels Utrecht v Netherlands* (1986) 46 DR 200 (ECHR)), and 'attain a certain level of cogency, seriousness, cohesion and importance' (*Campbell and Cosans* (1982) HUDOC 25 February (ECHR)). The requirement of cohesion may explain the difficulties of Wicca and Druidry in receiving unequivocal recognition as religions under the Convention (see *X v UK*, (1977) 11 DR 55 (ECHR); *Chappell v United Kingdom* (1988) 10 EHRR 503 (ECHR); *Pendragon v United Kingdom* (1998) HUDOC 19 October (ECHR)). It may be that cohesion and comprehensiveness are not, however, necessary to claim Article 9 protection, as single issues can ground a claim (Evans, 1997 at 291–3).

Once a system has been found to fall within the ambit of Article 9, the most powerful protection is extended to the absolute right to freedom of belief. This right requires the State to respect the beliefs of the individual. In particular, it 'affords protection against indoctrination of religion by the State' (*Angelini v Sweden* (1988) 10 EHRR 123 (ECHR)), and can also require the State to protect the individual against such improper influence to change their beliefs (*Kokkinakis v Greece* (1994) 17 EHRR 397 (ECHR)). This right is unqualified – that is to say, the State cannot disregard the right in order to protect some other interest.

This is not as startling as may appear, however, as the right is basically internal: the right of the individual to be free of attempts to change their beliefs or indoctrinate them. Actions other than the simple holding of belief are manifestations of that belief, discussed below. It may be, however, that the ambit of this absolute right goes a little beyond the right not to be indoctrinated, 'brainwashed' or subject to autonomy infringing persuasion techniques. Reporting on article 18 of the ICCPR, as discussed above, the HRC stated that no one could be compelled to reveal his thoughts or adherance to a religion in terms that indicated this was a part of the absolute right to freedom of thought and belief (General Comment 22, para.3; Harris et al., 1995 at 361). The similarities between the ECHR and the ICCPR are so close as to make this of persuasive authority in understanding the scope of the ECHR.

There are strong policy reasons for wishing to restrict the power of the State to require individuals to provide information about their religious beliefs. As we can see from the Convention for the Protection of Individuals with Regard to Automatic Processing of Data 1981, religious affilation is sensitive information, and important to a State wishing to persecute a particular religious community efficiently. Even if that is not the purpose of the enquiry, members of religious communities which have historically been subjected to adverse action by the State in question may interpret it that way. More abstractly, an individual's thoughts and beliefs, rather than their actions, seem to be central to the concept of privacy. Perhaps the State should not be able to compel us to reveal what we think and believe, although it may seek to determine what we know and remember?

The problem with compacting this area into the absolute right to freedom of belief is that the State is thereby prevented from justifying such activity – even if there are strong arguments supporting its actions. For example, let us posit a religious community whose practices include a religious meeting at which rigorous steps are taken to ensure that only those who have made a commitment to the religion are present. During the meeting a sum of money is taken from a coat-pocket, in an area where only co-religionists were present. Arguably, if the police or courts require witness statements from those present, they are requiring them to state their religious beliefs, albeit indirectly. If this is absolutely prohibited, then the possible witnesses are able to refuse to assist the legal authorities, no matter how pressing the State interest in dealing with crime. It is possible to argue about whether the State is actually justified in requiring this information, but I would suggest that it is relatively easy to imagine an instance when the State would be justified in doing so, not least to protect the fundamental human rights of others. If there is an absolute right to remain silent on this point, however, justification is never possible within Article 9, although other parts of the ECHR may reduce the impact of this problem (for example, ECHR, art. 17).

The exclusion of this topic from the absolute right receives some support from the cases. The Commission has dealt with this issue, not as a religious right, but as primarily concerning the (qualified) right to privacy under Article 8. In *CJ, JJ and EJ v Poland* (1996) HUDOC 16 January (ECHR), the applicants argued that for a child to be required to opt out of religious education constituted a forced declaration of their religious convictions. The Commission found that a right to silence as to convictions was a personal right – a father could not complain that his childrens' declarations allowed inferences to be made as to his convictions. In relation to the children, the Commission noted that rights under Article 8 were not absolute, and in this case the opt-out did not amount to a violation of Article 8. In particular: '[t]he act of choice of religion or ethics as a school subject by its very nature entails, to a certain extent, a declaration as to the applicant's preferences, without necessarily revealing his or her religious beliefs or denomination'. The Commission did consider Article 9, but not in relation to the declaration, which they clearly saw as falling within the ambit of Article 8.

Of much greater practical importance than the absolute right, if only because it is more likely to be subject to State restriction and thus appeals to the ECHR, is the qualified right to manifest those beliefs. Manifestation of belief can take a number of forms. Most obviously, this includes religious worship (*Holy Monasteries v Greece* (1994) 20 EHRR 1 (ECHR)); educating oneself or others in the belief (*Kjeldsen, Busk Madsen and Pedersen v Denmark* (1976) 1 EHRR 711 (ECHR)); exercising a role in a religious community (*Hasan and Chaush v Bulgaria* (2000) HUDOC 26 October (ECHR)); proselytising, or attempting to spread the belief amongst others (*Arrowsmith v United Kingdom* (1978) 3 EHRR 218 (ECHR)); proclaiming belief publicly (*App.9820/82 v Sweden* (1982) 5 EHRR 297 (ECHR)); or observing dietary or similar prohibitions, including ritual slaughter (*The Jewish Liturgical Association Che'are Shalom ve Tsedek* (2000) HUDOC 27 June (ECHR)). These are unexceptional examples of manifesting religions historically present in the founding jurisdictions of the ECHR. A similar range can be found in The Declaration on the Elimination of All Forms of Intolerance and of Discrimination Based on Religion or Belief, 1981 which includes a non-exhaustive list of manifestations including worship and religious assembly, and the maintenance of places to do so; establishing charitable and humanitarian institutions; making, acquiring and using articles related to rites or customs; production of relevant publication; religious teaching; fundraising; training and appointment of religious leaders; observance of days of rest, holidays and religious ceremonies; and establishing communities (Declaration, art.6). How much further does manifestation extend?

In *Arrowsmith v United Kingdom* (1978) 3 EHRR 218 (ECHR) the applicant had been convicted under a United Kingdom statute for distributing leaflets intended to 'seduce' troops from their allegiance in relation to service in Northern Ireland. She claimed that this was a violation of her right to manifest her pacifism under Article 9. Not every part of the leaflet endorsed pacifist philosophy, and it did not constitute a general call for persons to give up all violence. The Commission noted: 'The Commission considers that the term "practise" as employed in Article 9(1) does not cover every act which is motivated or influenced by a religion or belief ... when the actions of individuals do not actually express the belief concerned they cannot be considered to be as such protected by Article 9(1), even when motivated or influenced by it' (ibid., para. 71).

Later cases support the view that religious motivation is not sufficient to bring Article 9 into effect – there must be some characteristic about the activity itself that is of a religious or conscientious nature. In *C v United Kingdom* (1983) 37 DR 142 (ECHR) the Commission saw the guarantee as protecting private 'acts which are intimately linked to [protected] attitudes, such as acts of worship or devotion which are aspects of the practice of religion or belief in a generally recognized form' (ibid., at 147). Thus, participating in an action designed to provoke a strike in public civil service (*App.10365/83 v Germany*, (1985) 7 EHRR 409 (ECHR)), refusing to perform administrative functions following from a position in a state religion (*Knudsen v Norway* (1985) 8 EHRR 45 (ECHR)), or to pay taxes towards state revenue used to fund objectionable purposes (*Bouessel de Bourg v France* (1993) 16 EHRR CD49 (ECHR)), or seeking the right to be killed during a terminal illness (*Pretty v UK* (2002) HUDOC 29 April (ECHR)) do not fall within Article 9. The behaviour must, rather, be 'the direct expression of a religious or philosophical conviction' (*Faclini v Switzerland*, (1993) 16 EHRR CD13 (ECHR), perhaps even an expression necessary under the religious system, rather than merely optional or desirable (Evans, 1999 at 394).

The construction placed on the applicant's actions by the ECHR organs is crucial in determining this. In *Stedman v United Kingdom* (1997) HUDOC 9 April (ECHR), for instance, the applicant had been dismissed for refusing to work on a Sunday, that day being a day of rest under her religion. The Commission found that although her refusal was religiously motivated, she had been dismissed for refusing to work particular hours rather than because of her religious beliefs as such. Similarly, in *van Den Dungen v Netherlands* (1995) HUDOC 22 February (ECHR), the applicant had been banned from the vicinity of an abortion clinic, where he had been addressing staff and patients, distributing leaflets, and attempting to dissuade those he addressed from involvement in abortions. This material included images of Christ, but the Commission held that: 'the applicant's activities were primarily aimed at persuading women not to have an abortion. The Commission considers that the activities at issue do not constitute the expression of a belief within the meaning of Article 9' (ibid., para.1).

Although a religious motivation may not suffice to bring an action within the protection of Article 9, it would seem to be a prerequisite – there must be some connection between the action and a belief system protected by the article. In *X and Church of Scientology v Sweden* (1979) 16 DR 68 (ECHR), the Commission considered whether placing an advertisement for an e-meter, a device central to the core practices of mainstream Scientology, constituted a manifestation of religion. The Commission felt not: 'the manifestation of a belief in practice does not confer protection on statements of purported religious belief which appear as selling "arguments" in advertisements of a purely commercial nature by a religious group ... the Commission would draw a distinction ... between advertisements which are merely "informational" or "descriptive" in character and commercial advertisements, offering objects for sale. Once an advertisement enters into the latter sphere .... [it is] more the manifestation of a desire to market goods for practice than the manifestation of a belief in practice' (ibid., at 72).

Once an activity is characterised as a manifestation of religion, it may still be restricted by the State. In the discussion of religious interests at the beginning of this chapter, I indicated that religious interests were not a trump value, but rather needed to be balanced with competing interests. Under Article 9, this is done primarily through the qualifications in Article 9(2). Under Article 9(2) manifestation may be restricted by limitations proscribed by law that are necessary in a democratic society in the interests of public safety, for the protection of public order, health or morals, or for the protection of the rights and freedoms of others. These restrictions are similar to those found in other Articles in the Convention, and have been applied in a similar way by the Commission and the Court (see Starmer, 1999 at 165–80).

The State must be able to point to a legal proscription on the manifestation, rather than simply pointing to factors justifying the restriction (see *Hasan and Chaush v Bulgaria* (2000) HUDOC 26 October (ECHR)). Where the State seeks to justify a legal restriction, the Court has recognised that its role is not to second-guess the domestic authorities (*Handyside v United Kingdom* (1979–80) 1 EHRR 737 (ECHR)), but rather to act as a Court of review, ensuring the decisions of local bodies fall within the national margin of appreciation (see generally Lavender, 1997). In *Wingrove v United Kingdom* (1997) 24 EHRR 1 (ECHR), while the Court stressed its ultimate responsibility to rule on compatibility with the Convention, it emphasised European diversity in this area, stressing that generally the State was in the best position to assess the demands of the vital forces within its jurisdiction. In particular instances, the importance of the manifestation being restricted may require a narrower margin – that is, a tighter control on the State's decision making. In *Manoussakis and Others v Greece* (1996) 23 EHRR 387 (ECHR), the applicants had been prosecuted and convicted for having established a place of worship without prior authorisation. The Court considered that 'in delimiting the extent of the margin of appreciation in the present case the Court must have regard to what is at stake, namely the need to secure true religious pluralism, an inherent feature of the notion of a democratic society' (ibid., para.44). In *Serif v Greece* (1999) HUDOC 14 December (ECHR), the Court took an extremely strong stance on State interference with disputes between religious communities, finding that criminalising a leadership role in a religious community could not be justified.

Although the argument for a tighter monitoring of especially significant interests seems a strong one, it is less clear that the religious diversity in Europe justifies a much lighter degree of monitoring in relation to other questions. On the contrary, it might be argued that this diversity increases the need for central monitoring. In *ISKCON v United Kingdom* (1994) 18 EHRR CD 133 (ECHR), for instance, the applicant argued that 'in an increasingly ethnically diverse Europe, the Commission should not hesitate, in a appropriate case, to adopt a narrow margin of appreciation under Article 9'.

Whatever the size of the margin of appreciation, the Court has been prepared to find that State action falls outside it, but it has not laid down much in the way of general principles that provide guidance as to how State action is to be assessed. A number of examples may, however, give a flavour of the Court's approach. In *Ahmad v United Kingdom* (1981) 4 EHRR 165 (ECHR), the applicant complained that he had been forced to resign from his full-time teaching post because he was refused permission to attend a mosque for the purposes of worship. The Commission found this restriction was permitted under Article 9(2) on the basis that 'the school authorities, in their treatment of the applicant's case on the basis of his contract ... had to have regard not only to his religious position, but also to the requirements of the education system as a whole' (ibid., para.19). In *Application 9820/82 v Sweden* (1982) 5 EHRR 297 (ECHR), the applicant had been convicted for insisting on repeatedly proclaiming in a loud voice the dangers of pornography, fornication, and alcohol. The Commission found that the violation of Article 9(1) was justified, noting that only shouting was restricted, rather than communication of his religious views generally. In *Chappell v United Kingdom* (1988) 10 EHRR 503 (ECHR), the applicant complained that the decision to close Stonehenge during the midsummer solstice and prevent Druids from practising their solstice ceremony was a violation of Article 9. The Commission avoided deciding whether Article 9 had been violated by finding that, even if it had, the action was justified as protecting 'the unique historical and archaeological importance of Stonehenge. The Commission concluded that the decision was a necessary public safety measure'. In the similar case of *Pendragon v United Kingdom* (1998) HUDOC 19 October (ECHR), which also concerned solstice celebrations at Stonehenge, the Commission preferred to found its decision exclusively on the need to keep public order. In *ISKCON v United Kingdom* (1994) 76A DR 90 (ECHR), the applicants had established a religious centre in a country manor, which was attracting increasing numbers of visitors. They argued that restrictions placed upon their use of the manor by planning controls constituted a violation of Article 9. The Commission found that the legislation as applied was aimed at protecting the rights of the residents of nearby villages, as well as protecting public order and health, and was justified. In *Williamson v United Kingdom* (1995) HUDOC 17 May (ECHR), a Church of England priest who claimed that the ordination of women within his Church violated his Article 9 rights failed, in part on the basis that the change was intended to reduce discrimination on grounds of gender. In *The Jewish Liturgical Association Cha'are Shalom ve Tsedek* (2000) HUDOC 27 June (ECHR), a restriction on lawful ritual slaughter to individuals associated with a particular branch of Judaism was found to be justified on the grounds of public health, in relation to the regulation of slaughterhouses, or public order, in relation to the regulation of orderly Church/State relations. In *Palau-Martinez v France*

((2003) HUDOC 16 December (ECHR)), a child custody decision against a Jehovah's Witness was found to violate her rights because 'a harsh analysis of the principles regarding child-rearing allegedly imposed by this religion' was not matched with consideration of her particular conduct. In *Agga v Greece* ((2002) HUDOC 17 October (ECHR)), bans on an individual presenting himself as a religious leader of a group that willingly followed him, and other measures to prevent division in leadership of a religious community, were disproportionate as a means of securing public order. In *Leyla Sakin v Turkey* ((2004) HUDOC 29 June (ECHR)) a university banned students from attending classes if wearing an Islamic headscarf or beard. The restriction was justified in the context of Turkey as protecting the rights and interests of others, and protecting public order by protecting secularism in a majority Islamic state.

The most difficult cases deal with conflicts between Convention entitlements of individuals, rather than the more explicit heads of State interest. In *Kokkinakis v Greece* (1994) 17 EHRR 397 (ECHR), the applicant, a Greek national and Jehovah's Witness, was invited into an Orthodox Christian's home and entered into a discussion with her. Her husband, a cantor of the Orthodox Church, called the police. The applicant was convicted of proselytism and fined. He claimed a violation of his right to manifest his religion under Article 9. The majority of the court recognised a tension between the interests of a believer in proselytising, and respect for the beliefs of non-believers. In particular, they drew an important distinction between proper and improper proselytism that, because it had not been considered in relation to the applicant, established a violation of Article 9: 'a distinction has to be drawn between bearing Christian witness and improper proselytism ... The latter represents a corruption or deformation of [true evangelism]. It may ... take the form of activities offering material or social advantages with a view to gaining new members for a Church or exerting improper pressure on people in distress or need; it may even entail the use of violence or brainwashing; more generally, it is not compatible with respect for the freedom of thought, conscience and religion of others' (ibid., para.48). Thus, the ECHR enshrines a right to proselytise, but limitations may legitimately be imposed on some methods of proselytising, particularly where power relationships exist external to the proselytising relationship (*Larissis and Others v Greece*, (1998) HUDOC 28 December (ECHR)). Indeed, the State has a duty to protect the freedom of the individual from infringement by such means – a positive duty not unusual in Convention jurisprudence.

In the later case of *Otto-Preminger-Institut v Austria* (1994) 19 EHRR 34 (ECHR), the court considered an application under the freedom of expression guarantee of Article 10. The applicant had announced public showings of a satirical film with a religious subject matter at a cinema. Before the first showing, the film was seized and later forfeited. The State sought to justify its action under Article 10(2) as being for the protection of the rights of others – in this case, in order to protect religious feelings. The Commission found that preserving religious peace was a legitimate aim, but that the action in this case had been disproportionate, and therefore not justified under Article 10(2). The case reached the court, which found that it was a legitimate Convention aim to 'protect the right of citizens not to be insulted in their religious feelings by the public expression of views of other persons' (ibid., at para. 48). In particular, they grounded this right in Article 9 of the Convention. On this basis, the court found that the applicant could be required to 'avoid as far as possible expressions that are gratuitously offensive to others and thus an infringement of their rights' (ibid., at para.49). The court considered that, given the high proportion of adherents of the religious system being satirised in the region, the restriction on the applicant was justified in this case. In this case, the court suggested that offending another's religious beliefs could restrict their manifestation of those beliefs because 'in extreme cases the effect of particular methods of opposing or denying religious beliefs can be such as to inhibit those who hold such beliefs from exercising their freedom to hold and express them' (ibid., para.47). Although later endorsed (for instance in *Refah Partisi v Turkey* (2002) HUDOC 17 October (ECHR)), this approach does not seem fully compatible with other cases, where an applicant had sought to argue that State action inhibited their religious life (e.g. *Logan v United Kingdom* (1996) 22 EHRR CD178 (ECHR), *Holy Monasteries v Greece*, (1994) 20 EHRR 1 (ECHR); *Paradis v Sweden* (1997) HUDOC 2 July (ECHR)). This raises the intriguing possibility that the court may be willing to frame Article 9 rights in broader terms when called upon to restrict the individual than when used as a protection against State power.

The specific restrictions allowed by Article 9(2) are supplemented by generally applicable provisions in the ECHR. Article 17 provides that Convention rights may not be used in order to destroy or limit the rights of others. This does not deprive individuals opposed to particular parts of the ECHR of their Convention rights, but instead serves to prevent them using the Convention as a shield from State action taken to protect the rights of others (*Lawless v Ireland (no.2)* (1961) 1 EHRR 13 (ECHR)). In *Glimmerveen and Hagenbeek v The Netherlands* (1979) 4 EHRR 260 (ECHR), the applicants were members of a party believing in the racial homogeneity of nations. They were convicted of distributing a leaflet inciting racial discrimination, and pleaded a violation of Article 10, although an Article 9 violation would seem to be as sound. The Commission found that Article 17 applied, as they were 'essentially seeking to use article 10 to provide a basis under the Convention for a right to engage in these activities which are, as shown above, contrary to the text and spirit of the Convention and which right, if granted, would contribute to the destruction of the rights and freedoms referred to above' (ibid., para.22). Additionally, the provisions of the Convention, including Article 9, can be disregarded in times of national emergency under Article 15. Given the extent of the qualification under Article 9, neither article is of very great practical importance to religious interests. Consider, for example, *Yanasik v Turkey* (1993) 16 EHRR CD5 (ECHR), where a student at a Turkish military academy, who was repeatedly disciplined for his involvement in Islamic fundamentalism, was finally dismissed. The Commission considered that the applicant had voluntarily undertaken restrictions on his rights when he entered the academy, analogous to becoming a minister in a State church, and therefore: 'considered that military discipline by its nature implied that certain limitations would be imposed on the rights and freedoms of military personnel which could not be imposed upon those of civilians. These limitations could include one prohibiting the military from engaging in Islamic fundamentalism, in views of its quasi-political aims'.

Article 9 is supplemented by an additional provision dealing with education. During the drafting process of the Convention, it was suggested that the rights protected should include rights related to the education of children. In order to ensure a speedy acceptance of the Convention as a whole these rights were excluded from the Convention, while further work was carried out on how best to frame them. In 1952, the First Protocol was completed, and made available to States for ratification. It states: 'No person shall be denied the right to education. In the exercise of any functions which it assumes in relation to education and teaching, the State shall respect the right of parents to ensure such education and teaching in conformity with their own religious and philosophical convictions' (ECHR Protocol 1, art.2)

Article 2 clearly includes philosophical convictions as well as religious beliefs, although it should be noted that this was a controversial point during drafting, a recommendation that it should be limited to religious education in conformity with the parent's creed being seriously considered (Robertson and Merills, 1993 at 218–19). As with Article 9, however, the limits on the convictions protected by the Article remain unclear. In *Belgian Linguistics Case* (1968) 1 EHRR 252 (ECHR), the court rejected an argument that the linguistic and cultural preferences of the parents in that case were protected by Article 2. In *Campbell and Cosans* (1982) HUDOC 25 February (ECHR) by contrast, the parents' objections to corporal punishment of their child amounted to philosophical convictions because they dealt with: 'a weighty and substantial aspect of human life and behaviour, namely the integrity of the person, the propriety or otherwise of the infliction of corporal punishment and the exclusion of the distress which risk of such punishment entails'.

It should be noted that the State is required to 'respect' the wishes of the parents. The parents cannot require the State to educate their children in a particular way (see *Family H v United Kingdom* (1984) 37 DR 105 (ECHR)), particularly if resources would be required to provide a particular form of education (see *W and Others v United Kingdom* (1984) 37 DR 96 (ECHR), *X v United Kingdom* (1978) 14 DR 179 (ECHR)). This does not provide parents with an absolute veto over the education their children receive in State schools, even where the content of the education meshes poorly with their religious or philosophical views. In the *Danish Sex Education* cases, parents objected to compulsory sex education lessons. The court held that the State had a responsibility for establishing the curriculum in its schools, and this entitled it to include information or knowledge of a directly, or indirectly, religious or philosophical nature, however: 'the State, in fulfilling the functions assumed by it in regard to education and teaching, must take care that the information or knowledge included in the curriculum is conveyed in an objective, critical and pluralistic manner. The State is forbidden to pursue an aim of indoctrination that might be considered as not respecting parents' religious and philosophical convictions. That is the limit that must not be exceeded'.

If Article 2 was restricted to the content of the curriculum it would provide a simple, but useful guarantee prohibiting the State from using the power of the State school system to propagate its own religious or philosophical convictions against the interests of dissenting communities, families, and individuals. It is clear, however, that the Article extends to other aspects of school life. In the corporal punishment case referred to above, for instance, the court stressed that education was wider than teaching and encompassed 'the whole process whereby, in any society, adults endeavour to transmit their beliefs, culture and other values to the young', and included discipline, which was: 'an integral part of the process whereby a school seeks to achieve the object for which it was established, including the development and moulding of the character and mental powers of its pupils'.

Other Regional Human Rights Documents

As well as the ECHR, there are a range of other regional human rights regimes including, relevant to our jurisdictions, the Inter-American System (Mower, 1991; Davidson, 1997); and the African Charter on Human and People's Rights (Murray, 2000; Murray and Evans, 2001). Both contain specific guarantees of religious rights, although neither has been as extensively developed as those under the ECHR.

The American Convention on Human Rights 1969 provides by Article 12 that everyone has the right to freedom of conscience and of religion. The right includes the freedom to maintain or change religion, as well as the freedom to profess or disseminate it individually or with others, in public or in private. This is subject to restrictions on manifestation very similar to those under the ECHR (Article 12(2)). There is an additional guarantee of the rights of those raising children to provide for a religious education in accord with their convictions (Article 12(4)).

The African Charter on Human and People's Rights 1981 provides for freedom of conscience, and the profession of and free practice of religion 'subject to law and order' (Article 8). The African Commission has reported that this protects religious communities that do not pose a threat to law and order from State harassment (*25/89, 47/90, 56/93, 100/93* (joined) *Free Legal Assistance Group and Others and Zaire*, para.45).

The Limitations of International Law

At the beginning of this chapter, I indicated that international law was not as directly applicable a form of law as national, or domestic, law. At this point it may be useful to address some of the implications of this distinction in relation to religious rights. The first question to address is how important international law can be in relation to religious interests, given its more detached status. There are three significant roles for international law in developing national law.

Firstly, international law can act as a check on State power where internal restriction have failed to operate properly. This is particularly true when the international guarantee is supplemented by a strong enforcement mechanism, capable of clearly showing that a violation of international law has occurred. The right of individual application under the ECHR is an example of such a mechanism, and has had a sizeable impact on domestic law. A useful example is *Dudgeon v United Kingdom* (1981) 4 EHRR 139 (ECHR). In that case, the applicant was a homosexual male resident in Northern Ireland. Domestic law in Northern Ireland absolutely prohibited some sexual acts between men. The European Court of Human Rights, as the body capable of giving a definitive interpretation of the ECHR, found that the domestic law constituted a violation of the applicant's right to privacy, and that the State was unable to justify this violation by reference to any of the permitted restrictions contained within the Convention. As a direct result of this finding, the law in Northern Ireland was amended to meet the requirements of the Convention (Homosexual Offences (Northern Ireland) Order 1982 (UK)).

This pressure to accept international standards is especially pronounced in regional human rights guarantees such as the ECHR, which constitute agreements between nations involved in developing broader and deeper economic and social ties. There is especial pressure on national governments to ensure the obligations are met. This element can be overstated. Nonetheless, the pressures concerning international human rights in general are present more firmly in a scheme linked so closely with regional policy, including economic aspirations.

Secondly, international law can act as a pressure for reform within the State (see Young, 1998), and serve as a tool by internal bodies seeking such reforms. In the Isle of Man, for instance, a number of domestic laws were *prima facie* contrary to the Convention. Although it had been rendered impossible to take these potential violations to the European Court of Human Rights, the incompatibility with international standards provided a powerful argument for domestic lawmakers. Eventually the potential violations were removed from Manx law, primarily in order to meet these international obligations (Edge, 1997 at 149–52).

Thirdly, international law can have some influence on the exercise of powers by domestic decision makers. Within the United Kingdom, for instance, the courts recognise that the government has agreed to be bound by international human rights obligations, particularly those under the Convention. As a consequence the courts may have some recourse to these obligations when seeking to interpret legislation. Where the statute that is to be interpreted is ambiguous, and could support an interpretation in line with these obligations, such an interpretation is to be preferred over readings of the statute that would cause the United Kingdom to violate its international obligations (*Salomon v Commissioners of Customs and Excise* [1967] 2 QB 116 (UK)). Additionally, the English courts may traditionally take account of treaty obligations when developing the common law.

International law has been seen by some legal scholars as a uniquely valuable foundation for the evaluation of domestic laws dealing with minority cultures. Poulter, for instance, makes use of the rules of international law in order: 'to escape from the criticism that, whenever English law refuses to countenance a minority tradition or ethnic practice, this amounts to a form of unjustified cultural imperialism' (Poulter, 1998 at 69). There is much to be said for this stance, when the focus is upon imperialism by a single legal system. Within the United Kingdom, for instance, we can find instances of ECHR values being turned to in the development of policy; and it is a commonplace for critiques of domestic law to begin with an evaluation of compliance with the ECHR (for example, Edge and Loughrey, 2001).

It becomes less convincing when we shift the focus of cultural imperialism away from the individual State to the human rights movement as a whole. We might see cultural imperialism as consisting of the imposition of cultural values upon individuals or communities which do not freely agree with those values. This raises two questions – does the international human rights regime have cultural values and, if it does, are they imposed upon others?

The answer to the first question must be yes. Even the cursory consideration of religious rights in this section demonstrates that the human rights regime embodies particular cultural assumptions, and creates particular values. The emphasis on individual autonomy, for instance in the Court's view of proper and improper proselytism, is a cultural value. The significance of gender equality in determining an objection against the ordination of women in the Church of England is another example. The comprehensiveness, cohesion, and claims for exclusivity of the human rights regime make it sensible to evaluate it as not just a bundle of cultural values, but an entire worldview. Spickard, for instance, has gone as far as to argue that 'human rights beliefs are essentially religious ... the human rights movement has its sacred histories and texts, its holy discourses, its rituals, its saints and its demons' (Spickard, 1999 at para. 1.10; see also Tan, 1997).

The answer to the second question is slightly more difficult, given the variety of sovereign States which have accepted the international guarantees, and the differing makeup of these States in terms of religious adherence. It is impossible to argue, however, that every form of religious belief and cultural tradition has been in a position to accept or reject the values contained therein. Even with the global documents, and even in relation to 'Christianity', 'Islam' and other religions with powerful positions in particular territories, the values accepted by members of those religions with State authority do not in any case, *ipso facto*, constitute the values of all those living within the territory.

In short, although the values of human rights guarantees may not represent a form of cultural imperialism by particular States or religious systems, we cannot conclude from this that they do not constitute such imperialism by the philosophies of the human rights guarantees themselves.

Religious Interests in Generally Applicable Domestic Guarantees

The Role of Generally Applicable Guarantees of Rights in Constitutions

In the first chapter, I indicated that sources within a domestic legal system could be placed in a hierarchy, with constitutional rules taking priority over other sources of law. Where a formal constitution exists, it is commonplace to find a set of generally applicable guarantees of fundamental rights – that is, a set of individual rights which may not lawfully be violated by the State. If such a right is involved this may require the courts to declare legislation to be invalid, or interpret it in an unusual way to avoid infringement; the legislature to gain a special majority supporting a measure which limits the right; and the executive to act in a way which respects the right. This section briefly reviews generally applicable guarantees of freedom of religion in our jurisdictions.

United Kingdom

In the earlier discussion of sources of law, I suggested that the United Kingdom and New Zealand were distinctive, in that both lacked a category of law which could be classed as 'the constitution', although both possess laws which deal with constitutional matters. In particular, in both systems protection of individual rights was effected by the normal legal and administrative mechanisms. This system of rights protection was subject to extensive criticism, and in 1998 Parliament legislated to provide mechanisms for enforcing the ECHR in the United Kingdom. Although falling short of a guarantee effective against all organs of the State, primarily because of the need to accommodate Parliamentary sovereignty, this new legislation constitutes the closest approximation to a positive guarantee of religious rights yet seen in the English jurisdiction (Bradney, 2000).

The Human Rights Act 1998 (UK) does not represent a fully-fledged British Bill of Rights, but rather seeks to incorporate the guarantees of the ECHR into English law (National Council for Civil Liberties, 1997). The content of the ECHR was discussed earlier in this chapter, but the mechanisms by which the HRA gives effect to the ECHR merit brief discussion. It is an oversimplification to say that the HRA 'incorporates' the ECHR into English law. Rather, it provides a number of distinct mechanisms by which English law may be brought into line with the ECHR. Additionally, the HRA contains a special clause dealing with religion, HRA 1998 s.13, which merits some discussion.

The two most significant enforcement mechanisms under the HRA are the new rule of statutory interpretation contained in s.3, and the new ground of challenging administrative action in s.6.

Section 3 introduces a new, and potent, principle to be used in interpreting statutes (Lester, 1999). Before the HRA, the courts would only look to the ECHR if legislation was ambiguous. The HRA shifts to a stronger position where 'so far as it is possible to do so, primary and subordinate legislation must be read and given effect in a way which is compatible with the Convention' (HRA 1998 s.3(1) (UK)). This rule is not an absolute prohibition on the Courts interpreting legislation as contrary to the Convention, however, as it: '(b) does not affect the validity, continuing operation or enforcement of any incompatible primary legislation; and (c) does not affect the validity, continuing operation or enforcement of any incompatible subordinate legislation if (disregarding any possibility of revocation) primary legislation prevents removal of the incompatibility' (HRA 1998 s.3(2)

(UK)). Where it is not possible to give a compatible interpretation to the legislation, it must be given full effect. Unlike, for instance, the system under the United States Constitution, the courts have no authority to ignore or strike out Acts of Parliament, or statutory instruments lawfully deriving authority from such Acts. If they are unable to make the legislation fit with the Convention (see Marshall, 2003), they must apply it as it stands (Butler, 2000). When applying such legislation, however, they may make a declaration that it is incompatible with the Convention, which can be used to speed corrective legislation through Parliament (Hardie, 1993).

Section 6 provides a new ground by which the Courts can overturn a particular decision by an administrative body. The actions of these bodies are regulated by administrative law. At common law, officials were not subject to review simply for failure to comply with the ECHR, although a decision which violated human norms might be subject to especially tight scrutiny (*Bugdaycay v Secretary of State for the Home Department* [1987] AC 514 (UK)). Section 6 provides that it is unlawful for a public authority to act in a way incompatible with the Convention, unless it was bound to act as it did by primary legislation, or was acting to give effect to primary legislation that was itself incompatible with the Convention. This applies only to public authorities; Manning and Kilpatrick, although accepting that this term remains to be properly developed, suggest that public authorities include the Crown, Crown servants, advisors to Ministers, persons and bodies exercising powers delegated by statutory power, and non-statutory bodies set up to undertake public functions; a body deriving its power exclusively from contract, or the consent of those subject to its powers, it not a public authority (Manning and Kilpatrick, 1998 at 102–6).

As well as these general provisions, a section was introduced to the HRA during its passage through Parliament specifically to allay the concerns of religious organisations (see Cumper, 2000a; Cumper, 2000b). At a late stage during the passage of the Human Rights Bill through Parliament, concern arose that its provisions would extend to the Church of England, and possibly to other religious bodies that have charitable status (Thorp, 1998). A number of bodies lobbied for an exclusion from the Bill for religious organisations exercising public functions, although some religious organisations, such as Christians for Human Rights, strongly objected to such exclusion. The fundamental concern was that: '[t]he Bill, instead of regarding Churches as autonomous bodies, as the European Court does, defines them as public bodies. They would therefore in unacceptable ways become subject to the authority of the civil courts for certain purposes' (Free Church of Scotland, 1998).

Particular manifestations of this concern arose in relation to possible requirements on the organisations to conduct same sex-weddings, employ non-co-religionists as teachers in religious schools, or appoint women bishops (see more broadly, Charlesworth, 1999). These concerns resulted in a variety of amendments being proposed in Parliament, the most radical of which would have resulted in the exclusion of religious organisations from the remit of the legislation, even where exercising a public function. In response, the Government sponsored an amendment to the Bill, removing this special treatment but adding reassurance in the form of section 13 of the Act. This provides: '(1) If a court's determination of any question arising under this Act might affect the exercise by a religious organisation (itself or its members collectively) of the Convention right to freedom of thought, conscience and religion, it must have particular regard to the importance of that right'. In his study of this section, Cumper suggests that the section is likely to have little legal effect in the short to medium term, due to the structure of Convention guarantees under Article 9 and the form of the HRA itself (Cumper, 2000b).

New Zealand

As I discussed in the previous chapter, New Zealand lacks an entrenched set of constitutional guarantees for fundamental rights. Instead, the Bill of Rights Act 1990, which was taken as the model for much of the United Kingdom's Human Rights Act 1998, seeks to balance the ultimate authority of the legislature with an improved emphasis on fundamental rights. Although section 7 of the Act provides mechanisms for heightened scrutiny of legislation which may be contrary to the rights in the Act (*Mangawaro Enterprises Ltd v Attorney-General* [1994] 2 NZLR 451 (NZ)), the key provision is section 6. Under this provision, where the court is able to interpret legislation it should prefer the interpretation which most meets the requirements of the Bill of Rights (*R v Poumako* (2000) 5 HRNZ 651 (NZ)). The courts are not able to force an interpretation on legislation which it could not otherwise bear (*Moonen* (1999) 5 HRNZ 224 (NZ)), and must enforce legislation even where it is contrary to the Bill of Rights (Bill of Rights Act 1990 s.4; *R v Bennett* (1993) 2 HRNZ 358 (NZ)). They may, however, disregard established interpretations of a clause (*Flickinger v Crown Colony of Hong Kong* [1991] 1 NZLR 349 (NZ)), although this consequence was not clear from the face of the Bill (Cooke of Thornden, 1997). In contrast to the Human Rights Act of the United Kingdom, there is no formal mechanism by which a court can declare a measure to be contrary to the Bill of Rights (Butler, 2000).

The Bill was modeled on the Canadian Charter (Taggart, 1998) and contains a number of substantive rights related to religious interests. Unusually, the Bill draws a sharp distinction between religious belief, and religious practice. Section 13 states the right to freedom of thought, conscience, religious and belief. Section 15 contains the right to manifest religion or belief in worship, observance, practice, or teaching, either individually or in community with others, and either in public or in private. This includes the right to determine the religious education and upbringing of children (*Re J (an infant)* [1996] 2 NZLR 134 (NZ)). Section 20 deals separately with community rights, guaranteeing the right of members of a minority, including a religious minority, to profess and practise the religion in community with other members of that minority. Section 19 contains a general non-discrimination guarantee whose relatively small range of grounds, which included religion, has been amended to include a very extensive list of grounds (Thompson, 1996). By section 5 the rights under the Bill are subject to such reasonable limits prescribed by law as can be demonstrably justified in a free and democratic society. This section has been used to restrictive religious practices (Ahdar, 1996).

The United States

As Ahdar has observed: '[n]on-Americans are fortunate that most of the religion and law conflicts that are likely to be tested in court have already been so in the United States. The American propensity towards litigation means that the supply of examples is not likely to dry up' (Ahdar, 2000 at 6–7). This section very briefly outlines the principal constitutional guarantees of freedom of religion in the United States.

The US legal system has a strong federal tradition, under which the power to make and apply laws is shared between central (Federal) government and local (State) government. The laws and constitutions of these individual States often provide legal protection for religious interests. For instance, the Human Rights Law 1968 of New York contains specific guarantees dealing with religious discrimination, including a prohibition on intentional religious discrimination, and a requirement that the need to observe particular holy days should be respected (see Becker, 1999). The most important guarantee of religious liberty, however, is contained in the First Amendment to the United States Constitution.

The US Constitution adopted in 1787 was the result of a number of compromises between the different States and groups within them (Hodder-Williams, 1988). Although the Constitution contained some guarantees that in effect provided for the protection of individual rights, there was no Bill of Rights 'of the sort which had already become a well-known feature of most, though not all, state constitutions' (Fellman, 1978 at 51). This deficiency was rectified very quickly, with the ratification by the States of the first ten amendments to the US Constitution, commonly referred to as the Bill of Rights, in 1791 (see McKay, 1993 at 39–50). Originally interpreted as limiting the power of the Federal government only, these rights, in particular the religious liberty guarantees under the First Amendment, have since been applied to limit the actions of the individual States (Cortner, 1981 at 279–301).

The First Amendment provides that 'Congress shall make no law respecting an establishment of religion, or prohibiting the free exercise thereof'. This provision contains two distinct, albeit related, clauses (McConnell, 2000). Firstly, there is the prohibition on the 'establishment of religion'. Secondly, there is the guarantee of 'free exercise' of religion. The meaning and application of these clauses remains contentious and has produced a massive amount of literature.

The two clauses probably share a common definition of religion. The text of the First Amendment only uses the word once, and practical problems would emerge if this word was to be given different definitions according to which clause is being considered by the court. In particular, a group that constituted a religion for free exercise purposes, but not for establishment purposes, would be in a privileged position in relation to groups that were religious under both definitions.

Effectively, it would be able to claim the protection offered by the free exercise clause without being subject to the restrictions on state linkage contained in the establishment clause (Ricks, 1993).

Identifying this shared definition, however, is extremely problematic. In *Davis v Beason* 133 US 333 (1890) (US), the Supreme Court, as the final arbiter on the meaning of the Constitution, stated that 'religion has reference to one's views of his relations to his Creator, and to the obligations they impose of reverence for his being and character, and of obedience to his will' (ibid., at 342). The Supreme Court has since rejected any requirement for a Supreme Being (*United States v Seeger*, 380 US 163 (1965) (US)) but has been reluctant to develop a comprehensive definition in its jurisprudence, perhaps because 'the content of the term is found in the history of the human race and is incapable of compression into a few words' (*United States v Kauten*, 133 F.2d. 703 (1943) (US)). The closest, although its exact precedential value is unclear, comes from *Seeger v United States* 380 US 163 (1965) (US), where the Court defined religion as: '[a] sincere and meaningful belief which occupies in the life of its possessor a place parallel to that filled by the God of those admittedly qualifying for the exemption ... This construction avoids imputing ... an intent to classify different religious beliefs, exempting some and excluding others' (ibid., at 176).

Looking to beliefs which are fairly clearly qualified under the clause, the term encompasses Buddhism and Taoism (*Torcaso v Watkins*, 367 US 488 (1961) (US)); ethical culture and secular humanism (*Seeger v United States* 380 US 163 (1965) (US)); Jehovah's Witnesses (*Cantwell v Connecticutt*, 310 US 296 (1940) (US)); Seventh Day Adventists (*Sherbert v Verner*, 374 US 398 (1963) (US)); the Amish (*Wisconsin v Yoder*, 406 US 205 (1972) (US)); Native American religions (*Bowen v Roy*, 476 US 693 (1986) US)); some forms of Transcendental Meditation (*Malnak v Yogi*, 592 F.2d 197 (US)); Scientology (*Founding Church of Scientology v United States*, 409 F.2d. 1146 (US)); Judaism (*Braunfeld v Brown*, 366 US 599 (1961) (US)); animism, paganism and Wicca (*ACLU Nebraska Foundation v City of Plattsmouth Nebraska*, 2004 WL 298965 (2004) (US)) and the Church of Jesus Christ of the Latter Day Saints (*Corporation of Presiding Bishop v Amos*, 483 US 327 (1987) (US)). The term also includes less formalised belief systems, as it is not necessary to belong to an organised church, sect, or denomination in order to be able to claim rights under the First Amendment (*Frazee v. Illinois Dept. of Employment Security*, 489 US 829 (1989) (US)). In *United States v Ballard* 322 US 78 (1944) (US), a set of claims that Jesus had shook Ballard's hand, and that St Germain had appeared to Ballard to commission him to convey messages and heal, was entitled to the protection of the First Amendment. Single-faceted ideologies, however, such as vegetarianism or Social Darwinism, may not be protected (*Africa v Pennsylvania*, 662 F.2d. 1025 (US)). Nor, it seems, will choices that are 'merely philosophical and personal rather than religious' (*Wisconsin v Yoder*, 406 US 205 (1972) (US)); or claims that are so unusual as to be clearly non-religious in motivation. The latter may be better viewed as a reflection on the need for sincerity in putting forward beliefs, rather than constituting part of the religious belief itself. Consider, for instance, *United States v Kuch* 288 F. Supp. 439 (US), where the

Neo-American Church, whose central tenets mandated around the use of psychedelic substances, had official songs including 'Puff the Magic Dragon'. The Court noted that Kuch had failed to establish the Church was a religion, as 'one gains the inescapable impression that the membership is mocking established institutions, playing with words and totally irreverent in any sense of the term' (ibid., at 144).

There is a considerable body of academic commentary seeking to draw out a more coherent, and comprehensive, definition of religion, but nothing approaching any consensus as to what the term means. It should be noted, however, that the term is clearly capable of encompassing some form of beliefs that do not involve statements as to metaphysical reality. This may be a consequence of the wording of the First Amendment that in contrast with, for instance, the European Convention on Human Rights does not provide any express protection for conviction or belief (Marshall, 2000).

Turning to the establishment clause, the First Amendment, originally intended to restrict the power of the Federal government, was aimed at preventing the establishment of a national State Church. It has developed into a prohibition on establishment at both Federal and State level. Establishment is a complex concept, but the Supreme Court has stated that: '[n]either [federal nor state governments] can pass laws which aid one religion, aid all religions, or prefer one religion over another. Neither can force or influence a person to go to or to remain away from church against this will or force him to profess a belief or disbelief in any religion. No person can be punished for entertaining or professing religious beliefs or disbeliefs, for church attendance or non-attendance. No tax in any amount, large or small, can be levied to support any religious activities or institutions, whatever they may be called, or whatever form they may adopt to teach or practice religion. Neither a state nor the Federal Government can, openly or secretly, participate in the affairs of any religious organizations or groups and vice versa' (*Everson v. Board of Education*, 330 US 1 (US) at 15–16).

Thus, State endorsement of particular religious tenets is not permitted (*County of Allegheny v. American Civil Liberties Union Greater Pittsburgh Chapter*, 492 US 573 (1989) (US)), nor is the prohibition of teachings arguably contrary to Biblical tenets, for instance Darwinism (*Edwards v. Aguillard*, 482 US 578 (1987) (US)). This constitutional separation leaves considerable areas of uncertainty in the relationship between religious organisations and the State. For instance, some State involvement in supporting religious education is permitted, but it is easy to go too far. Additionally, while the State may not endorse particular religious tenets, it is not establishment for the State to retain ceremonial deism, for instance in dating official documents 'in the year of our Lord' or calling upon God during legislative and judicial ceremonies (Epstein, 1996).

Nonetheless, although the details of the separation of religious organisation and State can be difficult to determine, the general philosophy is clear. The State should not become too closely entangled with any religious organisation, nor should religious organisations become too closely entangled with the State. To allow entanglement would lead to bad government in a country where every religion is a minority religion (Laycock, 1996; Stein, 2000). The importance of avoiding this entanglement can justify even restrictions on the free exercise of religion by individuals (*Locke v Davey*, 124 S.Ct. 1307 (2004) (US)). The contrast with both English law, and the obligations under the European Convention on Human Rights, is marked.

Turning to the free exercise clause, the key debate here is the extent to which the free exercise clause places an additional limit on the State (Cartyer, 1993). In *Reynolds v United States* 98 US 145 (1878) (US), the Supreme Court had to consider whether a law criminalising polygamy, the practice of which was demanded by the Church of Jesus Christ of the Latter Day Saints at that time, restricted free exercise when applied to a Mormon man. The Supreme Court ruled that the First Amendment prohibited any law against mere opinion, but did not protect 'actions which were in violation of social duties or subversive of good order' (ibid., at 164). In a later polygamy case, the Supreme Court reiterated the exclusion of acts from the First Amendment (*Davis v Beason*, 133 US 333 (1890) (US)).

In *Cantwell v Connecticutt* 310 US 296 (1940) (US), the Supreme Court accepted that acts could be entitled to the protection of the First Amendment. In that case a Jehovah's Witness and his children were prosecuted for soliciting religious contributions without a state certificate authorising them to do so. The Supreme Court found that this was a violation of the First Amendment. As Justice Roberts noted, free exercise 'embraces two concepts – freedom to believe and freedom to act. The first is absolute, but in the nature of things the second cannot be' (ibid., at 303–4). In *Sherbert v Verner* 374 US 398 (1963) (US), the Supreme Court endorsed this acceptance of actions, and explored the legitimate restrictions upon this freedom to act – for State action to comply with the First Amendment there must either be no infringement of religion, or a compelling state interest justifying the burden on religion.

This approach aims to deal with substantive neutrality – that is, the impact of laws on the religious adherent, even when those laws are, on the face of it, neutral and applicable to everyone within the jurisdiction. An alternative, and now dominant, theme in the Supreme Court jurisprudence concentrates on formal neutrality (Conkle, 2000). In *Employment Division v Smith* 494 US 872 (1990) (US), the Supreme Court were required, albeit indirectly, to consider whether a free exercise argument could protect the ingestion of peyote, a hallucinogen controlled by the relevant Criminal Code. The Court found that: 'generally applicable, religion-neutral laws that have the effect of burdening a particular religious practice need not be justified by a compelling governmental interest' (ibid., at 886). Thus, laws that incidentally burden religion do not per se violate the free exercise clause (*America Family Association Ltd v FCC*, 365 F.3d. 1156 (2004) (US)).

This decision was extensively criticised, and the US Congress enacted the Religious Freedom Restoration Act 1993 (see Drinan and Huffman, 1993), which was intended to revive the test developed by *Sherbert v Verner*. The US Constitution strictly divides the exercise of judicial, legislative, and executive powers, however, and this legislation was later found to be an infringement of the separation of legislative and judicial powers, and hence invalid (Sheffer, 1998). Following the survival of *Smith*, commentators have begun to take seriously the question of whether the religion clauses of the US Constitution, as interpreted by the Supreme Court, need revision (for example, Greenawalt, 1998; George, 1998).

Even in the light of *Smith*, however, free exercise retains some meaning. In *Church of the Lukumi Babalu Aye, Inc. v City of Hileah* 113 S.Ct. 2217, 2227 (1993) (US) a unanimous Supreme Court upheld a free exercise claim against a criminal law (Cornwell, 1994). In that case members of the Santeria religion wished to build a church in Hileah. Santeria practises include animal sacrifice. In an attempt to stop the sect from building a church, the city passed an ordinance criminalising the ritual sacrifice of animals, but not the slaughtering of animals *simpliciter*. The law punishing animal cruelty, including animal sacrifice which was not intended primarily for consumption as food, was rejected on the basis that it had both the purpose and effect of restricting religious conduct, and did not address non-religious conduct causing similar harms.

Canada

The Canadian legal systems share a close common heritage with the English legal system. In particular, like the United Kingdom, the predominant approach towards rights protection in Canada did not make use of generally applicable guarantees of fundamental rights. Beginning with the Canadian Bill of Rights (Constitution Act 1982, Pt.I (Can.)), a shift in the Canadian legal system culminated in the Canadian Charter of Rights and Freedoms (Beatty, 1995 at 61–102). The Canadian Charter, which begins with a statement that 'Canada is founded upon the principles that recognize the supremacy of God and the rule of law' (Canadian Charter, preamble (Can.)), guarantees in article 2(a) that '[e]veryone has ... freedom of thought conscience and belief' (see Swinton, 1996; Horwitz, 1996). Like the other provisions of the Charter, this is subject to 'such reasonable limits prescribed by law as can be demonstrably justified in a free and democratic society' (Article 1). In determining whether a limit meets this criteria the legislative object must constitute a pressing and substantial concern, and must be proportionate to the effects. In gauging proportionality: 'the limiting measures must be carefully designed, or rationally connected, to the objective; they must impair the right as little as possible; and their effects must not so severely trench on individual or group rights that the legislative objective, albeit important, is nevertheless, outweighed by the abridgement of rights' (*Edward Books and Art Ltd v R* (1986) 35 DLR (4th) 1 at 41 (Can.)). Additionally Article 15 provides: 'Every individual is equal before the and under the law and has the right to the equal protection and equal benefit of the law without discrimination based on race, national or ethnic origin, colour, religion, sex, age, or mental or physical disability'.

The obligations under the Charter bind both the national government and the authorities of the individual provinces (Article 32). Although the Charter is a relatively strong human rights guarantee, it can be over-ridden by the Canadian or provincial legislatures by express declaration that a contrary provision is to operate notwithstanding the Charter (Article 33). The Supreme Court of Canada has taken the approach that the rights outlined in the Charter are living rights – an approach we have already seen in relationship to the development of the ECHR. In developing the religious rights under the Charter the Supreme Court has made extensive use of US jurisprudence on the First Amendment (Manfredi, 1993).

The Supreme Court has considered the meaning of the guarantee under s.2(a) of the Charter in two key cases, both dealing with Sunday trading laws. In *R v Big M Drug Mart Ltd* (1985) 18 DLR (4th) 321 (Can.) a Canadian law had been used to impose a criminal penalty upon a corporation that had traded on a Sunday. The Court found that the legislation did not have a secular purpose, but rather a religious one – compelling sabbatical observance. This purpose was contrary to the Charter, as it: 'works a form of coercion inimical to the spirit of the Charter and the dignity of all non-Christians. In proclaiming the standards of the Christian faith, the Act creates a climate hostile to, and gives the appearance of discrimination against, non-Christian Canadians. It takes religious values rooted in Christian morality and, using the force of the State, translates them into a positive law binding on believers and non-believers alike. The theological content of the legislation remains as a subtle and constant reminder to religious minorities within the country of their differences with, and alienation from, the dominant religious culture' (ibid., at 354).

At a minimum, freedom of conscience and religion prevented the government from coercing individuals to affirm a specific religious belief or to manifest a specific religious practice for a sectarian purpose, including manifestation by coerced inaction. As the purpose of the legislation was an unconstitutional one, it was not necessary to consider its effects, as effects could never be relied upon to save legislation with an invalid purpose; neither was it necessary to consider justifications under s.1 of the Charter, as the purpose was not to gain the benefits of those justifications. Thus, the legislation infringed upon the freedom of conscience and religion identified by s.2(a) of the Charter.

The court returned to Sunday trading laws in *Edward Books and Art Ltd v R* (1986) 35 DLR (4th) 1 (Can.). In this case a provincial law required some retail businesses to be closed on particular days, including Sunday. Some retailers were exempt from this limit if they closed on Saturday instead. In sharp contrast to *Big M*, the court found that although the purpose of the legislation was an acceptable, secular one, its effects might still be contrary to Article 2(a). The article prohibited coercive burdens, above the trivial or insubstantial, upon freedom of religion. These burdens could be 'direct or indirect, intentional or unintentional, foreseeable or unforeseeable', so long as they fell upon the 'profoundly personal beliefs that govern one's perception of oneself, humankind, nature, and in some cases, a higher or different order of being' (ibid., at 34). The court found that the impact of the legislation was to place a non-trivial coercive burden upon the religious freedom of Jews and Seventh Day Adventists in particular, but that the burden could be upheld under s.1 of the Charter. The Newfoundland Court of Appeal, in reviewing these cases, considered that 'conformity to a statutory obligation which merely coincides with the dictates of a particular religion does not in itself amount to compulsion to engage in religious practices' (*R v Peddle*, 1989 CarswellNFld 38 (Can.)).

In conclusion, the provisions of the Canadian Charter Article 2(a), although not identical to the constitutional provisions of the US constitution, are close in scope and reach to those guarantees. Although this provision of the Charter has yet to produce as much in the way of commentary, the decisions of the Supreme Court of Canada benefit, in particular, from the explicit and modern form of the constitutional document they are required to consider, in contrast to the US First Amendment.

Australia

Like the jurisdictions of the United States, the Australian jurisdictions share many characteristics with the English legal system. These are more pronounced in many areas, as the Australian jurisdictions, in the absence of an abrupt moment of legal independence, continued to draw strongly upon English law and developments for longer than the United States jurisdictions. As with the United States, Australia possesses a federal system, with central authority vested in the Commonwealth of Australia, but substantial authority remaining in the States (Zines, 1977; Hanks, 1996 at 228–84). Particular laws at the State and Commonwealth level may serve to protect the religious interest (for instance the anti-discrimination laws discussed in Thornton, 1990 at 88–101). Additionally, there is an important constitutional provision limiting the power of the Commonwealth.

Section 116 of the Australian Constitution provides: 'The Commonwealth shall not make any law for establishing any religion, or for imposing any religious observance, or for prohibiting the free exercise of any religion, and no religious test shall be required as a qualification for any office or public trust under the Commonwealth'. Although this provision has strong resemblances to the First Amendment to the United States Constitution, there are very significant differences. In *ex rel Black* (1981) 146 CLR 559 (Aust.), the High Court of Australia considered whether assistance to non-governmental, religious, schools violated the prohibition on establishment. Counsel made extensive use of authorities on the First Amendment, but this approach was not accepted by the majority of the High Court. Although they were prepared to accept that US material could be useful where the Constitution was ambiguous, in relation to s.116: 'not merely is there a difference between the Australian text and the language of the relevant provisions of the Bill of Rights, but that language has received an interpretation before the adoption of our Constitution. It later had further and at times different interpretations. The adoption of such divergent language thus has a more than usual significance' (ibid., at 578–9).

The first significant difference between the two is the scope and nature of the obligation. In contrast to the US provision, this section binds only the Commonwealth authorities exercising federal authority. The individual states of Australia are not bound by this provision, nor is the Commonwealth when legislating for the non-State territories (*Kruger & Ors v The Commonwealth Of*

Australia; Bray & Ors v The Commonwealth Of Australia (1997) 190 CLR 1 (Aust.)). The original form of s.116 would have bound the States also, but this was amended during the passage of the legislation, with the express purpose of leaving the powers of the States to make laws concerning religion intact (Official Record of the Debates of the Australasian Federal Convention, (Melbourne), 2 March 1898, vol V at 1769).

One judge of the High Court has noted that: 'It makes no sense to speak of a constitutional right to religious freedom in a context in which the Constitution clearly postulates that the States may enact laws in derogation of that right' (Guardon J. in *Kruger & Ors v The Commonwealth Of Australia; Bray & Ors v The Commonwealth Of Australia* (1997) 190 CLR 1 (Aust.)). This emphasis on limiting the power of the Federal authorities, rather than protecting religious rights regardless of the legal source of the limitation, can also be found in the early history of the First Amendment to the US Constitution, although as I have noted the guarantees have now pervaded the US system.

Secondly, this emphasis on s.116 as a limit on legislative competence, rather than a guarantee of individual rights, has restricted the guarantee to legislative purpose. The section 'is directed to the making of law. It is not dealing with the administration of law', although administration can be evidence of a breach of the law 'not because of the manner of the administration but because the statute, properly construed, authorises it' (*ex rel Black* (1981) 146 CLR 559 (Aust.) at 581). On one view, the section deals only with laws which in terms ban religious practices, so that 'a law requiring a man to do an act which his religion forbids ... does not come within the prohibition of s.116' (*Kryger v Williams* (1912) 15 CLR 366 (Aust.) at 369). A more modern view is that the section can extend beyond laws that on their face ban religion, but the courts must be able to find that a purpose of the law was one prohibited by s.116. As Gaudron J put it in *Kruger & Ors v The Commonwealth Of Australia; Bray & Ors v The Commonwealth Of Australia* (1997) 190 CLR 1 (Aust.), 'purpose is the criteria and the sole criteria selected by s.116 for invalidity ... [a law will not violate the section if] it is necessary to attain some overriding public purpose or to satisfy some pressing social need. Nor will it have that purpose if it is a law for some specific purpose unconnected with the free exercise of religion and only incidentally affects that freedom.' Thus, the guarantees in the provision only serve to prevent legislation that has a prohibited purpose, rather than a prohibited effect. Although this guarantee is relatively narrow, it does provide some protection for religious freedom, including the freedom of atheists (*Adelaide Company of Jehovah's Witnesses Inc v The Commonwealth*, (1943) 67 CLR 1161 (Aust.)).

The most general guarantees are the bar on the Commonwealth establishing any religion; and on prohibiting free exercise of religion. Establishing has been extensively discussed by the High Court of Australia, and has been construed narrowly as involving 'the entrenchment of a religion as a feature of and identified with the body politic, in this instance the Commonwealth', or constituting 'a particular religion or religious body as a state religion or state church' (*ex rel Black* (1981) 146 CLR 559 (Aust.)). It does not constitute a blanket prohibition on the giving of aid or encouragement to religion, or the indirect furtherance of religious organisation practices. Free exercise prevents only those legislative acts that unduly infringe religious freedom (Lumb and Ryan, 1977 at 362–5; cf. Latham, 1952).

Because of the limited scope of the Australian constitutional guarantee, and the small size of the Australian jurisdictions, there is less useful case law and commentary than is to be found within the US jurisdictions (but see Richardson, 1995; New South Wales Anti-Discrimination Board, 1984; Sheen, 1995).

South Africa

As the most modern of the constitutions discussed in this text, the structure of the South African Constitutional guarantees is much more fully developed, and explicit, than that of say the United States. Against that, because the Constitution has only been in effect since 1997 the volume of authoritative decisions of the Constitutional Court, and associated commentary, is comparatively small.

The Constitution begins with a reference to theism, and van der Vyver has seen both this preamble and a number of substantive provisions as a testimony to theism (van der Vyver, 1999 at 649–52). Although, as we will see, the relationship between religion and State is not one of rigid separation, a particular religious stance does not seem to form one of the fundamental values of the Constitution as stated in section 1 (McLean, 1996).

The central guarantees of religious interests are contained in s.15. Section 15(1) states the right to freedom of conscience, religion, thought, and belief. This is, in essence, a liberty right analogous to the United States right of free exercise. It does not, however, imply a special restriction on establishment of religion, beyond that necessary to avoid unfair discrimination on the grounds of religion (*S v Solberg*, 1997 (10) BCLR 1348 (SA)). A restriction analogous to the United States establishment clause was expressly rejected by the drafters of the constitution (Freedman, 2000 at 113). Instead, 'religion is not perceived as a governmental taboo, but rather the South African Constitution requires evenhandedness in official dealing relating to religion and religious institutions' (van der Vyver, 1999 at 671). This is illustrated by section 15(2), which permits religious observance by State and state-aided institutions provided it follows rules laid down by appropriate public authorities, is conducted on an equitable basis, and attendance is free and voluntary. Section 15(3) provides, in rather convoluted language, that the section does not prevent the legislature from recognising marriages, and resolution of family matters more generally, under a system of religious law. Van der Vyver sees this section as emerging from a controversy concerning polygamy and notes that, although polygamous customary African marriages have been recognised by legislation, there has been no similar recognition for Hindu and Muslim polygamous marriages (van der Vyver, 1999 at 660–3). Moosa has suggested that such recognition could promote social reform within these communities, by bringing polygamous practices into the constitutional forum (Moosa, 1998).

Section 15 is supplemented on specific areas by other generally applicable rights in the Constitution. Section 3 includes within the linguistic rights 'Arabic, Hebrew, Sanskrit and other languages used for religious purposes in South Africa'. Section 9 contains a number of broad guarantees of nondiscrimination and equality, capable of binding private organisations such as religious bodies (van der Vyver, 2000), including prohibition of unfair discrimination on the grounds of 'religion, conscience, belief'. Section 16, containing a general guarantee of freedom of expression, does not apply to advocacy of hatred based on race, ethnicity, gender or religion where it constitutes incitement to cause some harm. Section 35 guarantees that detained persons, including prisoners serving a sentence, the right to communicate with and be visited by their chosen religious counselor. Section 31 contains a novel recognition of community religious interests, amongst them, recognition of other forms of community. It provides that persons belonging to a religious community may not be denied the right to practice their religion with other members of that community; or to form, join, and maintain religious organisations.

All of these positive rights are subject to an overarching limitation clause, section 36. This section provides that the rights may be limited by laws of general application when the limit is reasonable and justifiable in an open and democratic society based on the value of human dignity, equality, and freedom (Meyerson, 1997). In making this judgement, regard should be had to all relevant facts, including (a) the nature of the right; (b) the importance of the purpose of the limitation; (c) the nature and extent of the limitation; (d) the relationship between the limitation and its purpose; and (e) less restrictive means to achieve the purpose.

Are Generally Applicable Religious Guarantees Useful?

The primary advantage of a generally applicable religious guarantee is that it provides a constant level of background consideration for religious interests. The lack of such a guarantee increases: 'the ever-present potential of the majority, indirectly and unthinkingly, to discriminate against the religious practices of a minority. Regulations and restrictions which are not intended to discriminate against religious practice, and are applied uniformly, may nevertheless in their effect discriminate to the extent of imposing an intolerable burden on the adherents of a particular religion' (Malcolm, 1996 at 981). So, if the drafter of a regulation on hygiene in the meat industry is unaware of the dietary codes of a very small religious community with little or no tradition of accommodation by the State, members of that community can have recourse to the overarching guarantees to secure consideration of their religious interests.

Chapter 3

The State and the Individual

The Nature of the Problems

Although there are differences in the balance between the private sector and public sector in our jurisdictions, in all of them the State is an extremely powerful agent – far more so than even a large corporation. The State is thus in a position both to threaten the religious interests of individuals, and to protect those interests from others.

In the first category, a State may create legislation explicitly intended to suppress particular religious activities – for instance, a provision punishing membership of a particular religious group with imprisonment or execution. In practice, within the jurisdictions we are concerned with, this form of explicit suppression is comparatively rare. Much more common is the situation where a State creates a law intended to apply to everyone, but which has a particular impact upon an individual because of their religious beliefs. Consider, for instance, a law requiring parents to have children of a certain age vaccinated, subject to criminal punishment if they wilfully disobey. If particular parents have religious beliefs which prohibit vaccination, they will be faced with a dilemma as to whether to act contrary to their religious beliefs or, on the face of it, to violate national law. If the parents choose to disobey the generally applicable rule, the State must then choose between allowing the disobedience to go unpunished, punishing the parents for their religiously motivated conduct, or exempting them from a scheme intended to further the public good. These are not easy choices to make, as we will see in relation to prohibitions against religious drug use and duties to perform military service and pay taxation.

In the second category, a State may restrict the freedom of other individuals and private associations to take action prejudicial to the religious interests of an individual. Although it is easy to focus upon the rights and entitlements of the religious individual who is being protected – particularly for writers and readers with an especial interest in that area – it must be remembered that State intervention will be at the expense of others. If the State prohibits public meetings intended to create a feeling of fear and insecurity amongst the Muslim community the freedom of the organisers is thereby restricted. In that example, the correct balance of interests may be so obvious that we hardly consider the anti-Islamic activists to have an interest that should be considered. But what of a small employer who finds their ability to allocate duties to their employees restricted by the religious duties of those employees, which the State will intervene to protect? We explore the issues raised by this form of State action by considering proselytism under the European Convention on Human Rights. The State which declines to use its power to indoctrinate members of minority communities may be distrustful of activities by private individuals which threaten to cause an individual to transfer from one community to another. In some European States, proselytism is regulated by national law, with improper forms of proselytism being prohibited.

Disobeying Generally Applicable Prohibitions

When we consider an individual disobeying the law for religious purposes, one of the first scenarios that come to mind is that of a conscientious objector to all forms of warfare refusing to answer a call to military service. This is, to some extent, something of a special case. The pacifist is refusing to carry out a positive duty placed upon them by the State – that is, a duty to do something. Although positive duties have become more common with the expansion of the State during the twentieth century, many legal obligations upon the individual are negative – that is, a duty to refrain from particular conduct. For instance, the State may prohibit unfair discrimination on the grounds of sexual orientation – in doing so, it places individuals and organisations covered by the prohibition under a duty not to discriminate on such grounds (Cruz, 1994).

These generally applicable laws may raise significant issues in relation to what I earlier identified as manifestation interests. For instance, a religious individual may see differential treatment between homosexual and heterosexual couples as a manifestation of their individual beliefs, and their community values. During the passage of the Human Rights Act 1998 through the UK legislature, for instance, some religious organisations and leaders were concerned that they would be required to accept homosexual marriages, contrary to their views of doctrine (Edge, 2001 at 93–4; Charlesworth, 1999).

Some 'generally applicable' laws are actually nothing of the sort, but are rather carefully crafted prohibitions aimed at restricting the activities of one particular religious community. In such a case, we might expect the courts to be particularly alert to the possibility that the law in question is unjustifiably damaging to religious interests and, where the domestic legal system empowers them to do so, willing to declare the law to be void as contrary to the fundamental rights of the individual. The United States provides a particularly good example of this. In *Church of the Lukumi Babalu Aye, Inc. v City of Hialeah* 113 S.Ct. 2217 (1993) (US) the Church's Santeria practices included animal sacrifice by trained priests during religious rituals. In 1987 the Church leased land within Hialeah, in order to establish a place of worship, and publicised their practice of animal sacrifice. As a result of an emergency meeting the city council passed local laws devised to prohibit this animal sacrifice. Was this a violation of First Amendment religious rights? The Supreme Court found that it was. On the basis of the wording of the law, its effect, and its history, it was clear that the law had been passed in order to suppress the Santeria religion. As it was intended to restrict religious practices because of their religious inspiration, it could not be said to be either neutral or of general application. Accordingly, the State was required to justify the restriction by reference to a compelling governmental interest. The law in question failed to meet the, deliberately, high standard this set (Cornwell, 1994).

Similarly, some generally applicable laws contain within themselves exemptions for religious purposes. For instance, the Criminal Justice Act 1988 s.139 (UK) deals with the possession of bladed weapons in a public place. Subsection (5)(b) provides a specific defence for any person who proves that they had the weapon 'for religious reasons'. Originally intended to address the needs of Sikhs, this provision was later applied to a pagan who wore a sword as part of their religious practices. In a number of United States jurisdictions, the legislature has provided exemptions to child abuse and manslaughter rules where the harm has followed from prayer-treatment (Treene, 1993). In some cases, however, the lawmakers may not have addressed their minds to the needs of a particular religious community; or the community may have lacked the political strength to secure a specific exemption. As Scalia J put it in *Smith*, discussed below, 'it may fairly be said that leaving accommodation to the political process will place at a relative disadvantage those religious practices that are not widely engaged in'.

This leaves us with the most difficult problem – if the State has created a law which is genuinely meant to apply to everyone, and whose purpose is not to suppress or restrict religious activities, can an individual claim a special exemption from that law for religious purposes? In other words, if an individual is accused of violating a generally applicable prohibition intended to advance a legitimate secular interest, can they claim the right to do so on the basis of their religious beliefs? Allowing the individual to ignore the prohibition will not only risk defeating the legitimate purpose upon which the prohibition is based, but may also be 'unfair to those who have to abide by the law and potentially dangerous to social cohesion' (Evans, 2001 at 168–9); while requiring compliance may put an unjustly onerous burden upon the individual.

The issues raised by generally applicable laws and religious practices are usefully illustrated by religiously motivated drug use cases in three of our jurisdictions: the United States, England, and South Africa.

Religious Drug Use in the US, England, and South Africa

A number of religious traditions have sought to question prohibitions on the use of psychoactive drugs, on the basis that their use is a religious practice within that tradition. In the US, religious practices were specifically recognised by the Act of Congress which implemented the prohibition of alcohol. The Act provided an exemption for wine used for sacramental purposes, or like religious rites. The wine was to be supplied only to 'a rabbi, minister of the gospel, priest or an officer duly authorized for the purpose by any church or congregation' (Volstead Act 1919 s.6 (US)). The sacramental purposes exemption proved extremely popular. Reporting in 1925 the Department of Research and Education for the Federal Council of the Churches of Christ reported that wine had been withdrawn for sacramental purposes in very large quantities – 2,139,000 gallons in 1922; 2,503,500 in 1923;

and 2,944,700 in 1924. There were undoubtedly concerns that wine withdrawn for sacramental purposes was being used for the secular purpose of entertainment (Kobler, 1974 at 250–1). Similar concerns have arisen in relation to claims for religious exemption for other substances, most notably in *United States v Kuch*, 288 F.Supp. 439 (US). In that case, the defendant sought to defend charges related to the supply of cannabis and LSD by reference to his role in the Neo-American Church. One tenet of this Church was that psychedelic substances were sacramental foods. The courts were prepared to find that this was not a bona fide Church, however, making use of the Church's motto ('Victory over Horseshit!'), symbol (a three-eyed toad), and official hymns ('Puff, the Magic Dragon' and 'Row, row, row your boat').

Before 1990 there had been a number of freedom of religion challenges to drug prohibitions in US courts, usefully reviewed by Brown (Brown, 1983). These included claims to the use of peyote by members of the Native American Church (*State v Big Sheep*, 75 Mont. 219, 243 P. 1067 (1926) (US); *People v Woody*, 61 Cal. 2d 716 (1964) (US)), and others (*In Re Grady* 61 Cal.2d 887 (1964) (US)); cannabis (marijuana) use on the basis of biblical texts (*People v Mitchell*, 244 Cal.App. 2d 176 (1966) (US)), the teachings of the Ethiopian Zion Coptic Church (*US v Middleton*, 690 F.2d. 820 (1982)), more diffuse beliefs (*People v Collins*, 273 Cal.App. 2d. 486 (1969) (US)), and worship of cannabis itself (*People v Mullins*, 50 Cal.App. 3d 61 (1975) (US)). The strongest line of authorities gave some protection to use of peyote by members of the Native American Church, while not extending such protection to other religious communities or substances (Brown, 1983 at 143), while other authorities suggested that free exercise of religion could never allow use of prohibited drugs (for instance, *State v Bullard*, 267 N.C. 599 (1966) (US); *State v Randall*, 540 S.W.2d. 156 (1976) (US)). The issue was dealt with by the Supreme Court, at length, in *Employment Division v Smith*, 494 US 872 (1990) (US).

In that case, Smith and a colleague were dismissed by a private drug rehabilitation organisation because they had ingested peyote during a ceremony of the Native American Church. They then applied for unemployment compensation, which was denied by the State of Oregon on the basis that they had been dismissed for work-related misconduct. The Supreme Court held that the State could prohibit sacramental peyote use without violating the free exercise guarantees of the Constitution, and consequently could refuse unemployment benefits to persons discharged for such use. A law which sought to ban peyote use solely because of its religious motivation would be contrary to the Constitution, but the situation was different where an otherwise constitutional criminal law which was not directed at religious practice incidentally forbade an act that the religion required. In such a case, the State did not have to defend its ban by reference to a compelling governmental interest. It was constitutionally permissible to exempt sacramental peyote use from the operation of the drug laws, but it was not constitutionally required.

Scalia J, giving the leading judgement of the court, feared that to find otherwise would be to create 'a private right to ignore generally applicable laws'. In particular, 'if "compelling interest" really means what it says (and watering it down here would subvert its rigor in the other fields where it is applied), many laws will not meet the test. Any society adopting such a system would be courting anarchy, but that danger increases in direct proportion to the society's diversity of religious beliefs, and its determination to coerce or suppress none of them. Precisely because "we are a cosmopolitan nation made up of people of almost every conceivable religious preference", and precisely because we value and protect that religious divergence, we cannot afford the luxury of deeming presumptively invalid, as applied to the religious objector, every regulation of conduct that does not protect an interest of the highest order'.

The significance of *Smith* was not simply that the ban on peyote use for religious purposes was upheld, but that it was done so without requiring a justification by the State of the impact upon the religious defendant. As I mentioned in the discussion of the US Constitution in Chapter 2, this was an immensely controversial decision, which led to a number of attempts by the Congress to reduce its effect. The most general measure, aimed at changing the Court's ruling on how to approach generally applicable neutral measures, was itself ruled unconstitutional by the Court. A more specific measure was also enacted to permit peyote use by Native Americans in connection with the practice of a traditional Indian religion (American Indian Religious Freedom Act Amendments 1994 (US)).

This measure does not, however, protect the peyote use of non-Native American co-religionists (Santangelo, 1995); or of members of other religions; or other drug use. This raises claims based on religious discrimination, rather than simply a religious right to sacramental drug use. If members of the Native American Church are entitled to sacramental drug use, is it unconstitutional religious discrimination not to allow sacramental use of cannabis by Rastafarians? This point was considered by a State court in *State v McBride*, 955 P.2d. 133 (1988) (US). The court was prepared to distinguish between the two communities on three grounds (Taylor, 1998). Firstly, peyote was used in limited quantities and during specific ceremonies by the NAC, whereas Rastafari use of cannabis was found to be unlimited – making it much more difficult to regulate if religious use was allowed. Secondly, abuse of peyote was far less common than abuse of cannabis – again making it more difficult to properly regulate religious cannabis use. Thirdly, and a point stressed by the court, the US has a special duty to respect the political and cultural integrity of Native Americans. The court did not consider an argument based on discrimination against Rastafarians when compared with Churches which used wine in sacramental services.

The US position, then, is that prohibition of drug use which incidentally bans a particular religious practice will not be subject to scrutiny on the basis of religious rights. It is open to the legislatures, however, to create religious exemptions to drug legislation if this is desired.

Turning to England, the only substantial challenges to the prohibition of drugs on religious grounds concern cannabis use by Rastafari. Soon after the Human Rights Act 1998 came into force, a Rastafarian charged with possession of cannabis with intent to supply sought to argue that his religious rights under Article 9 of the ECHR would be infringed he were convicted. The trial judge did not consider the case on its merits, but left the possibility of a clash between the domestic law on drugs and the rights under Article 9 open (Loveland, 2001). Later the same year, a similar case reached the Court of Appeal.

In *Taylor* [2001] EWCA Crim 2263 (UK), later endorsed in *Andrews* [2004] EWCA Crim 947 (UK), the defendant had been observed by police officers to approach a Rastafarian temple, and upon being searched was found to be carrying a number of small parcels of cannabis. More cannabis was found in his car. Upon arrest he indicated that he was a Rastafarian, and that the cannabis was part of his religion. During questioning he expanded on this by explaining that the cannabis had been prepared for a regular act of worship at the temple. At his trial, the defendant argued that the proceedings should be stayed if the Crown accepted the truth of his statements; or that the jury had to be satisfied either that the cannabis was not intended for religious purpose, or if it was that the criminal proceedings were not a necessary and proportionate measure effecting a legitimate aim. Effectively, the defendant was arguing that his acts should be interpreted as a manifestation of religion under ECHR Article 9, and the criminal proceedings needed to be justified under Article 9(2).

At the trial, the prosecution conceded without argument that Rastafarianism was a religion, and that the drugs were all destined for religious purposes. The court moved from this to the conclusion that Article 9 was implicated. It may be, however, that this was too uncritical. Stavros has discussed generally applicable prohibitions in relation to both the ECHR and the US Constitution (Stavros, 1997). He sees a distinction in the ECHR jurisprudence based on the intimacy of the link between the religious belief and the practice. He argues that 'manifestation' is much easier to find where the law being queried is aimed at religious activity. Where the law is generally applicable, the ECHR requires a much clearer proof that the practice is a direct manifestation of the religious belief. That said, once this has been established, the State is required to balance the legitimate interest advanced by the rule against 'the demands which religion makes on some persons affected by this rule' (Stavros, 1997 at 619). In deciding whether a proper balance has been struck, the ECHR exercises much closer scrutiny over specifically religious laws than generally applicable laws which implicate religious interests. He concludes that, as with the United States Supreme Court, 'although in theory the Commission has never excluded the possibility that such claims could succeed under Article 9 of the Convention, in practice it is very reluctant to accept that a person has the right, because of his or her religious beliefs, not to comply with a law which was meant to apply to everybody and which was enacted with no religious considerations in mind' (Stavros, 1997 at 622).

Taking Article 9 to be involved, the trial judge found that Article 9(2) justified the prohibition, and thus the criminal proceedings. In doing so, he stated that the proper test was whether there was a pressing social need, and whether the prohibition bore a reasonable relationship to the end pursued. This was admittedly a very complex matter for a trial judge to decide, but he was able to make use of a number of international conventions aimed at restricting psychotropic substances (see further Boister, 2001). These indicated an international consensus for an unqualified ban on the possession of cannabis as necessary to prevent public health and safety dangers arising from the drug. If he were wrong, and the prosecution was contrary to the ECHR, the English statute could not be reinterpreted so as to comply with it, and he was required to enforce it.

Rose LJ delivered the only judgement in the Court of Appeal. He noted that this was not a case of possession of cannabis for private religious use, but of supply for religious use. He accepted for the purposes of the appeal that Article 9 issues were raised by the case, but it is clear from the judgement that this could be an open issue at a later date. The key issue in the case was whether any prima facie violation was justified. Rose LJ considered *Smith*, and the South African case of *Prince* discussed below, before coming to the conclusion that the trial judge had been justified in relying upon the international conventions in concluding that Article 9(2) was satisfied. Accordingly, the conviction of the defendant was affirmed. His sentence of twelve months' imprisonment was, however, reduced as being manifestly excessive for such an offence committed for religious purposes rather than for profit.

In contrast to the US position, then, although the result was effectively the same, the English Court of Appeal did engage in a process of scrutiny of the law as enforced against a religious defendant. It was not, however, very far reaching. Rather than making use of medical, sociological, and religious data peculiar to cannabis and to Rastafarians, as suggested by counsel for the defendant, the key issue of proportionality was answered by reference to international legal documents of general application.

These cases contrast sharply with the decision of a closely-divided Constitutional Court of South Africa in *Prince v The President of the Law Society of the Cape of Good Hope and Others* 2002(2) SA 794 (SA) (see also *Prince v President of the Cape Law Society and Others* 2001 (2) SA 388 (SA)). In this case, Prince wished to become an attorney. He satisfied the requirements for entry into the profession, but had a number of convictions for possession of cannabis. During the application process he expressed his intention to continue using cannabis, such use being inspired by his Rastafari religion. The Law Society concluded that he was not a fit and proper person to become an attorney, and refused to allow him to proceed in the qualification process. Prince did not seek to challenge the constitutionality of the prohibition on cannabis use generally, but instead argued that the prohibition went too far by including use required by the Rastafari religion. Evidence was heard from Professor Carole Diana Yawney on the cultural and religious practices of Rastafari.

A large minority of the court agreed. Ngcobo J, with the support of Mokgoro and Sachs JJ and Madlanga AJ (four justices in all) found that the status of Rastafarianism as a religion under the South African Constitution was not disputed; that the use of cannabis was an essential element of individual meditation and collective reasoning; that cannabis had particular medical effects, including harmful psychological dependence if smoked. Ngcobo J stressed that Rastafari made use of cannabis in different ways, including many which did not involve smoking. Officials opposing Prince's case argued that, while the prohibition was a restriction on his right to freedom of religion, it was justifiable under s.36 of the Constitution as essential to the war on drugs, and to ensure South Africa met its international obligations. Additionally, a religious exemption for Rastafari alone would be difficult to administer. Ngcobo J stressed the importance of religious rights, particularly in a diverse democracy based on human dignity, equality, and freedom. In this case 'the existence of the law which effectively punishes the practice of the Rastafari religion degrades and devalues the followers of the Rastafari religion in our society. It is a palpable invasion of their dignity. It strikes at the very core of their human dignity. It says that their religion is not worthy of protection. The impact of the limition is profound indeed' (para. 51). Accordingly, while recognising the significance of the war on drugs, a properly crafted religious exemption could allow the State to achieve its legitimate aims without restricting the religious rights of Rastafari to the extent the absolute prohibition did. Ngcobo J was not concerned with the content of such an exemption – that was a matter for the legislature – but was prepared to hold that the current law, lacking any exemption, was unconstitutionally broad.

A bare majority of the court reached the opposite conclusion. Chaskalson CJ gave a joint judgement with Ackerman and Kriegler JJ, which was concurred in by Goldstone and Yacoob JJ (for a total of five justices). Chaskalson interpreted the factual context of the case differently, placing more stress on the prevalence of cannabis use in Rastafari life, and its lack of regulation by doctrines or organisational structures. While in agreement with Ngcobo J that the prohibition limited the religious rights of Rastafari, the makers of this judgement considered it to be a justifiable limitation under section 36 of the Constitution. A blanket ban on drug use, regardless of the harm caused by a particular instance of use, facilitated enforcement of legislation aimed at dealing with harmful drugs. In particular, in contrast with the structured use of peyote discussed by the minority judgement in the US case of *Smith*, there 'is no objective way in which a law enforcement official could distinguish between the use of cannabis for religious purposes and the use of cannabis for recreation' (para. 130). The practical problems of administering a religious exemption would be exacerbated by the organisational structures of Rastafarianism, and the need to encompass religious claims by non-Rastafarians. Accordingly, the legislation was a constitutionally valid limitation on Prince's religious rights.

Although in all three cases, claims to a legal right to religious drug use failed, the three reveal important differences in approach. In particular, the majority in *Smith* were unwilling to find that neutral, generally applicable, drug laws needed to be justified by the State, and certainly not that they were subject to strict scrutiny. The Court of Appeal in *Taylor* were prepared to acknowledge that the restriction needed to be justified by the State, but were then satisfied with a low level of, strictly formal, legal evidence. The Constitutional Court in *Prince* undertook a serious, detailed, consideration of the case, and its religious context, before concluding that the restriction was justifiable.

Refusing a Positive Duty to Act

In the previous section, we considered the position of the individual who was subject to a prohibition, a duty not to act. The complexities are further increased when the individual is under a duty not merely to refrain from doing what they believe to be right, but from actively engaging in activity they believe to be wrong. Consider, for instance, a religious pacifist who regards involvement in warfare, including preparing for defensive war, as contrary to their religious beliefs. If required to serve in the armed forces themselves, they may every day be required to act contrary to their religious beliefs. Even if exempt from conscription, or in a State with purely voluntary armed forces, they see a clear link between their provision of resources to the State through general taxation, and the maintenance and employment of armed forces, their regular payments of taxes may similarly be seen as requiring them to collude with an enterprise they believe to be morally repugnant. A situation may be created where the State must either tolerate a considerable amount of law breaking by those unwilling to perform their duties, punish them for this refusal, or create some form of accommodation of these objections (see Braithwaite, 1995).

In this section, we consider objection to both military service, and to payment of taxes. In both examples, the individual is seeking to avoid a duty to carry out a duty seen by the State as essential to its fundamental interests. In relation to compulsory military service, if all those liable were to be exempt, the established mechanisms for national defence would cease to function; similarly, if none of those liable were to pay taxes, the State would no longer possess the resources needed to carry out its functions. Not only does the State possess clear interests in imposing the positive duty upon its citizens, but citizens possess secular incentives to avoid the duties. In the case of military service, the citizen may seek to escape the hardships of conscription, and the risk of injury or death in case of conflict; in the case of taxation, the citizen may wish to keep a larger proportion of their income for disposal as they see fit. These are areas, then, where the State has a particular interest in ensuring general compliance; the insincere claimant has clear benefits to be gained by achieving exemption; and the sincere claimant's religious interests may be particularly engaged.

Conscientious Objection to Military Service under the ECHR

Conscientious objection to military service is often seen as the classic example of refusal of a legal duty for religious reasons (Hammer, 2001 at 186–7). When a State decides that it should adopt compulsory military service, it will be faced with a variety of decisions concerning conscientious objection. Bibbings has given a useful analysis of the approach taken in the United Kingdom during both World Wars (Bibbing, 1995). In 1916 there was considerable debate as to whether conscription should be introduced, and the Military Service Act 1916, introducing conscription, included an exemption for conscientious objectors (Military Service Act 1916 s.2(1)(d) (UK)). Those who succeeded in claiming an exemption could receive partial exemption, which excluded them only from combatant duties; conditional exemption, which required them to undertake alternative work of national importance; or absolute exemption, which required no substitute work. The legal provisions were poorly defined, and administered by tribunals rather than courts. By the start of the Second World War, conscription and exemption for conscientious objectors were both established concepts. The relevant legislation provided the same possible exemptions for conscientious objectors (National Service (Armed Forces) Act 1939 s.5 (UK)). The scheme was more clearly defined by statute, and administered by tribunals including legally trained members.

The UK systems, then, recognised that a sincere conscientious objection might be met by a variety of responses from the State – in some cases it could be accommodated by non-combatant military duties, or duties of equivalent importance to the State during its time of war; in others, no substitute duty should be given. They did not, however, explicitly deal with the question of specific objection – that is, the situation where the claimant does not absolutely rule out the possibility of fighting, but either believes that the conflict in question should not be fought (*Gillette v United States*, 401 US 437 (1971) (US)), or that they should remain free to judge the merits of any particular conflict (*United States v Macintosh*, 283 US 605 (1931) (US)). Neither did the schemes on their face deal with the way in which a claimant proves they are entitled to an exemption – for instance, whether they were required to be part of a defined religious community with clearly documented pacifist doctrines (see *United States v Seeger*, 380 US 163 (1964) (US)). A statutory scheme for conscription can, however, address these issues.

Increasingly, however, States are subject to the constraints of international law in framing their policy and legislation. Evans has outlined the development of conscientious objection under the ECHR (Evans, 2001 at 170–9). Initially, the Commission took the view that Article 9 did not require States to recognise conscientious objectors, as the Convention explicitly foresaw the possibility of compelling such objectors to serve (*Grandrath v Federal Republic of Germany*, App. 2299/64, 10 Y.B. E.C.H.R. 626 (1966) (ECHR)). Article 4 prohibits slavery and related restrictions on the individual. The provision does not extend to 'any service of a military character or, in the case of conscientious objectors *in countries where they are recognised*, service exacted instead of compulsory military service' (ECHR, art.4(3)). Although the way in which a State chose to implement any alternate service was not entirely unfettered by the ECHR (*Autio v Finland*, App.17086/90, 72 E.C.H.R. D&R 245 (1990) (ECHR)), there was no right to substitute service, and certainly no right to avoid even substitute service.

A number of extra-judicial developments, however, increasingly undermined an approach that excluded Article 9 from the area. In particular, in 1976 the Parliamentary Assembly of the Council of Europe called on member States to comply with principles governing conscientious objection which recognised the implication of Article 9 rights (Evans, 2001 at 175). In the 1990s, conscientious objection was placed more firmly within Article 9. In *Thlimmenos v Greece* (2000) HUDOC 6 April (ECHR) a Jehovah's Witness had refused to enlist in the army for religious reasons, and as a result had served two years' imprisonment. He was later refused entry into the accounting profession on the basis of his conviction for a serious criminal offence. This was found to be in violation of Articles 9 and 14 read together, because of the discriminatory nature of applying the rule to this particular instance. The majority of the Commission noted, however, that due to the lack of any alternate service when Thlimmenos was convicted he was faced 'with the choice of either serving in the armed forces or being convicted. In these circumstances, the Commission considers that the applicant's conviction amounted to an interference with his right to manifest his religion'.

Conscientious Objection to Taxation in the US

Flowers has considered conscientious objection in relation to the payment of taxes (Flowers, 1993). The issue has arisen in a variety of contexts. In relation to social security benefits, for instance, Congress has recognised that members of the Old Order Amish conscientiously object to the State taking responsibility for caring for the aged and infirm, and so self-employed adherents should not be compelled to participate in the programme (Flowers, 1993, 711–2). The Supreme Court has, however, ruled that there is no constitutional right of non-participation beyond the scope of the self-employed, so that an Amish employer cannot refuse to withold social security tax from their employee's wage, or to pay the employer's share of the taxes (*United States v Lee*, 455 US 252 (1982) (US)). The statutory exemption for the self-employed has itself been interpreted narrowly (for example, *Hughes v Commissioners*, 81 TC 683 (1983) (US)). In both cases, the courts were concerned that accommodation of religion should not compromise fiscal stability and efficient administration.

Social security is a comparatively recent state activity, and the hypothecated taxation used in the US and elsewhere is unusual. What of where a religious individual refuses to pay taxes to the government in order to prevent State support for an activity the individual objects to? The issue goes beyond objection to warfare (consider *DiCarlo v Commissioner*, 280 TCM (CCH) (1992) (UK)), but cases in the US do cluster in that area. In *United States v Lee*, the court noted that it would be impossible to distinguish between taxes for military purposes and the government's general programme of taxation. Even if it were possible, allowing individuals to select those taxes they were willing to pay could destroy the State's ability to function (*Autenrieth v Cullen*, 418 F.2d 586 (1969) (US)), and so could not be compared with exemption from military service (*Muste v Commissioner*, 35 T.C. 913 (1961) (US)). There is an obvious concern that witholding of taxes may be insincere, and intended for personal benefit, but even attempts to divert that proportion of the taxes due to a different charitable or public project have failed – it is for the State to determine how to dispose of tax revenue, not the tax payer (for example, *Russell v Commissioner*, 60 T.C. 942 (1973) (US)).

Seeking Protection for Religious Difference: Improper Proselytism under the European Convention on Human Rights

In the preceding sections, the State sought obedience to generally applicable laws in order to protect State interests. We can see some State interests as being primarily the interests of the organs and personnel of the State – for instance, the collection of revenue in order to fund State structures. But even here, the assumption in our jurisdictions is that the State by its existence provides some benefits to individuals within its territory. The role of the State in benefiting individuals is clearer in the discussion of prohibited drugs earlier in the chapter. Although on some definitions use of such drugs is a crime without a victim – so that we cannot find an individual whose interests are protected by the restriction on the freedom of the prospective drug user – this was not the approach taken even by the sophisticated Constitutional Court in *Prince*. Rather, the court concluded that harms would happen to individual members of the State collectively if the 'war against drugs' was to be hampered to the extent a religious exemption would require. So, generally applicable laws might be seen as providing a diffuse level of protection to individuals throughout the territory.

On occasion, however, particular individuals may make more specific claims for protection by the State. These can include claims for protection of religious interests. In some instances, these will be claims against State action itself – so that we could interpret *Prince* and *Smith* as defendants seeking the protection of the respective courts from the actions of the legislatures and executives of the territories. Often, however, these will be claims for protection against the actions of a private individual or organisation.

The application of fundamental rights to non-State actors is a complex issue in States which seek to provide substantial protection for a private sector of economic, social, and cultural life (see Clapham, 1993). Fundamental rights may be explicitly extended to bind non-State actors, but even here we would expect to find a distinction between the obligations of State and non-State actors. We can find this in the Constitution of South Africa 1996 s.8, which provides by ss.(1) that '[t]he Bill of Rights applies to all law, and binds the legislature, the executive, the judiciary and all organs of state'; while ss.(2) states '[a] provision of the Bill of Rights binds a natural or a juristic person if, and to the extent that, it is applicable, taking into account the nature of the right and the nature of any duty imposed by the right'.

Even where a fundamental guarantee does not bind private individuals, the State may sometimes be to blame for allowing violations of the fundamental rights by such private individuals. We can see this under the ECHR in particular. As an international instrument, the ECHR does not directly bind non-state bodies such as individuals and corporations. The State may be found to have violated the Convention if it permits such individuals to violate another's fundamental rights, however, but it is that permission, rather than the acts of the individual, which are reviewed. For instance, if the State did not legally prohibit murder, and a private individual killed another person, the State would be liable under the ECHR for legally permitting the deprivation of life contrary to Article 2. As a result of this feature of the ECHR, the impact of the Human Rights Act 1998 (UK) on relationships between private individuals has been a subject of considerable academic debate (for example, Addo, 1990; Hunt, 1998; Buseton, 2000; Wade, 2000).

Rather more straightforward, however, are the instances when, guided by the same values as those underpinning the fundamental guarantees, the State has chosen to implement particular laws protecting religious interests from the actions of private individuals. A frequently contentious issue is the borderline between attempting to convert others to one's religious beliefs, which is a lawful manifestation of religion protected by religious liberty guarantees; and indoctrination of others, which may constitute a violation of their fundamental religious right to hold their current beliefs freely.

In a pair of related cases, the European Court of Human Rights has explored the legal limits of proselytism. In *Kokkinakis* v *Greece* (1994) 17 EHRR 397 (ECHR), the court considered a claim by a Jehovah's Witness who had been imprisoned by the Greek State for proselytism (see further Edge, 1995). In 1986, the applicant and his wife, both active Jehovah's Witnesses, persuaded the wife of the local cantor to allow them into her home, whereupon they began to discuss religious matters. Her husband immediately contacted the police, who arrested the couple on charges of proselytism. The couple were convicted of the offence, although Mrs Kokkinakis' conviction was quashed on appeal. The relevant provision of Greek law defined proselytism as: 'any direct or indirect attempt to intrude on the religious beliefs of a person of a different religious persuasion, with the aim of undermining those beliefs, either by any kind of inducement or promise of an inducement or moral support or material assistance, or by fraudulent means or by taking advantage of his inexperience, trust, need, low intellect or naiveté'.

The majority of the Greek appellate Court found that the applicants' conduct had satisfied this definition, although it was clear that no extreme methods of enticement, such as bribery, threats, or 'brainwashing', were employed. Before the European Court of Human Rights, Greece accepted that the offence of proselytism was an interference with the right under Article 9(1), but argued that the interference was justified under Article 9(2).

The majority of the court found that the restriction upon the applicant was not necessary in a democratic society. They drew a sharp dividing line between 'bearing Christian witness and improper proselytism'. The former was 'a corruption or deformation' of the latter, which could be evidenced, inter alia, by offering material or social advantages with a view to gaining new members of the Church, by exerting improper pressure on persons in distress or need, or by use of violence or, to adopt the terminology of the court, 'brainwashing'. Improper proselytism was incompatible with respect for the freedom of religion of others, and therefore could legitimately be regulated by the State. The court held that at no point had it been shown that the defendant's behaviour constituted improper proselytism, therefore it had not been shown that the infringement was necessary, and therefore Article 9 had been violated.

In coming to this conclusion, the majority of the court enunciated an important view of autonomy in relation to proselytism and conversion. They cited with approval a 1956 report of the World Council of Churches dealing with improper proselytism. Although they expressly avoided giving a complete definition of improper proselytism, it would appear that they endorsed a definition which included putting 'improper pressure on people in distress or need'. It should be noted that the distinguishing feature of this form of improper proselytism is the target of the pressure, rather than the pressure itself, as other forms of improper pressure such as bribery and violence are dealt with elsewhere in the definition. Thus, the majority would seem to recognise that religious autonomy can be impaired by distress or need as well, it would seem to follow, as by more permanent characteristics such as age and incapacity.

The majority of the court, and a number of the dissenting judgements, also see proselytism as potentially dangerous. Judge Valticos' dissenting opinion makes it clear that he views the predator/prey relationship as the paradigm of conversion. His narrative of the incident, which differs from the majority of the court, brings out an image of the missionary as predator: 'On the one hand, we have a specialist in conversion, a martyr of the criminal courts whose earlier convictions have served only to harden him in his militancy, and, on the other hand, the ideal victim, a naive woman, the wife of a cantor in the Orthodox Church (if he manages to convert her, what a triumph!). He swoops on her, trumpets that he has good news for her (the play on words is obvious, but no doubt not to her), manages to get himself let in and, as an experienced commercial traveller and cunning purveyor of a faith he wants to spread, expounds to her his intellectual wares cunningly wrapped up in a mantle of universal peace and radiant happiness. Who, indeed, would not like peace and happiness? But [is] this the mere exposition of Mr Kokkinakis' beliefs or is it not rather an attempt to beguile the simple soul of the cantor's wife? Does the Convention afford its protection to such undertakings? Certainly not' (ibid., at 430–1).

The other judges in the court, including the majority, do not take such an extreme, or demonised and sexualised, view of the proselytism transaction. It is clear, however, that proselytism is seen as balancing the rights of the believer to seek to convert an unbeliever, against the right of the unbeliever to be left alone. But this is a limited model of religious freedom, in that it neglects the importance of conversion as a benefit to the convert. Restrictions on proselytism carry with them the assumption that development of the personality is best carried out within the existing belief system, whatever it may be, rather than any other religion which may be brought to the target's attention by a proselytiser. On a related point, religious experience, including the experience of atheists and agnostics, may be a personal search for truth (see Marshall, 1994). Given that neither the State nor the European Court of Human Rights has the jurisdiction to determine this personal truth, all that is required is for the State and Court to allow the individual to conduct their own search. This search is best carried out when a free market of ideas in the religious field exists. Thus, restrictions on proselytism affect not only the right of the proselytiser to spread their faith, but also the right of the target to undertake their search for truth. Personal truth can involve a change of faith, rather than the simple retention of faith described in the paradigm.

The courts' reservations concerning proselytism extend so far as to indicate that the State has a duty to protect the individual from improper proselytism of the kind listed above. The principal justification for restricting improper proselytism was that it constituted an infringement of the rights of the target. If the State fails to restrict such proselytism, it is in violation of the Convention for failing to adequately protect the target's rights. The majority of the court found nothing objectionable about providing such protection through a specific offence of religious proselytism.

The European Court of Human Rights returned to proselytism in another case concerning Greece, that of *Larissis and Others v Greece*, (1998) 27 EHRR 329 (ECHR). In this case the applicants were members of the Pentecostal Church, and officers in the Greek Air Force. They were convicted of the offence of proselytism both against subordinates in the Air Force, and against a number of civilians. It was accepted that their conviction and punishment for the crime constituted an interference with their religious rights under Article 9, and the principal question for the court was whether the restriction, to protect the rights and interests of others, was necessary in a democratic society. In relation to the subordinate airmen the court found that 'the hierarchical structures which are a feature of life in the armed forces may colour every aspect of the relations between military personnel, making it difficult for a subordinate to rebuff the approaches of an individual of superior rank or to withdraw from a conversation initiated by him. Thus, what would in the civilian world be seen as an innocuous exchange of ideas which the recipient is free to accept or reject, may, within the confines of military life, be viewed as a form of harassment or the application of undue pressure in abuse of power' (ibid., para. 51). Accordingly, although the court found that the charges in relation to civilians were not justified, they upheld the convictions for proselytism against subordinates in the Air Force.

Conclusions

As the discussion in this chapter shows, the State can have a powerful impact upon the life of a religious person. It is capable of restricting their religious practices by reference to other goals which it wishes to pursue – for instance preventing Rastafari from using cannabis in order to pursue a policy against non-medicinal drug use. It is capable of placing their religious interests above these general goals – for instance allowing conscientious objectors to avoid military service. It is also capable of acting to restrain the activities of others in order to protect these religious interests – as we see for instance in relation to proselytism.

Ultimately, it is a question of balance. The State cannot give ultimate priority to religious convictions, unless it wishes to sanction, at the extreme, involuntary human sacrifice. It cannot ignore the special hardship of a religious person restrained from acting according to their principles unless it wishes to restrict religion to the field of personal belief rather than activity. But striking the balance between the claims of religious individuals and the interests of others remains a difficult task.

Religious individuals, however, are not the end of the story. The State also interacts with religious communities and organisations, raising a different set of concerns.

Chapter 4

The State and the Religious Organisation

The Nature of the Problems

In the preceding chapter, I focused on the interaction between the State and the private individual. In practice, of course, most religious traditions have a communal element. There may be particular religious practices which can only be carried out together with co-religionists. Even if this is not the case, individuals who identify with one another may well seek to form associations to advance their common interests.

Religious organisations raise significant concerns for the interaction of law and religion, which may usefully be summarised under the broad heading of entanglement. If the State seeks to be neutral between religions, and to allow members of a variety of traditions to be full members of the State, then it cannot become excessively associated with a single religious tradition or organisation. If the State seeks to allow exercise of religious rights at a community level, rather than restricting religious freedom to a private activity, then it cannot excessively restrict the formation and operation of religious organisations. If the State seeks to become a partner with religious organisations in furthering public policy, for instance by involving Church groups in the delivery of social and practical care for the poor, then it needs to be aware of the impact of this partnership upon the religious organisation in question, and upon those not included in the partnership.

Entanglement is an abiding concern of the United States constitution, but is a concern even for States which lack a formal restriction on the establishment of religion, such as the United Kingdom. In this chapter we consider five different areas of potential entanglement.

Firstly, we consider the formal involvement of religious organisations in the State and, at the international level, in international organisations. The principal focus here is the distinctive mechanism for representing the Church of England in the United Kingdom Parliament. Secondly, we consider schemes for the recognition, and registration, of religious organisations by the State. The principal focus here is the influential, but extremely controversial, model for religious registration in Russia. Thirdly, we consider the conferment upon religious organisations of the fiscal and legal benefits associated with charitable status. The principal focus here is the administration and formulation of United Kingdom charity law. Fourthly, we consider the enforcement of legal rights against religious organisations by private individuals. Here, we focus upon the employment of ministers in the UK, and liability for clergy misconduct in the US. Finally, the chapter concludes with a consideration of a particular sort of community resource – sacred places. The focus here is upon sacred buildings in the United Kingdom, including buildings which are also a family dwelling, and sacred landscapes in the United States, particularly in relation to Native American religious practices.

Organisational Involvement in the Domestic Constitution and International Organisations

A substantial body of academic work on the interaction of law and religion focuses on issues of 'Church and State' – indeed, the latter term is sometimes used to refer to the interaction more generally. A fundamental concern of these discussions is the appropriate relationship between religious organisations and the State. How far should the State enter into a partnership with a particular religious organisation or group of organisations? How should the State treat religious organisations, or the religious individual, who are excluded from these partnerships? Religious organisations also need to consider how far they should become involved in the State, and what the implications of that involvement for them will be.

From the State perspective, we have already considered the importance of constitutional rules dealing with fundamental religious rights. Additionally, many constitutions lay down the relationship between the State and particular religious organisations; or religious organisations more broadly. Inevitably, these will reflect the social positions of the organisations at the time the constitution is drafted.

A useful example is that of Ireland, which has been considered by Hogan (Hogan, 1987). He notes that the 1937 Constitution contains an article guaranteeing freedom of religion, prohibiting the State from endowing any religion, prohibiting religious discrimination both generally and in the area of education in particular, and guaranteeing the autonomy of religious denominations (Irish Constitution 1937 art. 44 (Ireland)). At the same time, however, the Constitution 'recognizes the special position of the Holy Catholic Apostolic and Roman Church as the guardian of the Faith professed by the great majority of the citizens' (Irish Constitution 1937 art.2 (Ireland)). The tension between these provisions was resolved, until 1963, with interpretations that prioritised the Catholic Church and Catholic values (Hogan, 1987 at 56–63). After that date, the balance shifted more towards the non-discrimination values in article 44, to a point where Hogan sees an 'absence of any overt discrimination or favouritism on the part of the State in religious matters' (ibid., at 73).

Not all European states have a national Church, and some States are actively working to reduce the legal strength of historical ties (see for instance Stegeby, 1999). Many, however, prefer to maintain a special relationship with a national Church. This has been accepted as compatible with the ECHR so long as it does not result in damage to the Article 9 rights of non-members (*Darby v Sweden* (1989) HUDOC 9 May, para. 37 (ECHR)).

An alternative to constitutional recognition is a constitutional bar on the State entering into a special relationship with any religious organisation. In Australia, for instance, the federal government is unable to 'make any law for establishing any religion' (Commonwealth of Australia Constitution Act 1900 s.116 (Aust.)). This constitutional limitation is directed at laws which are intended to give the religion an 'established' status, and does not prohibit laws which unintentionally have the same effect (*Kruger and Others v The Commonwealth of Australia* (1997) 190 CLR 1 (Aust.)).

A more pervasive limit on establishment can be found in the US Constitution, which states that 'Congress shall make no law respecting an establishment of religion, or prohibiting the free exercise therof' (United States Constitution, First Amendment (US)). This clause was originally intended to prevent the establishment of a national State Church, rather than preventing individual States from forming special links with particular religious organisations. It has developed, however, into a strong requirement that all elements of the US State avoid excessive entanglement with religious organisations. The Supreme Court has stated that government bodies cannot 'pass laws which aid one religion, aid all religions, or prefer one religion over another ... No tax in any amount, large or small, can be levied to support any religious activities or organisation, whatever they may be called, or whatever form they may adopt to teach or practice religion. Neither a state nor the Federal Government can, openly or secretly, participate in the affairs of any religious organisations or groups or vice versa' (*Everson v Board of Education*, 330 US 1, 15-16 (1947) (US)). A rigid prohibition on entanglement of Church and State can pose problems of its own as the State seeks to engage in action within a social context where religion plays an important role – as a consideration of the detailed jurisprudence and commentary on public schooling in the United States shows (see *Consideration of Reports Submitted by State Parties under Article 40 of the Covenant, Initial Report of State Parties, Addendum, USA*, UN Doc. CCPR/C/81/Add.4 (1994) para. 564–71).

In the case study that follows, we consider a particularly strong form of State entanglement with a religious organisation, where the national legislature is composed, in part, of officials within a particular religious organisation.

Religious Representation in the UK

The United Kingdom is generally understood to have at least one 'Established' or State Church – the Church of England. It is not always clear what is meant by 'Established' in this sense, but it is often used to describe a complex set of rights, duties, privileges, and obligations which apply to the Church of England, and to the Church of England alone (see Edge, 1998). A distinctive example of this is the place of representatives of the Church of England in the United Kingdom Parliament.

Within Parliament, the House of Lords no longer has authority equal to the House of Commons. The Lords do not have the authority to amend, reject or delay money bills, and most other legislation may receive the Royal Assent without the consent of the House of Lords, if the Commons is determined to put the legislation through (Parliament Act 1911 (UK), Parliament Act 1947 (UK)). The House of Lords is currently in the process of being reformed, although its final composition remains to be determined (see generally, Shell, 2004).

The current House contains a number of Lords Spiritual. The Lords Spiritual are members of the hierarchy of the Church of England. Originally, all Bishops of the Church of England sat in the Lords, but the increase in the number of bishoprics was not met by an increase in the number of seats. Today, both Archbishops, the Bishops of London, Westminster and Durham, and the twenty-one most senior of the remaining Bishops sit in the House of Lords (Bishoprics Act 1878 (UK)). They retain their position so long as they hold their bishopric, effectively retiring from both roles before the age of seventy (Ecclesiastical Offices (Age Limit) Measure 1975 (UK); Bishops (Retirement) Measure 1986 (UK)). It is possible for other religious organisations to gain a voice in the Lords through the appointment of a life peer with strong links to the organisation (McEldowney, 1994 at 55). Although these are sometimes seen as being appointments of religious representatives, in a recent review Weller identified them as having 'been solely on the basis of a recognition of the individual concerned, rather than as part of an explicit attempt to reflect the wider range of religious traditions and communities now present in our increasingly pluralising society' (Weller, 1999 at para. 6.5). Even if it is possible to have religious representation through this mechanism, however, there are significant differences between this peer and a Lord Spiritual. A life peer effectively retains their position for life, so would remain in the Lords even if they ceased to be a member of their original religious organisation or community, while a Lord Spiritual who ceases to hold their position in the Church of England hierarchy loses their place in the Lords. The appointment of a Lord Spiritual is effectively automatic, and as of right to the most senior Bishops, while appointment of life peers to function as religious representatives is *ad hoc* and at the discretion of the political figures recommending the creation of life peers. It follows that the selection of which religious figure to appoint as a representative of a religious organisation or community can be contentious (see Newman, 1997).

There have been a number of studies of the way in which the Lords Spiritual work in the House of Lords. In particular, we have the general study of the House of Lords by Bromhead (Bromhead, 1958), the important review of the Lords Spiritual by Weare (Weare, 1966), the study of the Lords Spiritual by Drewry and Brock (Drewry and Brock, 1971), and the detailed study of them between 1979 and 1987 published by Brown in 1994 (Brown, 1994). Additionally, as part of a broader study of religious representation in legislatures, Edge and Pearce considered the Lords Spiritual (Edge and Pearce, 2003). These studies allow us to draw out the key characteristics of religious representation through the Lords Spiritual.

Firstly, the fundamental justification for their place in the Lords is their role as religious representatives. Although it is possible to argue that they entered the Lords as Barons, and so constitute merely a 'hangover from the middle ages' (Russell and Hazell, 2000 at 17), this historical explanation – if valid – is no longer the prime justification for their presence (DATF, 1999 at 24). Rather, they sit as representatives of the Church of England (see House of Lords Precedence Act 1539 s.3 (UK); Welsh Church Act 1914 s.2(2) (UK)). Although summoned individually, they sit by virtue of their ecclesiastical office, rather than as individuals chosen to assist Parliament because of their personal characteristics. Although complicated by the role of Royal patronage – exercised on the binding advice of the Prime Minister – in making the appointment, it is fair to say that the Lords Spiritual are appointed by the Church of England itself. Once a Bishop has been appointed by the Church's own procedures, albeit procedures involving State actors, there is no discretion in any State actor as to whether a Bishop becomes a member of the Lords.

Secondly, they sit as representatives of an Established Church, the Church of England. In her recent discussion of the issue, Smith sees this as central to understanding the role of the Lords Spiritual (Smith, 2002), and it has informed many considerations of reform of that role (for instance Bryce, 1918). Although they sit as representatives on one Christian organisation, however, they do appear to have a weak interdenominational role. I use weak in the sense that although other denominations have no control over appointment or removal of the Lords Spiritual, once appointed the Lords may feel that they have a duty to represent the interests of other Christian denominations. Bromhead saw the contributions of Archbishop Fisher, for instance, as 'on behalf of the Church, and perhaps organised Christianity in general' (Bromhead, 1958). Brown saw more than 60 per cent of Bishops' interventions between 1979 and 1987 as involving Church or Christian interests (Brown, 1994). In a recent passage quoted in the following paragraph, the Church of England describes its role in Parliament as encompassing speaking for other denominations.

Thirdly, the Lords Spiritual may also have a weak inter-religious role. Certainly this is a role that has been claimed by the Church of England itself. In a detailed response to the Royal Commission considering reform of the House of Lords, it argued: 'Bishops will be found speaking not just for the Church of England but for its partners in other Christian churches, and for people of other faiths and none' (Church of England, 1994 at 4). There is evidence in recent debates of attempts to represent non-Christian religious interests (for instance, Bishop of Chelmsford, HL Deb 24.10.2001 col. 1075–77 (UK)). Accordingly, while some commentators have doubted the willingness or ability of the Bishops to fully perform an inter-religious role (Medhurst, 1999), the possibility that the Lords Spiritual carry out this role needs to be left open.

Fourthly, there are twenty-six Lords Spiritual, who accordingly are able to sit as corporate rather than individual representatives. This should not be overstated, and in particular it would be erroneous to view the bishops' bench as equivalent to a political party, with a party line and an interest in the number of votes cast on central issues. The Church of England has described the bishops as 'primarily independent local leaders' (Church of England, op.cit., at 6). In his consideration of their group life, Brown comes close to endorsing those who saw their group behaviour as 'both inconsistent and spasmodic' (Brown, op.cit., at 106). This comes from an institutional priority for a bishop speaking on an issue of concern, 'no matter what he may actually say' (ibid., at 108). Similarly, the bishops do not sit in groups, or vote in large numbers, even on key debates. With their range of other duties across England, the emphasis is upon ensuring a representation, not upon a volume of attendance. Although the Lords Spiritual constitute around 4 per cent of the membership of the House of Lords, they rarely sit or vote in large numbers. To illustrate this, Brown's study of 1979–87 found one vote which was decided by the votes of the Lords Spiritual present, but he observed that if all the Lords Spiritual had voted with the bishop who attended, this would have risen to 63 (Brown, op.cit., at 108–10).

Fifthly, the Lords Spiritual appear from the secondary sources to have a distinctive role in debates. They are entitled to contribute to all the work of the House, and since the 1960s have done so (Weare, op.cit., at 210; Cranmer, 2001). We can see a special focus on the law of the Church of England, moral issues, and a voice distinct from political parties. Commentary tends to take for granted the role of the bishops in dealing with ecclesiastical business before the House, but this has been seen by others as sufficiently important to justify their presence in the House (Archer, 1999 at 402). Commentators, and the Church itself, have repeatedly seen the Lords Spiritual as bringing a special voice to bear on moral issues. In his discussion of the Lords Spiritual, Weare saw some bishops as limiting their contributions to moral or social welfare or education (Weare, op.cit., at 209). Drewry and Brock likewise saw a role developing in relation to social, ethical, and moral issues – in practise a very broad category (Drewry and Brock, op.cit.). Winetrobe and Gay, writing in 1999, saw a continuing involvement in social and moral matters (Wintrobe and Gay, 1999). The Church saw the bishops as bringing a thoughtful concern with ethical principles to bear on all public and private issues (Church of England, op.cit., at 6). In the most recent consideration of the issue, Smith saw the debate over the Lords Spiritual as constructing them as specialists able to provide the House with expertise when discussing social, philosophical, and theological issues (Smith, op.cit., at 111). The non-partisan nature of the Lords Spiritual, at least in the twentieth century, is also stressed by the sources. Doubts have been expressed as to whether the Church of England will have its own, partisan, political agenda (DATF, op.cit., at 25). In any case, it should be noted that non-partisan does not mean non-political, and that the backgrounds of the bishops may be seen as closing off some lines of argument (Laski, 1925). During the passage of the Reform Bill of 1832, for instance, their work in the Lords 'cast them in the role of the most entrenched reactionaries. The palace of the Bishop of Bristol was burned down, and the Archbishop of Canterbury was assaulted with a dead cat' (Archer, op.cit., at 401).

Finally, it may be that the Lords Spiritual are able to use moral or religious modes of argumentation with greater ease than other members of the legislature (Goodrich, 1997). If this is the case, it is unlikely to take the form of detailed theological analysis. Rather, they seek to offer 'a voice of spiritual and moral concern' (Church of England, op.cit., at 11), using their role 'if not for the expounding of theology then at least for the articulation of a wide cultural concensus based historically on the Christian tradition' (Archer, op.cit., at 401).

In recent years, the composition of the House of Lords has been a matter of intense political debate in the United Kingdom. Although primarily focused on the right of hereditary peers to sit in the national legislature – a right which was extensively modified by legislation in 1999 – there has been some consideration of religious representation. In particular, at one time the possibility of extending religious representation beyond the Church of England was actively explored by the government. The practical problems of extending representation to other communities and organisations are, however, likely to make this impossible. We are then left with the question of whether, given that not all religious organisations can be entitled to a place in the national legislature, it is just for a single religious organisation to be so entitled (see Edge and Pearce, 2004).

Organisational Involvement in the International Arena

In domestic constitutions, the role of religious organisations has long been recognised – if only because the drafters were keen to ensure that they did not discharge any formal role within the legal order of the State. It will be recalled, however, that the central focus of international law was historically the sovereign State. With the growth of the human rights movement in the twentieth century, the rights of the individual – or rather the duty of the State to protect those rights – became an important focus of international law. Where does the religious organisation fit in?

Any organisation, whatever its precise legal status, is an association of individuals. One way to view a religious organisation, then, is as a mechanism by which those individuals exercise their religious rights. For instance, an individual member of a religious community may be unable to afford a place for worship, and so support an organisation owning and maintaining such a facility; or may wish to support proselytism but be unable to actively proselytise themselves, and so form an organisation with that as their goal. Viewed that way, a number of legal systems have recognised the importance of religious organisations to religious rights. A useful example is the ECHR.

Associating with co-religionists may itself be a fundamental part of freedom of religion for the individual. In *Manoussakis and Others v Greece* ((1996) 23 EHRR 397 (ECHR)) the Court was particularly concerned that domestic law had been used to prevent Jehovah's Witnesses from establishing and operating a place of worship. A number of other cases have recognised the importance of religious organisations to individuals. The ECHR goes further, however, in recognising that religious organisations themselves may have religious rights. In *Holy Monasteries v Greece* ((1994) 20 EHRR 1 (ECHR)), for instance, a number of Greek monasteries were able to bring an application based, in part, on the religious rights under Article 9. The Court described the objectives of the monasteries as 'essentially ecclesiastical and spiritual ones' (ibid., at para. 49). The test appears to be whether the organisation has as an aim the exercise of religious rights by its members, so need not be a church or close analog. In *Kustannus Oy Vapaa Ajattelija Ab and Others v Finland* ((1996) 2 ECHR CD69 (ECHR)) the organisation was a publishing company formed with the primary aim of publishing and selling books reflecting and promoting freethinking ideals. The government claimed that the organisation was not a religious or philosophical community, nor a non-profit body, but rather a commercial company which accordingly could not claim Article 9 rights. The Commission disagreed, finding that as a body formed for promoting the rights of freethinkers, it could claim Article 9 rights.

It is probably best to think of such organisational religious rights as claimed 'on behalf of its members' (*Hautanemi et al v Sweden* (1996) 22 EHRR CD155 (ECHR)). There are, however, clear practical benefits in allowing religious organisations to exercise religious rights, particularly when it comes to claiming such rights before a court or similar body. In particular, given how serious an endeavour recourse to law is, a religious organisation may be best placed to take responsibility for organising, funding, and maintaining an allegation of a violation which primarily affects the group life of its members, and may have little impact on any particular individual.

In one instance, however, a religious organisation has a status beyond simply making human rights claims on behalf of its memberships. The Holy See possesses international legal personality (Abdhullah, 1996). As a result, the Catholic Church is entitled to a particular place in international gatherings, sitting as a sovereign State rather than as a non-governmental organisation, for instance in the Organisation for Security and Cooperation in Europe, and the United Nations High Commission for Refugees. With a territorial area of 109 acres, and a population of less than 800 persons, this sovereign state enters into international agreements and sends and receives diplomatic representatives to the 174 states with which it has formal diplomatic relations.

State Involvement in the Organisation: Registration and Recognition in Russia

To some extent concerns over entanglement between religious organisations and States are a matter of degree rather than kind – even the hardest separation of Church and State, as it is often put, presupposes that the State can identify an entity as a Church that needs to be kept separate. This act of identification is, itself, an act of entanglement. Many States go further than simply identifying an organisation as one involving religious rights, and have schemes whereby formal identification as a religious organisation carries with it a variety of benefits. In Denmark, for instance, recognition results in taxation rights, and easier access to State funds for cultural activities (Riis, 1999 at para. 4.3), while the Slovak Republic provides substantial support to registered churches and religious organisations (Mulik, 1998).

Registration can raise concerns when religious organisations are restricted in their religious activities if they fail, or are unable, to register. In *Christian Association of Jehovah's Witnesses v Bulgaria*, (((1997) HUDOC 3 July (ECHR)) the Bulgarian system had been considered by the Commission. In 1994, reflecting broader developments in relation to registration of denominations, Bulgarian law was changed to require religious associations to register subject to the consent of the Council of Ministers. The Association applied vigorously for registration, but heard nothing more until the press reported that registration had been refused. As a consequence of this non-registration, or non-recognition, meetings of the Association were disrupted and prohibited, religious materials seized or prevented from being brought into the country, members required to agree not to preach, and non-national members expelled from the country for their involvement with the Association.

In a more recent judgement, that of *Metropolitan Church of Bessarabia v Moldova* (2001) HUDOC 13 December (ECHR), the Court considered a registration scheme which prevented unregistered religions from operating – ministers could not carry out religious services, nor members meet to practise their religion. A refusal to register the applicant church was, therefore, an infringement of its Article 9 rights. The Court accepted that a registration scheme could be justified on the basis of public order and safety, but found the scheme in question was not justifiable. The judgement was a strong one, with the State criticised for having 'failed to discharge the duty of neutrality and impartiality' (ibid., para. 123), and the scale of the restrictions on activities was stressed. The State was found, unanimously, to have violated Article 9.

Registration may, however, consist primarily of an entitlement to benefits beyond the bare exercise of fundamental religious rights. Two concerns are raised as soon as registration goes beyond mere administrative recognition to the conferment of substantial benefits. Firstly, are different categories of religious organisation recognised, with some categories carrying higher privileges? Austria, for instance, distinguishes between communities recognised as legal persons only, and those given special status as public law corporations (Miner, 1998; Potz, 1998); while Spain allows 'deeply rooted' registered organisations to enter into special agreements with the State (de Codes, 1998). Secondly, what criteria are used in determining whether an organisation is entitled to register? In Armenia, for instance, groups may gain official recognition if they are based on historically recognised holy scriptures, their doctrines form part of the international religious-ecclesiastical communities, and they are sufficiently large (Boyle and Sheen, 1997 at 268–9). Thirdly, how closely is the State involved in monitoring religious organisations once they have been registered?

Although registration schemes are widespread in Europe, the best known, and perhaps most controversial, is the Russian scheme. From the commentary, the opposition of Lekhel (Lekhel, 1999) and Brossart (Brossart, 1999) is particularly useful. Firstly, some background.

As Bourdeaux points out, Russia and its associated territories have long been religiously diverse (Bourdeaux, 1999). In pre-Revolutionary Russia, however, the Orthodox Church was seen as central to Russian life, and after 1721 was categorised as a department of the State. It was not until 1905 that non-Orthodox religious groups received a degree of tolerance. During the Soviet period Russia was a secular, anti-religious state where Orthodoxy was reduced to the same, uncomfortable, position as other religions. Religion was, generally, tolerated as an individual, personal, matter which should not disturb public life, or find expression in corporate activities. After the Second World War there was some increase in tolerance, but the State remained actively involved in regulating religious organisations. Groups were required to register to exist, and 'when the State perceived certain religious communities as undesirable for any reason, it simply refused to register them. Any activities by such unregistered groups resulted in criminal and civil sanctions to their members' (Lekhel, 1999 at 179–80).

Late Soviet and early Russian legislation on religion was notably less strict. In 1990 Soviet and Russian legislation both contained a combination of religious rights and a system to allow religious organisations to acquire key rights by registration (*O Svobode Sovest I Religioznykh Organizatsiialek*, 1990 (41, 813) (Soviet); *Zakon RSFSR O Svobode Veroispovedanii*, 1990 (21, 267–71) (Russia)). As a result of this comparatively liberal scheme, by September 1993 9,489 religious organisations had registered in Russia.

Easy registration had, however, led to an influx of foreign missionaries with good resources and experience in proselytising, and the growth of a number of stigmatised religious groups. This led the Orthodox Church to lobby for legislation to resist the growth of non-Orthodox religious communities. An initial Bill failed in 1993, after President Yeltsin vetoed it as contrary to international law and the equal rights of Russian citizens of different faiths. In 1997 a similar Bill was put forward again, and although Yeltsin vetoed this Bill too, he indicated that a compromise might be possible. The Bill was revised, and became law (*Federal'Nyi Zakon O Svobode Sovesti I O Religioznyh Ob'Edineniyh*, 1997 (39, 4465)). The registration scheme at the centre of the 1997 law can be analysed against the questions identified earlier.

Firstly, are different categories of religious organisation recognised, with some categories carrying higher privileges? The 1997 law distinguishes between religious groups and religious organisations. Religious groups are subject to monitoring by the State, but do not need to register formally, or to fill out regular reports to the State. They are, however, limited in their rights to conduct religious ceremonies and to teach religion, and are not a juristic person (art.7). Religious groups may not be formed by non-citizens. Religious organisations, on the other hand, are juristic persons (art.8), and receive preferential tax treatment and access to cultural and educational funds (art. 4(3)).

Secondly, what criteria are used in determining whether an organisation is entitled to register? The scheme is complex, so for simplicity let us focus on an organisation seeking registration as a national religious organisation. The applicant must state the full name of their organisation, which must be used in all their activities, and may only include 'Russia' if they have operated legally in Russia for at least fifty years. They will need to provide a charter, which includes the organisation's purposes, prospective activities, structure, sources of income, procedures for amending the charter, and a number of formal requirements to allow State monitoring (art.10). Registration may not be refused simply on the grounds that the religion is undesirable (art.12(2)). It may be refused, however, if the aims and activities of the organisation are linked with the infringement of the Russian constitution, the organisation is not religious, the charter is insufficient or inauthentic, another organisation of the same name already exists on the register, or a founding member is not legally competent (art.12). To be eligible for national registration, a national organisation must have at least three local, registered, organisations, each consisting of ten adult members who reside in the same locality (art.8). At this local level there is a strong distinction between established and more recent religious communities. To gain full registration as a local organisation the applicant must produce 'a document that confirms the existence of that religious group on the given territory for no less than fifteen years' (art.11(5)). Given the official persecution of some religious groups in 1982, this may be difficult to prove even for communities who were present at the time. A local organisation unable to prove the length of their stay may register with reduced rights, but in such a case the registration must be repeated each year until the fifteen-year point is reached (art.27).

Thirdly, how closely is the State involved in monitoring religious organisations once they have been registered? All religious groups, including those who are not eligible for registration, are subject to monitoring by the State. Registered religious organisations are most closely monitored, with reporting duties. The State is not, however, restricted to passively receiving information on the activities of a religious organisation. Instead, it is empowered to liquidate religious organisations under certain conditions – causing the religious organisation to lose juristic personality and its property to be distributed in accordance with its charter (art.14). In some ways, the most interesting of these is systematic contravention of the registered purposes set out in the charter – if a religious organisation strays too far from the charter without amending it, it may be liquidated. An organisation may also be dissolved, or its activities banned, on a wide range of grounds. These include 'the undermining of social order and security or threats to the security of the State; actions aimed at forcibly changing the foundations of the Constitutional structure or destroying the unity of the Russian Federation; the creation of armed units; propaganda of war, the igniting of social, racial, national or religious dissension or hatred between people; forcing a family to disintegrate; the infringement of the person, the rights and freedom of a citizen; the infliction of damage established in accordance with the law on the morality or health of citizens, including the use of narcotic or psychoactive substances, hypnosis, the performance of depraved or other disorderly activities in connection with their religious activities; encouraging suicide or the refusal on religious grounds of medical help to persons in life-endangering or health-endangering conditions; hindering the receiving of compulsory education; forcing members and followers of the religious association or other persons to alienate property which belongs to them for the use of the religious association; hindering people from leaving a religious association by threatening harm to their lives, health, property if there is a danger of this threat actually being carried out, or by using force or other illegal actions; inciting citizens to refuse to fulfill their civil obligations established by law, or to perform other disorderly actions'.

Both Lekhel and Brossart agree that the 1997 law restricts religious liberty.

Where they differ is the extent to which this restriction can be justified as necessary for Russia at this particular point in its history. Lekhel views the 1997 law as 'a formidable tool in the hands of the State to control the activities of religious communities, and to perpetuate distinctions and inequalities between them' (Lekhel, 1997 at 204). He sees the 1997 law as arising from five moral ideals in Russian history – all-encompassing State control; the absence of the idea of inalienable rights; great affinity between Church and State; the role of Orthodoxy as part of national identity; and xenophobia (Lekhel, 1999). These ideals do not constitute an objective justification for the restrictions on religious liberty both on the face of the 1997 law, and likely to arise from its application by officials left with a considerable degree of discretion. He is supported here by Basova, who notes considerable bias in the application of the law (Basova, 2000).

Brossart, on the other hand, recognises that the law will impact upon religious liberty, but sees it as justified because of the special position of Russia. He places particular weight on the cultural value of traditional faiths to Russia, the 'inability of Russians to discern between legitimate religions and hucksters' (Brossart, 1999 at 310), the growth and operation of 'cults' taking advantage of the spiritual vacuumn left by communism, and the need to protect a reviving indigenous religious culture. Taken together these protective needs justify some restrictions on individuals and organisations, but only 'as long and to the extent that the historical moment lasts' (ibid., at 316).

The Russian law, and the surrounding debate, illustrates a number of key points concerning registration schemes. Firstly, the detail of registration can be extremely significant in assessing its impact. The fifteen-year rule in relation to the registration of local religious organisations is a good example. Secondly, the administrative system of registration can place structural pressures upon the religious community seeking registration. In the Russian case, internal structures making it difficult to produce a suitable Charter might be amended in order to secure registration. A similar issue was discussed in *Canae Catholic Church v Greece* ((1997) HUDOC 16 December (ECHR)). The applicant had been denied legal personality by the Greek courts, despite having been in existence and operating as a legal person for a very considerable time. The Government suggested that the Church could have taken steps to acquire legal personality once it realised there was a difference of opinion. The Court disagreed, noting 'the difficulties of adapting a church to that kind of structure and the procedural problems which might arise in the event of litigation'. Thirdly, registration pressures may even go beyond the structural to the doctrinal. Article 14 of the Russian law, for instance, could pose some interesting issues to Rastafari who wish to make use of cannabis in a religious context. We have seen earlier how such drug use would be unlawful in the United Kingdom, United States, and South Africa. In the Russian context, such teachings may render the organisation liable to dissolution because of the 'use of … narcotic substances'. Fourthly, registration becomes a critical point of legitimisation – marginal groups seek registration as a marker of their legitimacy both socially and as a 'real' religion, while their opponents contest such registration for exactly this reason.

Organisational Involvement in State Initiatives: Religious Charities in the UK

As we have seen above, a number of countries have adopted a system of registration for religious organisations, where a failure to register may restrict the activities of the organisation, while successful registration may not only remove these restrictions but involve the conferment of benefits by the State. The United Kingdom lacks a system for religious registration, but it is possible for religious organisations to seek charitable status. Since 1960, the most straightforward way to take advantage of charitable status has been through registration with the Charity Commission (Charities Act 1960 (UK), now Charities Act 1993 (UK)). It is possible for religious organisations to function without charitable status, and so some may choose not to register with the Charity Commission. Registration, however, carries with it a substantial number of legal and financial benefits, not least in relation to taxation (Quint and Spring, 1999 at 156–8).

The principal body concerned with determining charitable status is the Charity Commission (see further Edge and Loughrey, 2001). The Commission works within a statutory framework, and within the context of previous decisions by the courts concerning charitable status. In practice, however, few applicants for charitable status challenge their decisions in the courts and the Commission has increasingly begun to look to its own earlier decisions for establishing charity law.

In considering whether an organisation is charitable, the Commission will first consider whether it falls within one of the four heads of charity – 'trusts for the relief of poverty; trusts for the advancement of education; trusts for the advancement of religion; and trusts for other purposes beneficial to the community' (*IRC v Pemsel* [1891] AC 531 (UK)). Religious organisations have traditionally been significant providers of charity in all its heads (Barker, 1999 at 304), but the most significant for our purposes is that of advancement of religion. Three significant issues arise – is the organisation associated with religion, will it advance religion, and in doing so will it provide a public benefit?

In the past, charity law was openly used to support approved forms of religion and spirituality, with the courts distinguishing between the State Church and 'the schisms of nonconformity, the errors of Rome, or the infidelity of Judaism or heathenism' (Newark, 1946 at 235). In that context, a purpose is religious if it is in accordance with the teachings of the Church of England (see further Bromley and Bromley, 1999). Modern charity law, however, seeks to engage with religious plurality, ideally so that 'the law does not now favour one religion over another' (*Varsani v Jesari* [1998] 3 All ER 273 (UK)). Since the nineteenth century the courts have accepted that religion can include non-Anglican forms of Christianity (for example, *Thornton v Howe* (1862) 31 Beav 14 (UK)), and non-Christian religions such as Judaism (for example, *Re Michel's Trust* (1860) 28 Beav 39 (UK)). The Charity Commission has also registered, for instance, Hindu, Buddhist, Sikh, Bahai, Zoroastrian, and Jain groups.

Neither the courts nor the Commission have, however, taken every moral or even spiritual stance as sufficient to constitute a religious purpose. In *Re South Place Ethical Society* ([1980] 3 All ER 918 (UK)) an organisation was refused charitable status because, although it was concerned with 'the cultivation of a rational religious sentiment', it was non-theistic. In making this finding, the court was placing itself clearly within a strong line of authority stressing the need for theism in the belief system to be advanced. Thus, the courts have clearly excluded atheisms from the scope of religion for the law of charity.

The Commission seem to have generally abided by this limitation, although the registration of some Buddhist charities may provide food for thought. They have, on the whole, interpreted theism liberally – although belief in a supernatural principle is not sufficient, there is no need for belief in 'a personal creator god of the traditional monotheistic religions'. They have, however, added a further requirement. In a decision rejecting an application from the Church of Scientology the Commission stated that religion involved an element of worship, which they defined as conduct which indicated reverence or veneration for the supreme being and submission to the object worshipped (Charity Commission, 1999). Accepting the teachings of a religion, and seeking to put them into effect, was insufficient. Accordingly, they found that the central practices of auditing and training by the Church of Scientology were not worship, and therefore Scientology was not a religion for charitable purposes.

There may be a further limit on the definition of religion. In *Re Watson* ([1973] 1 WLR 1472) it was suggested that belief systems which were adverse to the foundations of all religion, and subversive of all morality, were not charities. This could exclude some theistic belief systems where a supreme being is worshipped (consider Picarda, 1983).

Having established that a particular system is a religious one, it is necessary to show that the work of the organisation will advance that religion. In *Keren Kayemeth Le Jisroel Ltd. v Commissioners of Inland Revenue* ([1932] AC 650 (UK)) the House of Lords were required to consider whether a company whose main object was the settlement of Jews in Palestine, Syria, and other lands in Asia was established for charitable purposes. One of the grounds for seeking charitable recognition was that the company was formed for the advancement of religion. The main judgement was delivered by Lord Tomlin, who noted that the territories indicated included some which 'could not on any view be treated as included in the region covered by the description in Genesis', and was prepared to find the company was not formed for the advancement of religion on that basis. He was also prepared to reject the argument on the more general grounds that there was nothing about the activity which was of itself religious – the religious motives of the founders of the company were not sufficient to convert the activity into one advancing religion.

Advancement, therefore, is regarded objectively by the Courts – it is not enough that the creator of the organisation had a religious motivation, which could be rephrased as a belief that their actions will advance their religion.

The Courts have made some attempt to provide a definition of this legal term. The most commonly cited definitions come from the lower Courts in *Keren Kayemeth Le Jisroel Ltd.*, although they were neither adopted nor rejected by the House. That case poses some interesting problems for any legal definition of advancement. The House very firmly rejected the view of the founder of the organisation as decisive on this point. Yet, at the same time Lord Tomlin looked into the beliefs of Judaism as a whole as an alternate ground for rejecting the appeal. In other words, the courts will reject the views of those believers involved in founding the organisation, but will look into the views of believers in the same faith generally, in order to decide this issue. This may be a practical approach where the faith is large, but poses some problems where it is very small – at the most extreme, what if *every* believer in a particular faith is a founder of the organisation? It also illustrates the tendency of the courts to assume a particular model for religious organisation and practice.

The lower courts may have taken a different stance, and assumed that advancement for any religion can be judged by certain common criteria. At first instance, Rowlatt J suggested: '[t]he promotion of religion means the promotion of the spiritual teaching of the religious body concerned and the maintenance of the spirit of its doctrines and observances' (ibid., at 469). In the Court of Appeal, Lord Hanworth MR preferred: '[t]he promotion of religion means the promotion of spiritual teaching in a wide sense, and the maintenance of the doctrines on which it rests, and the observances that serve to promote and manifest it – not merely a foundation or cause to which it can be related' (ibid., at 477).

These definitions were cited with approval in *Re Thackrah,* ([1939] 2 All ER 4 (UK)) where Bennett J was required to consider whether the unincorporated Oxford group could be regarded as being directed towards the advancement of religion, and therefore able to take a legacy to the Secretary of the Group as a charitable gift for its purposes. Bennett J considered that '[i]t may seek to bind people together by religious bonds, and no doubt it does, but that is not what is meant by "the promotion of religion" as that phrase is understood in these courts'. A slightly more detailed definition was put forward in *United Grand Lodge of Ancient Free and Accepted Masons of England v Holborn Borough Council* ([1957] 1 WLR 1080 (UK)) where Donovan J refused charitable status to freemasons, noting that: '[t]here is no religious instruction, no programme for the persuasion of unbelievers, no religious supervision to see that its members remain active and constant to the various religions that they may profess, no holding of religious services, no pastoral or missionary work of any kind'.

It is, however, difficult to find a coherent approach to the question of advancement, as illustrated by *In Re Pardoe* ([1906] 2 Ch. 184 (UK)). There, a legacy was left to the ringers of a church to ring bells on the anniversary of the restoration of the monarchy. Kekewich J was prepared to draw what seems a tenuous link between this gift and the advancement of religion: 'As I understand it, the object of the gift was that the restoration of the monarchy should be brought back to the memories of those who listened to the ringing of the bells, and, the testatrix speaks of it as a happy restoration, about which, of course, no Englishman can express a doubt at the present moment. The notion of the testator evidently is that it shall bring back happy thoughts; and, seeing that this is to be brought about by listening to a peal of bells rung in a church tower, I think that those happy thoughts necessarily constitute a feeling of gratitude to the Giver of all good gifts.

I think I can see that in the testatrix's mind, as expressed in her words. If that is so, I do not think there is any doubt that it is a charitable gift'.

In conclusion, advancement of religion is a more difficult issue in English law than may at first appear. The courts have clearly rejected treating the views of the creators of the organisation as decisive, and may have taken this to its logical end by excluding the views of co-religionists, at least at the initial stage. The initial stage appears to be judging the activity against very broad headings imported from traditional religious values within the English jurisdiction. Only when the practice may fall within those headings does attention shift to the value of the religion in question. Thus, in *Keren Kayemeth*, settlement in the Promised Lands could fall within the category of religious observance, so it remained to see whether, in the context of Judaism, the activity proposed in the case really was religious observance.

The final test is whether the advancement of religion will provide the public with a benefit. It should be recalled that charitable status is intended to promote philanthropy, which Bromley defines as 'the social objectives which the State and the law seek to fund and address through the voluntary contributions and activities of citizens, and which the State will encourage and protect by extending legal and fiscal advantages to individuals and institutions funding and carrying out these objectives' (Bromley, 1993 at 66). All charities must, therefore, show that the public is benefiting in some way from their activities.

Haddock sees public benefits accuring from religious trusts in three different categories (Haddock, 2001). First order benefits are those material and spiritual benefits which accrue through metaphysical means from the performance of the activities. Second order benefits are the edification and inspiration to be gained by the public from the worship of God by others. An element of public interaction is the key here – either through the public being able to engage in the activity themselves, or through members of a smaller group who do so providing an example and mixing in society. Third order benefits are benefits of an exclusively secular nature which 'provide various ... civic benefits' (ibid., at 152).

In relation to first order benefits, the courts are faced with a dilemma here. If a particular religion teaches that a solitary spiritual practice will postpone the end of the world, this would seem to be a benefit to the public. But it can only be proven if the court is prepared to accept the belief system of the applicant – something which may be seen as endangering neutrality between religious claims. One solution would be to move the test for public benefit from the objective to the subjective (Picarda, 1993). In such a case, the court would accept that it 'has no right to interfere with the conscience of a donor who made a gift in favour of what he believes to be in advancement of his religion and for the welfare of his community or of mankind' (*Jamshedji Cursetji v Soonabi* [1907] ILR 33 Bomb 122 (India)). As we have seen in relation to the advancement question, however, the courts prefer to keep issues of charitable status objective.

A number of principles have guided the courts and the Commission in deciding whether advancing a religion in a particular way will provide a public benefit. Purely private, or familial, benefits will not satisfy the test as they 'can lead to no public advantage, and can benefit or solace only the family itself' (*Yeap Cheah Neo v Ong Cheng Neo* (1875) 6 LR PC 381 (UK)). A benefit will not be recognised for the public as a whole if it relies upon metaphysical causation, for instance prayers by cloistered nuns to benefit the world as a whole (*Gilmour v Coates* [1949] AC 426 (UK)). A public benefit may be recognised where the religious benefit is directly available only to a small group – as Cross J said in *Neville Estates Ltd v Madden* ([1962] 1 Ch 832 (UK)): 'the court is entitled to assume that some benefit accrues to the public from attendance at places of worship of persons who live in this world and mix with their fellow citizens'. The Commission appear to work on the basis that advancing any religion is prima facie beneficial, and then look for an element of interaction with the public to ensure that this benefit is of a public nature (Edge and Loughrey, 2001 at 47–51). A link between the two is assumed (Haddock, 2001). Evidence may, however, be presented that there is insufficient public interaction – a ground upon which a number of applications have failed – or even that advancing a particular religion would be contrary to the public benefit (Longley, 1993).

The difficulties of determining whether a particular religion should receive charitable status, and the dangers of excessive entanglement with the State associated with such a determination, have led me in the past to recommend the abolition of charitable status for religions (Edge, 1995). Although criticising this stance as insufficiently reflecting the public benefits of religious activities, Barker endorses this call, with the important refinement that '[r]eligious organisations, defined in such a way as to take account of the relevant articles of the Human Rights Act 1998, could be provided with the fiscal and other benefits which are necessary/desirable in order to facilitate the work they do without bringing them within a future charity law regime' (Barker, 1999 at 314).

Claims Against Religious Organisations: Clergy Issues

Claims by Clergy in the United Kingdom

Once it is established that an individual is employed by a religious organisation then, on the whole, employment rights can be enforced against that organisation as against any other employer. There are important exceptions to this general rule in relation to discrimination norms (see further Vickers, 2003a; Vickers, 2003b). This section, however, considers a prior issue – when is an adherent carrying out work for their religious organisation an employee?

Employment status is a contentious area of employment law generally, and it may be over simplistic to identify one aspect of status as particularly difficult, or to assume that a decision as to status is the same whether the status will serve to protect the individual, or to provide them with an entitlement to financial benefits. Nonetheless, a review of the cases concerning the employment of ministers of religion leaves the impression that throughout the last century the English courts attempted to exclude ministers from the increasingly complex pattern of law dealing with employees (see Brodin, 1996). Although drawn from a variety of contexts, including worker compensation and the law of dismissal, they seek to address a single core question – when is a minister of religion an employee of their religious organisation? (see further Petchey, 2003).

The first line of cases to consider constructs the minister as an office-holder, to the exclusion of the operation of any contract, let alone a contract of employment. In the so-called *Curate's Case* (*In re National Insurance Act 1911, On Employment of Church of England Curates* [1912] 2 Ch. 563 (UK)) Parker J was required to consider whether a curate, or a licensed curate, fell within the social security scheme as an employee. A few points regarding licensed curates need to be extracted to understand this case. Firstly, a curate must enter into an agreement with the vicar on whose behalf they are to exercise their duties, which must be accepted by the Bishop. Secondly, the curate receives a stipend assigned by the Bishop as a charge on the benefice, that is, the income associated with the post held by the vicar. Thirdly, the vicar cannot dismiss the curate without the Bishop's permission, nor may the curate resign without – at the very least – giving previous notice to the Bishop. Finally, the structure for appointment and maintenance of curates operates under the law of the Church of England, including the Pluralities Act 1838.

Parker J concluded that 'the position of curate is the position of a person who holds an ecclesiastical office, and not the position of a person whose duties and rights are defined by contract at all' (ibid. at 568–9). He considered that whether the court looked to appointment, dismissal, or the duty owed by the curate, there was no contract of service. On the first two points, the judgement can be criticised for considering the position of the vicar and concluding that, since the Bishop appoints and dismisses, there was no evidence of a contract of service. The vicar appears an inapt choice of ultimate employer, being more closely analogous to a supervisor, and these points simply strengthen the case for the Bishop being an employer, and thus the curate being an employee.

On the third point, Parker J found that the duties of a curate were 'in no way defined by any contract of employment between him and any one else ... the duty which he owes to the vicar is not a duty which he owes because of contract, but a duty which he owes to an ecclesiastical superior ... an authority which can be exercised by virtue of the ecclesiastical jurisdiction' (ibid., at 569–70). This emphasis on the ecclesiastical jurisdiction, together with the exclusion of a contractual basis for the duties of the curate, serve to place this case firmly within the context of the Church of England. Other religious organisations, in the absence of specific legislation, derive their authority from contract (see Woolman, 1986).

From the *Curate's Case*, it appears possible to exclude entirely the operation of contract, and thus of a contract of employment, where the party is an office-holder under ecclesiastical law – that is, the law of the Church of England (*President of the Methodist Conference v Parfitt* [1983] 3 All ER 747 (UK)). The principle was rejected by Professor Rideout in *Coker v Diocese of Southwark* (*Coker v Diocese of Southwark* [1995] 1 ICR 563 (UK)). On appeal against his decision, however, the Tribunal considered: 'the law to be plainly established by the highest authority: a priest of the Church of England appointed to an assistant curact is not as a result of that appointment employed under a contract of service, but is the holder of an ecclesiastical office, although it is conceivable, but by no means clear, that circumstances might exist in a particular case which showed that such a curate was indeed employed by some person or other' (*Diocese of Southwark v Coker* [1996] 1 ICR 897 (UK)).

Thus, one ground for excluding a minister of religion from the status of employee is that s/he is an office-holder of the Church of England, so that the relationship with the Church of England is governed by ecclesiastical law, rather than general employment law. This ecclesiastical law approach only works where the minister is appointed within the Church of England. An alternative approach, based on the absence of an intention to form a legally binding contract, has developed in cases where this ground could not be applied, for instance those involving other Christian and non-Christian organisations.

The earliest, and perhaps most interesting, case where this can be seen is *Rogers v Booth* ([1937] 2 All ER 751 (UK)), where an officer in the Salvation Army sustained injuries while working in the Army Hall. She claimed under the Workman's Compensation Act, and her counsel argued that, while the *Curate's Case* showed Church of England clergy were creatures of ecclesiastical law, the 'position of an officer of the Salvation Army is defined solely by his [sic] agreement with the General of the Army' (ibid., at 752). The Salvation Army regulations for the conduct and discipline of its officers contained contractarian language, such as: 'Officership in the Army, with participation in its privileges, carries with it continued obligation to abide by the undertakings entered into (see Appendix I) and to seek, to the best of the officer's ability, the accomplishment of the Army's great purposes' (ibid., at 753).

Appendix I set out a number of more specific undertakings, which were embodied in the very detailed application form the intending officer was required to sign. The Appendix included a pledge, when on active service for the Army, to work not less than nine hours every day; and an agreement that there was no contract with the Army, and no entitlement to wages, although there was a scale of allowances that would normally be paid.

On the basis of the ethos of the Salvation Army, its pre-eminently spiritual character, and this document, Wilfred Greene MR found that: 'the necessary contractual element which is required before a contract of service can be found is entirely absent. The parties, when they enter into a relationship of that kind, are not intending to confer upon one another rights and obligations which are capable of enforcement in a court of law' (ibid., at 754).

It is undoubtedly possible to exclude an individual from the status of employee by finding that, due to an absence of the intention to form a legal relationship, there was no contract of employment. The further legal question raised here, however, concerns evidence. Is there a presumption that a minister of religion and their religious organisation do not intend the relationship to be a contractual one? In *President of the Methodist Conference v Parfitt* Dillon LJ indicated that the spiritual nature of the relationship between a minister and their religious organisation would always be important in determining whether a contractual relationship arose. In particular: 'I have no hesitation in concluding that the relationship between a church and a minister of religion is not apt, in the absence of a clear indication of a contrary intention in the document, to be regulated by a contract of service' (op.cit., at 754). In *Santokh Singh v Guru Nanak Gurdwara* ([1990] ICR 309 (UK)), Neill LJ referred to this passage as 'a principle', which was to operate in the absence of indicators of a contract of employment. As the EAT had taken account of this, along with the constitution of the religious organisation, oral evidence, and all the other circumstances of the case, the Court of Appeal was not prepared to question its decision that the appellant was not an employee. This pair of Court of Appeal decisions suggests that there is indeed a presumption against an intention to create legal relations where a minister and Church are concerned.

Thus, a further ground for excluding a minister of religion from the status of employee is that they have no contractual relations with the Church, due to an absence of intention to form legal relations, and thus the relationship is not governed by general employment law.

The two lines of argument developed above, although subject to criticism, have the merit of being developed in the context of existing law. A third line of argument does not, however, draw so explicitly upon particular legal doctrines, and may indeed suggest a special exemption from the general rules for this category of worker. In the Court of Appeal decision of *President of the Methodist Conference v Parfitt* Dillon LJ, in stressing the spiritual nature of the relationship between a Methodist minister and his Church, noted that '[i]n the spiritual sense, the minister sets out to serve God as his master' (op.cit at 752).

This concept was applied in *Davies v Presbyterian Church of Wales*, before the House of Lords. Lord Templeman considered that: 'The duties owed by the pastor to the church are not contractual or enforceable. A pastor is called and accepts the call. He does not devote his working life but his whole life to the church and his religion. His duties are defined and his activities are dictated not by contract but by conscience. He is the servant of God. If his manner of serving God is not acceptable to the church, then his pastorate can be brought to an end by the church in accordance with the rules. The law will ensure that a pastor is not deprived of his salaried pastorate save in accordance with the provisions of the book of rules but an industrial tribunal cannot determine whether a reasonable church would sever the link between minister and congregation' (op.cit at 329).

It appears, therefore, that the cases have developed three different ways of excluding a contract of employment from the relationship between a minister and their religious organisation. It remains to consider the policy behind these rules, which exclude a substantial number of persons from the category of employee, despite sharing 'incidents of the relationship between a minister and the church ... similar to any other employee' (Woolman, 1986 at 357). There are two elements in the rules as applied to most religious organisations that need to be justified. Firstly, the possibility of a religious organisation excluding a full-time, paid, worker from employee status through lack of intention to form legal relations. Secondly, the presumption that ministers of religion and their religious organisations did not intend to form legal relations.

Particular religious groups may have strong objections to the position of their clergy being regulated by the State, even if the content of that regulation was identical. Others may find it both inaccurate, and in some senses insulting, for their ministry to be regarded as an employment rather than a life-embracing vocation. If the minister and their organisation genuinely agree that the State should have no role in regulating their relationship, why should the State interfere? (cf. Morris, 2001).

Consideration of this point may be aided by noting the possible extent of this doctrine. In *Ahmad v Embassy of Pakistan* (Unreported, London South Industrial Tribunal August 20, 1984) (UK)) the Industrial Tribunal found, inter alia, that as there was no priesthood in Islam, the applicant's duties included non-spiritual ones, and the council of the London Mosque Trust was a 'secular' one, the case could be distinguished from *Parfitt*, and the Imam regarded as an employee. This case seems wrong. There is no reason why these principles should be limited to an identifiable clergy making up only a small proportion of adherents of the faith. In particular, these principles could be applied to religious organisations which treat all members as having made a commitment to the religious organisation similar to that which the cases see as arising for clergy in a Christian faith – a full-time, total life commitment (consider Thomas, 1981). A religious community organised around, say, a small factory could evoke the principles discussed in an attempt to exclude some legal rules. Indeed, the wording of the documents discussed in *Rogers v Booth* could easily be adapted to other religious organisations seeking a full-time commitment from members without the status of employee. It is possible that, if this commitment primarily took the form of commercial activity, the Courts would find it fell outside this principle. Nonetheless, a religious community of adherents to a particular religion, perhaps living and working in common to provide resources for their religious duties, may well be able to make use of the cases on ministers of religion.

So, what policy reasons are there for not allowing the religious adherent/minister and the religious organisation to agree to exclude the operation of employment law?

First, if the religious organisation claims some unique over-riding feature, such as the only route to survival after death, then the differential in power between the prospective minister and the religious organisation may be so great as to render any agreement less than free. Additionally, if the religious organisation claims exclusivity, the prospective minister may not have the option of seeking another religious organisation that is happy to accept the provisions of employment law. If a believer in the doctrines of the Catholic Church, for instance, wishes to become a minister, it is difficult to see what route he has other than to become a minister of the Catholic Church.

Strong although this argument is, to accept it is to make serious inroads into the free exercise of religion in favour of a State supported view of the relationship between the individual minister and the State. The State could not, while respecting freedom of religion, require a community of believers to accept as minister someone who did not share their beliefs. If one of the beliefs, perhaps even a religious belief, of this community is that their ministers should not be able to make use of State employment law, than the State should not intervene to prevent manifestation of that belief through the organisation set up by the religious community.

Second, even if the minister freely consents to the exclusion of employment law at the beginning of their connection with the religious organisation, this view may change. This will be of particular importance if, for instance, a minister has spent their entire working life in the religious organisation, and is then dismissed from the organisation for some reason which general employment law would restrict. This is simply a refinement of the previous point, and subject to the same criticisms.

Third, the courts would have considerable reservations about placing such authority over the relationship solely in the hands of a commercial organisation – indeed, those reservations are the basis for the special rules of employment law – and the same reservations should apply to religious organisations that adopt an analogous structure. Rideout puts it strongly: 'Of course the church is able to enforce its authority. So is almost any organisation, from a members' club through a trade union to any employer. But this authority does not protect the party who does not possess it. The employer owns a property right in the premises upon which the industrial activity is conducted and that property right would give an employer considerable authority over his employees. He could effectively terminate their engagements by refusing them access to the premises. The employee has no authority and, consequently, no protection under such a system. The assumption that an agreement to work gives rise to a contract is nothing more than a device by which the courts assumed jurisdiction over that agreement' (*Coker v Diocese of Southwark*, op.cit.).

Once again, while accepting the weight of this argument, how does the State intervene to safeguard the rights of the minister without infringing not only the religious practices of the organisation, but also those of the minister? Religious believers have the right to make decisions that will result in their deaths as an exercise in their individual autonomy, for instance by refusing life-saving blood transfusions. It might seem curious if they could not similarly make decisions that will result in later impoverishment.

Fourth, by allowing religious organisations to exclude themselves from many provisions of modern employment law, it could be argued that the religious liberty of would-be ministers is damaged. In a different context Rutherford has identified three mechanisms by which this could occur – discouraging individuals from becoming ministers because they are required to forfeit state conferred rights; pressuring individuals who are unwilling, or unable, to conform with the requirements of the ministry to change their faith in order to pursue their calling; and limiting access to the views of those groups disfavoured by the religious organisations policy (Rutherford, 1989). Although these are strong arguments, they seem to place the balance too strongly on the side of the individual, rather than the less intense interests of the individuals who make up the group.

In conclusion, if a minister and religious organisation agree that the relationship shall not carry with it the implications of a contract, in particular of a contract of employment, this is an agreement that the State should respect. It is less easy, however, to justify a presumption of exclusion. The arguments in favour of such a presumption can be summarised briefly.

Firstly, the tasks undertaken by a minister are not easily fitted within a structure derived from the commercially orientated context of employment law. In particular, the minister has spiritual duties and undertakes spiritual tasks. Unless a religious organisation has structured itself to accommodate employment law, and expressed an intention that the law should regulate the relationship, it should not be applied to those carrying out such spiritual duties. Rideout is extremely dismissive of any special pleading for spiritual duties: 'the courts, in these earlier cases, considered that the spiritual quality of the relationship could not be regulated by contract. Contract can produce the organisational situation in which the spiritual duties are performed. It cannot, of course, produce the necessary state of mind for those duties to be carried out effectively. No more, however, can any contract of service produce the necessary trust and confidence between the parties' (*Coker v Diocese of Southwark*, op.cit., at 571).

There is, however, some force in this contention. The breach or otherwise of some spiritual duties could be determined by the courts – for instance, an obligation to lead particular services, to provide education in the doctrines and practices of the faith, or to visit coreligionists in hospital and deliver pastoral care, or 'to carry out [their] duties in a spirit of openness befitting a religious foundation' (*Neary and Neary v Dean of Westminster* [1999] IRLR 288 at para. 17, 19 (UK)). But other spiritual duties might be harder to evaluate – for instance, an obligation to protect a particular building from demonic attack, or to ensure the beneficial reincarnation of local coreligionists. Similarly, the obligations of some ministers appear to extend far beyond the normal bounds of an employment contract – including perhaps an obligation to serve as a minister for life, or regulate every aspect of personal life according to a set of rules. The best response to such problems is not, however, to exclude any possibility of a contract between the parties, but to recognise that only some parts of the relationship are intended as legally enforceable.

Secondly, the courts may prefer to become involved in such disputes within a religious organisation only by invitation. This would help to preserve a religious space for adherents. It would also avoid the possibility that stigmatised faiths, or faiths primarily followed by groups historically subject to racial discrimination, would feel that their religious values were not being respected by a legal system dominated by other religions or traditions. In short, it could be a pluralism-enhancing measure. The flaw with this approach, however, is that the area that such a presumption seeks to regulate is not homogenous. It might be sensible to say that in some traditions a legal relationship between minister and organisation is uncommon. But the first task for the court would be to determine whether the organisation in question fell within such a tradition. Determining this question would go a long way towards determining, on the facts of the case, the issue that the presumption was intended to resolve. Given the rich variety of religious structures, any general presumption seems far too broad an approach. Given the constitutional structures of the United Kingdom, it is not an approach mandated by a State based, as opposed to religion based, restriction on State involvement in this form of dispute. By contrast, in his review of United States jurisprudence Garry concludes that: '[c]laims between clergy and church, though categorized as secular or employment disputes, often involve the relationship between a clergyperson and his or her superior and the dictates of the ecclesiastical law of the religious organization. Matters involving religious clergy, as a matter of law, should not be reviewed by civil courts. To find otherwise would secularise the entire governing structure of a church and the relationship between the church and its clergy. Such a result would jeopardize the traditional patterns of separation of church and state and the free exercise of religion within America's organized churches' (Garry, 1992 at 191).

In conclusion, although there is considerable sense in the courts being reluctant to find an intention to create legal relations between minister and religious organisation, determining whether there is such an intention in a particular case is far too complex a task to be assisted by even a preliminary presumption. Rather, the court should have regard to all the evidence available to it in determining this point. The Courts have shown a willingness to consider evidence such as constitutions and doctrines of the religious organisation; documents provided to would-be ministers; the process by which ministers enter into their commitment; the functions to be carried out by the minister; and the extent of the obligations upon the minister. Even if the absence of such a presumption led to an increase – probably temporary – in the number of ministers who were found to be employees, the practical consequences are likely to be fairly small. The theoretical consequences, however, are rather greater. By allowing for the possibility of religious organisations opting out of some State values concerning the workplace, a plurality of potentially monist spaces is created within employment law. By requiring evidence that both parties agreed to involvement in this form of space, and in most cases to the loss of some legal entitlements of the individual against their religious organisation, some protection is afforded to the individual. At the very least, the religious organisation will need to convince the court that there was no intention to create legal relations, and will need to make this clear to prospective non-employees.

Claims for the Misconduct of Religious Professionals in the United States

Shupe defines clergy malfeasance as 'the exploitation and abuse of a religious group's believers by trusted elites and leaders of that religion' (Shupe 1998a at 1). This definition is clearly capable of application to the (perhaps fictive) sort of organisations which are the concern of the anti-cult movement, which Shupe has also written on (see for instance Shupe and Bromley, 1994). It is, however, applicable to any religious organisation – as Shupe puts it in the same collection: 'with power differentials inherent in religious organisations, the opportunity structures for exploiting that power by leaders are never going to disappear in any religion of which we can conceive' (Shupe, 1998b). In the United States these issues have recently arisen particularly in relation to the Catholic Church (see Jenkins, 1998), but is not limited to any particular religious group. Iadicola has, however, suggested that some organisations are more prone to clergy malfeasance: 'a religious organisation most likely to experience clergy malfeasance would have hierarchical internal and external power structures, charismatic leadership, and highly unstable normative doctrine. Clergy malfeasance is least likely to occur in an organisation with more egalitarian internal and external power structures, a legal/rational leadership, and highly stable doctrine' (Iadicola, 1998 at 228).

This power can be abused deliberately, for instance through economic exploitation, 'excessive monitoring and controlling of member's livelihoods, resources and lifestyles to enrich that leader, either in money or power' (Shupe, 1998a at 7), or for sexual purposes. Some forms of these exploitations may be prima facie lawful in the State, but may be considered unacceptable by the religious organisation itself – for instance a sexual relationship between a celibate priest and an adult member of their congregation.

There are two significant issues to consider, given our current organisational focus, both based in civil law. Firstly, how far can the organisation itself be made liable for the deliberate misconduct of a cleric, perhaps one acting against the laws and policies of the organisation? Secondly, how far can the organisation be made liable for the negligent misconduct of such a cleric? For instance, if a cleric undertakes counselling of a member of their community, but does it so badly that as a result the counsellee commits suicide, can the organisation be held liable?

In either case, religious liberty issues may be raised by the involvement of the State in relationships within the religious communities. In the United States, the Supreme Court has traditionally deferred to religious organisations themselves on 'religious or ecclesiastical disputes' (*Watson v Jones*, 80 US (13 Wall) 679 (1872) (US)). To do otherwise would require the US Courts to become involved in doctrinal theology and religious law, depriving the religious community of the right to do so themselves, and becoming entangled in a relationship which the parties do not intend to be governed by the State as supreme arbiter. This has led to the US courts renouncing a role in relation to disciplining clergy (*Putman v Vath*, 340 US S.2d 26 (1976) (US)), and appointment decisions within clerical structures (*Kaufmann v Sheehan*, 707 F.2d 355 (1983)). Garry puts the position too baldly when he says 'matters involving religious clergy, as a matter of law, should not be reviewed by civil courts' (Garry, 1992 at 191). In context, however, he is primarily concerned with claims by clergy against the Church when, in a secular context, the Church would be an employer with whom the employee is in dispute. He does not propose a 'benefit of clergy' exempting such ecclesiastical figures from the control of State laws, and US courts have been happy to find liability for deliberate wrongdoing by clergy (see Lehman, 1990). Nonetheless, the US Courts have been aware that cases involving clergy acting as such need to be dealt with thoughtfully, as they need to avoid evaluating the religious or doctrinal content of the cleric's beliefs.

In relation to deliberate misconduct, the clearest example is where a cleric has committed sexual acts with an individual under their pastoral care. In some cases, for instance where the individual is a child, these sexual acts will be of themselves unlawful in both a criminal and a civil sense. The cleric will be subject to criminal sanctions, and liable in civil law to pay compensation to the victim. In these cases, the victim may wish to attach civil liability to the religious organisation more broadly – particularly, to be pragmatic, where the cleric themselves lacks the financial resources to compensate the victim. Victims have not, however, always been able to recover from the organisation. A preliminary problem is establishing that the organisation can ever be liable, vicariously, for the actions of the cleric. In some cases, the relationship between the organisation and the cleric may be so far away from the supervisory model of the corporation/employee that the action will fail. If the organisation is vicariously liable, it may have little defence where the conduct was endorsed, or at least accepted, by the organisation's teachings. For instance, if a religious organisation taught the acceptability of sex between adults and children, it may be liable if a cleric puts this teaching into effect. Where the cleric's actions are explicitly contrary to the teachings and policies of the organisation, however, it is harder to argue that he was acting within his duties, and a number of cases have failed on just this ground (for example, *Rita v Roman Catholic Archbishop*, 232 Cal.Rptr. 128 (1988) (US)). This is not to say that a religious organisation can simply ignore paedophile clerics, for instance. It may be liable directly for negligent hiring of a cleric where it knew, or should have known, of a propensity for sexual misconduct (for example, *Mrozka v Archdiocese of St. Paul and Minneapolis*, 482 N.W. 2d. 806 (1992) (US)). This could be a way to establish liability where an organisation can be shown to have a record of failing to remove offending clerics from the clergy, but instead moving them to a different post (see for instance Krebs, 1998).

A more difficult form of deliberate misconduct is where the conduct is unacceptable to the religious organisation, but – apart from the position of the cleric – is accepted in the broader society. The clearest example is a sexual relationship between a cleric and a parishioner. This may be unacceptable within the organisation, particularly if it has rules concerning clerical celibacy, but is it unlawful? A number of courts have rejected claims based on such relationships on the grounds that US law no longer recognises amatory torts such as criminal conversation and seduction (for example, *Strock v Pressnell*, 527 N.E.2d. 1235 (1988)). If adults enter into consensual sexual relationships, that should not ground civil liability particularly by third parties treating another's sexuality as a form of property. As Villiers argues cogently, however, this case is not concerned with the formation of a sexual relationship in a private capacity, but with exploitation of a particular sort of relationship. Putting it at it's strongest, 'during an emotional or psychological crisis, many parishioners seek counselling from a local pastor. If such outreach for help results in abuse, it is especially contemptible because the perpetrator's power and authority are perceived as derived from God' (Villiers,

1996). Villiers therefore supports the decisions of a number of courts to find a fidicuary relationship – one where the fiduciary is bound to act in the best interests of the other person rather than of themselves – has created liability for the sexual conduct (for example, *Sanders v Casel View Baptist Church*, 898 F.Supp. 1169 (1995) (US), but see contrary cases such as *Schmidt v Bishop*, 779 F.Supp. 321 (1999) (US)).

Turning from deliberate misconduct, what of where a cleric has negligently failed to perform their duties in a capable fashion, and as a result their parishioner has suffered loss? The classic case, although perhaps an extreme one, is *Nally v Grace Community Church of the Valley* (763 P.2d. 94 (1988) (US)). Here the nontherapist councillors of the Church offered pastoral counselling to members 'in matters of faith, doctrine, and the application of Christian principles'. This pastoral counselling was used to engage with a variety of 'emotional problems' including addictions and mental illnesses such as depression and schizophrenia. Nally was receiving pastoral counselling when he committed suicide, having informed two of his pastors of previous suicide attempts, expressed regret that he had not succeeded in the latest attempt, and asked one counsellor whether Christians who committed suicide would nonetheless be saved. Did the Church have a duty of care to Nally so that, when the pastors failed to take appropriate measures to safeguard him from suicide, the Church was civilly liable? The Californian Supreme Court held that no such duty existed, basing its reasoning on the requirements for a duty in general tort law, rather than any special constitutional issues raised by the Church setting. Nonetheless, *Nally* demonstrates the key problems with this sort of case.

Firstly, commentators considered that, if *Nally* had arisen in the context of professional, secular, counselling, liability for the failure to safeguard Nally would have been found. As Burton puts it: 'the consequence is that the less trained, and thus the most dangerous, are able to wield the same power with immunity. The public requires equal, if not more, protection from these individuals' (Burton, 1997). This concern may underpin the decision of some Courts to sever, where possible, religious duties from essentially secular counselling, even when carried out by a cleric recommended by the religious organisation. In *Dausch v Ryske* (52 F.3d. 1425 (1994) (US)), for instance, the plaintiff had entered into a counselling relationship with a cleric after being advised to do so by her Church. The cleric informed her that she was in need of secular counselling, and that he was qualified to provide her with it. During the course of her therapy, he initiated a sexual relationship with her. She brought an action for professional negligence and violation of the Illinois Sexual Exploitation in Psychotherapy Act. Judge Ripple found that although clergy malpractice per se was not a ground for action because of the Church/State issues, these did not apply where the conduct in question 'does not bear such a direct relationship to the doctrinal or organisational aspects of religious practice ... such activity can be proscribed by a legitimate regulation of general applicability designed to protect the health, safety or good morals of the community' (ibid., at 1432).

Secondly, if we are prepared to extend liability to religious counselling and pastoral care, how do we judge when the care is sub-standard? If I may use an

extreme example, how is the court to judge whether a prayer over the head of a
subject was carried out 'properly'? Burton sees this as being the biggest problem
with clergy malpractice suits, and sees three popular standards in the literature. The
Court may seek to separate pastoral counselling from the religious functions of the
cleric, and then hold them to a single standard, for instance applying comparable
standards to those of a secular psychologist (see Funston, 1983). Alternatively, but
in practice very similar, the cleric could be required to show an awareness of the
current state of the art in related areas such as psychology (see Burek, 1986).
Finally, the courts could enforce a standard based on the accepted care of clergy
within the religious organisation – effectively setting different, denominational,
standards of conduct for, for instance, Roman Catholic and Wiccan clergy.

Community Rights: Sacred Places

A key issue for religious communities in particular is access to, and regulation of,
sacred spaces and sacred places. For a place to be recognised, however, it must
have boundaries in physical space. There is some evidence that the law prefers to
engage with places which have concrete boundaries, rather than those whose
boundaries are less clearly defined, or more permeable. Consider, for instance,
places of worship. The least permeable places are those with a permanent physical
boundary and whose sole or paramount use is as a sacred space. An obvious
example is a dedicated church, temple, or chapel – '[b]eyond the metaphor, the
interior space of the church [is] quite literally 'walled off'' (Carmella, 1997 at
1226). More permeable are concrete spaces that are not solely sacred places, but
also have other substantial uses. A good example of this is a domestic dwelling
house that is also used for prayer meetings and religious discussion groups. The
most permeable are places which are bounded only on a temporary basis, perhaps
with no visible boundary separating the space from its surroundings. A good
example would be a Pagan circle in a field or other open space.

   The ability of religious communities to designate sacred sites, in particular
religious buildings and places of worship, is one of the keystones of religious
liberty (Reymond, 1995). Such sites can provide a nexus for community life,
especially acts of communal worship. Additionally, within a particular tradition a
designated sacred space may be essential for the religious life of individuals. Yet
the permanence of many traditions' sacred space, combined with a communal
function, has been the source of a number of clashes with planning authorities
responsible for regulating land use.

   Even if planning law is not used as a tool to limit the growth of a particular
religious community, it can still be used to discriminate between religious groups.
An obvious example is where a particular religious group is treated under special
planning rules, perhaps on the basis of its longer presence in the territory of the
State, or a special connection with the State. In the US case of *Islamic Center of
Mississippi v City of Starkeville*, (840 F.2d. 293 (1988) (US)) for instance, a
planning ordinance prohibited the use of buildings as places of worship within a

particular area, unless an exception was granted. The Islamic Center had been denied such an exemption, although twenty-five Christian churches were already operating in similarly regulated areas. The court found that the City government had failed to show that it had not favoured Christian churches over Muslim mosques, and its actions were found in violation of the US guarantees of freedom of religion.

In the remainder of this section we will discuss two examples of the interaction of law and religion in relation to sacred places. Firstly, we will consider the way in which buildings constituting a sacred place are regulated in United Kingdom law. Here the emphasis is upon dedicated religious buildings, for instance a church or a mosque, and upon permanent buildings which although used for other purposes – for instance as a family dwelling – also function as a religious building at some times. Secondly, we will consider the way in which United States law has dealt with less bounded claims to the sacredness of a place, particularly in relation to indigenous American religions which identify particular regions as sacred, rather than buildings upon those regions.

Sacred Buildings in the United Kingdom

The existence of buildings dedicated to religious traditions serve a variety of functions. As mentioned above, in some traditions particular forms of sacred space are essential for particular religious activities, or for structured communal worship. Additionally, such dedicated sites can constitute a clear statement of the existence of the religious community within the plural public space. It is unsurprising, then, that such dedicated buildings can be the focus of dispute over the place of minority religious communities in the territory of the State. In its report on Islamophobia in the United Kingdom, The Runnymede Trust identified opposition to the buildings of mosques as a specific example of 'bitterness and mistrust' in relations between Christians and Muslims (The Runnymede Trust, 1997 at 54–5). Additionally, because of their role as public buildings, and the antiquity and scale of some of the more established buildings, there can be a tension between the religious functions of such buildings, and their antiquarian, historical, and aesthetic public functions. As Richardson has noted in the US context: 'The purpose of historical preservation statutes is to preserve irreplaceable buildings having cultural, architectural, or historical significance. Churches often are distinctive or even unique in their architectural design and frequently are historically significant. Therefore, churches often will be designated as historic properties and will play an integral part in any historic preservation programme. The inclusion of churches within historic preservation statutes is especially important when a church is part of a historic district because the central idea is to preserve the area's integrity of design and setting. If churches were excluded from historic districts whenever the congregation evoked [religious liberty] claims, it would be difficult to preserve the unity of a historic district' (Richardson, 1985 at 418).

Buildings whose primary use is as a place of worship are exempted from the planning controls ordinarily applicable to buildings which are listed – by which I mean identified as of especial value for conservation purposes (Ecclesiastical Exemption (Listed Buildings and Conservation Areas) Order 1994 art 4). Such exempted buildings may be altered without government consent. This exemption does not apply to all places of worship, however, but only to those controlled by religious organisations with an internal regime for controlling use of such buildings. The paradigm of this is the Faculty jurisdiction of the Church of England, whose current form is in part the product of negotiations between the Church of England and the government department responsible for the conservation of important sites (see Leeder, 1997 at 224). Similar exemptions are also enjoyed by the Church in Wales, the Roman Catholic Church, the Methodist Church, the Baptist Unions of Great Britain and Wales, and the United Reformed Church (see further Last, 2002).

Although the exemption can be seen as an attempt by the State to provide a greater degree of autonomy within the community's own sacred space (Hill, 1995), the limitation of the exemption to only some religious organisations may be problematic. Government guidance, however, directs authorities considering non-exempt religious organisations' requests to take account of whether the changes are necessitated by a change in the worship needs of the congregation, a change in its size, or the accommodation of other activities to help ensure its continuing viability as a place of worship (PPG 15, para. 8.12 (UK)).

The most wide ranging consideration of religious interests in English planning law concerned the development of a place of worship by ISKCON (a branch of the Hindu faith), and reached the European Commission of Human Rights as *ISKCON v United Kingdom* ((1994) 18 EHRR CD133 (ECHR)). In 1973 ISKCON acquired a manor house. The house had previously been a nurses' residential college, and the local authority confirmed that its use as a residential theological college fell within the same use class, and so planning permission was not required. After that date, attendance at the property grew considerably. In 1983 ISKCON and the local authority entered into an agreement whereby ISKCON would limit attendance to less than 1000 people per day, except with the consent of the council, and the council licensed festival days, subject to conditions. In 1987 the local authority served an enforcement notice on ISKCON, on the basis that there had been a material change in the use of the land, constituting a breach of planning controls. In particular, the local authority alleged that, following repeated complaints by local residents, they had become aware that the 1000 person limit was being exceeded. They characterised the new use of the land as for 'the purposes of a residential educational college and a religious community and public worship and public entertainment in connection with religious festivals'. ISKCON appealed against the enforcement order, and the Inspector carried out a substantial enquiry, resulting in a 136-page report.

The Inspector made explicit his findings as to the practices of ISKCON; the importance of the manor as the only United Kingdom training centre for Hindu priests in that tradition; and the importance of the manor as a place of pilgrimage. He also summarised the extent to which the activities in the manor impinged on the local community, and the position of the manor as a listed building, within a

Conservation Area, itself within the Metropolitan Green Belt. The Inspector found that a breach of the planning controls had taken place, as the residents of the manor house lived as a religious community, the manor house was open for public worship, and that activities linked with festivals constituted public entertainment, having 'many of the attractions of a fete, and more besides'. He then moved to consider, in the most interesting part of his report, whether planning permission ought to be granted. In particular, did the importance of the Manor as a shrine and the need to provide places of worship for the Hindu population constitute very special circumstances that would justify development?

The Inspector recognised that the manor had become a special place of worship and pilgrimage for the Hindu community, one of only a very small number of Hindu places of worship in the region. It was of especial importance as the UK home of the founder of ISKCON. Also: '[n]o one could ignore the national and international concern, and the social issues posed by the possibility of restricting participation in the worship at the Manor and the celebration of the Hindu festivals'.

Having said that, the Inspector concluded that the scale of the manor's activities was incompatible with its setting: '[t]he intimate small scale closely built character of a home counties village simply cannot accommodate the crowds attracted to a tirtha in the Indian sub-continent'. Although recognising the interests of the Hindu community in the manor: 'it is necessary to weigh the needs of one group or interest against others, and needs of religious or ethnic minorities, however important, cannot necessarily be allowed to override those constraints which have to apply to everyone, in planning as in other matters, in the interest of a tolerant and free society in a small and crowded country'.

Accordingly, weighing the interests of the congregation, government policy on development in the area, and the disquiet and inconvenience to residents, he found that there was insufficient justification for setting aside the weight of policy as well as other specific and convincing planning objections. At a later date, the problem was resolved by construction of a new access to the Manor, and permission to use the Manor as a non-residential theological college and religious community, together with days of public worship (see further Poulter, 1998 at 271–4).

The first point to draw from this case, and the most obvious, is that a planning decision which recognises the importance of the religious interest, and the needs of a minority ethnic community, can still go against that community. The religious interest is not, and should not be, a trump value. It is simply one material factor to be considered when making planning decisions.

Secondly, the Inspector recognised the special importance of the manor amongst UK Hindu temples, but also recognised that if an alternative temple site were available, arguments for the current site would be weakened. The exact importance of the existence of an alternative site remains unclear, but a number of cases have recognised that, where an alternative site exists, its merits or demerits can be a material consideration. In a number of decisions on religious sites, one factor considered when rejecting planning permission was the possibility of the religious building being placed on a different site.

Thirdly, the Inspector's Report shows the importance of making individuals of every religious tradition feel that they share full citizenship. The Inspector stressed that similar objections would arise from 'any church of any faith or denomination in a small village ... which regularly attracted 1000-1500 people for late evening services on Sundays, and crowds of up to 12,000 for festivals three times a year'. By comparing the festivals with the meetings of Billy Graham the Inspector sought to reinforce, albeit clumsily, the same point. It is crucial that the planning decision carry with it no suggestion that metaphysical or social merits of the religious system in question was of any importance to the decision makers. Not all Inspectors' reports make it clear that the religious interest of the applicant was given full weight in refusing them planning permission (for example, *Cherwell D.C. v Vadivale* (1991) 6 P.A.D. 433 (UK)). This is especially important where the religious organisation is an unpopular one, as the concerns of those around them may be considered a material consideration.

A building may be permitted to function as a centre for a community under planning law, but United Kingdom law also recognises that a building may be a place of worship. Places of meeting for religious worship by any body or denomination other than the Church of England may be registered as such under the Places of Worship Registration Act 1855 (UK). Registration carries with it a number of practical benefits. A registered building is excepted from registration under the Charities Act, and is not liable to be rated. The criminal law regulating order within places of worship applies to the site (see Places of Religious Worship Act 1812 s.2 (UK), Liberty of Religious Worship Act 1855 s.1 (UK)). Additionally, although it is a criminal offence to regularly allow a building to be used by more than twenty persons for the purposes of worship, unless the building is a private dwelling house, this offence does not apply to registered places of worship (Places of Religious Worship Act 1812 s.12 (UK)). In order to gain these benefits, the place of worship must be duly registered.

Registration is carried out by the Registrar General for England and Wales (Places of Worship Registration Act 1855 (UK)). The Registrar keeps a list of all certified places of meeting, including their denomination and district, and this list is available to the public at a local level. Registration is not a purely administrative process, and the Registrar General must be satisfied that the place is a place of religious worship, used by an identifiable, settled body. The key case on this point is *ex parte Segerdal* ([1970] 3 All ER 886 (UK)). The Church of Scientology had sought to register a chapel on their grounds in East Grinstead as a place of worship, and the Registrar General refused to certify the chapel as a place of worship. The Church sought judicial review on the basis either that the Registrar General had no authority to decline an application for registration, or had used this authority incorrectly in this case. The case reached the Court of Appeal, where all three judges delivered judgements of interest. All three agreed in very similar terms that the role of the Registrar General was more than merely ministerial – he or she had to be satisfied that the place was one of religious worship.

In relation to the second question, Lord Denning rejected in very broad terms the arguments of the Church of Scientology, whose status as a religious community he appears to have doubted. He took the phrase 'religious worship' as a whole: 'It connotes to my mind a place of which the principle use is as a place where people come together as a congregation or assembly to do reverence to God. It need not be the God that the Christians worship. It may be another God, or an unknown God, but it must be reverence to a deity. There may be exceptions. For instance, Buddhist temples are properly described as places of meeting for religious worship. But, apart from exceptional cases of that kind ... it should be a place for the worship of God' (ibid., at 889–90).

Lord Denning saw Scientology as a philosophy, centred on the spirit of Man, containing nothing of reverence for God or a deity. When members of the Church of Scientology used prayer they did not use it 'in its proper sense, i.e. intercession to God', nor were their references to God used 'in any religious sense' (ibid., at 890). Thus, although Lord Denning did not seek to distinguish between 'religious' and 'worship' in his judgement, the general tenor is that the Church of Scientology failed because they were not a real religion.

The other two judges, however, focused on whether Scientology involved 'worship'. Winn LJ gives a brief, rambling, and confused judgement that may have done little to encourage the appellants. Concluding that 'without feeling that I am really able to understand the subject-matter of this appeal, I have formed, for what it may be worth, a possibly irrational, possibly ill-founded, but very definite opinion', he found that Scientology did not involve worship: 'if I am bound to define my terms, I mean to indicate that they do not humble themselves in reverence and recognition of the dominant power and control of any entity or being outside their own body and life' (ibid., at 891). Buckley LJ gives a much better reasoned argument for excluding Scientology's ceremonies from worship: 'Worship I take to be something which must have some, at least, of the following characteristics: submission to the object worshipped, veneration of that object, praise, thanksgiving, prayer or intercession ... I do not say that one would need to find every element in every act which could properly be described as worship, but when one finds an act which contains none of those elements, in my judgment, it cannot answer to the description of an act of worship ... the sort of ceremony which takes place ... is a ceremony of instruction in the tenets of this particular body, but it is not a ceremony which can properly be described as constituting worship' (ibid., at 892).

So far, we have considered the position of community places that function primarily as religious sites. What is the position of a place that has both a religious and a non-religious function? The central practical question here is how far religious worship, teaching, and related activities can take place in a dwelling house without requiring planning permission. In their review of a number of religious traditions Mazumdar and Mazumdar stress the importance of the home to many religious traditions as a site for religious activities, rituals, ceremonies, and prayers; religious instruction and learning; religiously mandated ways of cooking, sharing food, and maintaining food taboos; and ritual purification and bathing. Their conclusion, at least in relation to the communities they consider, is that: '[c]ontrary to the ethnocentric assumptions of the public-private dichotomy which devalues the home and its activities, home in religious societies is the locus of important social, economic and ritual activities' (Mazumdar and Mazumdar, 1999 at 167).

The home as a religious site is particularly important to those religious communities which place emphasis on the family as a religious unit; and those whose size, material resources, or organisational structures make dedicated premises impractical. Additionally, the religious beliefs of the community may lead to a preference for home worship. In *Christian Gospel Church Inc. v San Francisco* (896 F.2d. 1221 (1990) (US)), for instance, the congregation explained that home worship followed from their belief in the imminent coming of their saviour Jesus Christ, making non-residential structures unnecessary and contrary to their values; and their desire to be isolated from commercial establishments, making use of rented rooms undesirable.

Uses incidental to the enjoyment of the dwelling house as such do not constitute development of the land, and so do not require planning permission (Town and Country Planning Act 1990 s.55 (UK)). If the religious activity goes beyond this, however, it may constitute a material change of use, from residential to mixed residential/institutional, and thus require planning permission. In *ex parte Sarvan Singh Seera* ([1986] 53 P & CR 281 (UK)) the applicant owned a house in a residential suburb. A Sikh religious leader visiting the country suffered a heart attack, and stayed with the applicant to convalesce. Coreligionists in groups of around forty during the week, and up to one hundred on Sundays, came to pay their respects and chant prayers. The local council issued an enforcement order stating that there had been a change from residential to mixed residential/religious use, and thus a breach of planning control.

The leader recovered and left the house, but the applicant was concerned that the stop order would restrict his religious activities. In particular, it was traditional to hold prayer meetings on family occasions, which involved prolonged recitation of holy works, followed by chanting. He applied for review of the order on the grounds that it did not specify exactly what was prohibited, in particular that it failed to state what activities would be regarded as merely incidental to the enjoyment of the dwelling house. The order prohibited 'religious meetings and services ... and religious devotion otherwise than incidental to the enjoyment of the dwelling house as such'. In accepting this as sufficiently certain, the court placed a substantial burden upon the applicant. As one commentator noted, the applicant could hope for little in the way of compensation for this restriction on his religious activity if it was quashed. In the meantime, he was placed: 'in the difficult situation of having to decide how far to curtail his religious devotions. If in order to make sure he does not commit a criminal offence, he errs on the side of caution, he will have no redress ... It must be possible for the local planning authority to specify more precisely what activities it finds objectionable' (Anon, 1987).

If the religious interests of residents are to be given proper weight in the planning process, those responsible for enforcement should inform the resident what is acceptable in their situation, especially where the objectionable conduct consists of an increase in the volume of a use of a property, generally referred to as intensification, rather than the use simpliciter. To leave the border between acceptable and unacceptable behaviour undefined in an enforcement order is to expose religious activity to a chilling effect, one felt especially by those most eager to obey the law. In the US case of *State v Cameron* (498 A.2d. 1217 (1985) (US)), for instance, the New Jersey Supreme Court invalidated a provision prohibiting 'churches and similar places of worship' in a particular area because of its vagueness when applied to a residential home used for only a proportion of the week as a place of worship. If residents are to ensure their use of their property does not conflict with the law, it is clearly important for them to be able to predict what uses are likely to be considered incidental to the enjoyment of their dwelling house.

Sacred Places in the US: Indigenous American Religions and the US Landscape

I have suggested above that particular issues are raised by religious buildings, which are concrete (sometimes literally), bounded, areas which are owned by the religious community in question. A different set of concerns are raised by sacred places which are not bounded in the same way, and where the religious community is not in the traditional relationship to the land of an owner. Collins has studied these sort of places in four different jurisdictions, with a particular emphasis on the pre-colonisation, non-Christian, religious ethnicities of the United States, New Zealand, Australia and Canada (Collins, 2003). For Collins, the key question is how religious claims to sacred sites are dealt with where the land in question is publicly owned: 'privately owned land is more likely to have been developed in ways that are inconsistent with a continuing sacred site, while much government land remains in a relatively natural state' (ibid., at 241). In this context, although the Canadian experience is interesting (see further Hornborg, 1994), developments in the United States have been influenced not only by competing claims over the landscape, but by the constitutional concern of the United States to avoid the Establishment of religion.

Before the 1930s, US policy was hostile to the religious practices of Native American communities, and serious obstacles were placed in the way of continuation of Native American religions. Even after the explicit bans were lifted in 1934, the policy and legal environment was hostile to these religions. Following a period of increased activism, and two independent reviews of the area, Congress passed the American Indian Religious Freedom Act 1978 (US) (see Feldman, 2000). AIRFA did not create any rights which could be relied upon in litigation (*Lyng v Northwest Indian Cemetery Protective Association*, 485 US 439 (1988) (US)). It served, however, as a recognition of the need to better address the needs of Native American religious communities, and led to the development of policies accepting the importance of sacred sites to these communities (for instance, Executive Order 13007, 61 Fed.Reg. 26, 771 (1996) (US)).

Although Federal legislation does not as such give Native American communities rights over public land, it will be recalled that the US Constitution includes an amendment prohibiting the government from interfering with free exercise of religion, or establishing any religion. The way in which these rules have played out in this context is striking.

In relation to free exercise, on a number of occasions Native American communities have argued that proposed changes to public land will interfere with their free exercise of religion. A good example is *Lyng* (op.cit.), where the Forest Service planned to pave a logging road through an area traditionally used for Native American religious practices. These claims have been unsuccessful, although the courts have not always used the same reasoning to reject the claim. Thus there are judgements finding that free exercise does not require the government to provide an environment for carrying out religious practices (*Crow v Gullett*, 541 F. Supp. (1982) (US)); and that changes to the landscape will not restrict free exercise because the practices can be carried out elsewhere in the region (*Wilson v Block*, 708 F.2d. 735 (1983) (US)). The economic and political significance of public land has also been stressed. A line of cases have indicated that religious interests cannot bind the government in deciding how to make use of public land, as this would in effect allow private groups to establish control of public resources (for example, *Havasupai Tribe v US*, 752 F.Supp. 1471 (1990) (US)). More straightforwardly, the government interests in developing oil exploitation have been seen as a compelling government interest justifying restriction of free exercise (*Inupiat Community of the Arctic Slope v US*, 548 F.Supp. 182 (1984) (US)). Feldman sees this as being the key to understanding the cases: 'the compelling public interest in the economic benefits of tourism or the production of inexpensive public utilities typically has overridden religious claims. Sacred sites have proven particularly vulnerable because, as many argue, federal agencies ultimately serve as "partners" with developers or other interests' (Feldman, 2000 at 563).

Free exercise has not, then, provided much support for Native American religious practices and engagements with sacred landscapes (see further Lane, 2001). The prohibition on Establishment has, however, been used to prevent government action intended to protect Native American religious interests. A Navajo community had claimed that for the government to permit and encourage tourism on Rainbow Bridge infringed their free exercise of religion at the sacred site. The community proposed a number of compromises, including closing the site to the general public with reasonable notice when ceremonies were to be held. The court found that the access of others did not restrict free exercise, but to prohibit their access would create 'a government managed religious shrine', contrary to the Establishment clause (*Badoni v Higginson*, 638 F.2d. 172 (1980) (US)). This last point was built upon in a later case dealing with the Devil's Tower national monument. This Native American sacred site began to attract substantial numbers of recreational climbers (see further Linge, 2000). Following complaints from Native American communities, the Park Service adopted a policy of discouraging climbing during June, a key period in the religious calendar for the site. Although this ban was described as 'voluntary', the Park Service had the power to issue commercial climbing permits, and adopted a policy of not issuing such permits for June – in effect banning commercial climbing in that month (Linge, 2000 at 312).

A group of commercial climbing guides objected to this ban, alleging that it constituted religious favouritism contrary to the Establishment clause. A federal district judge agreed, and the Park Service was required to withdraw the ban, although they were permitted to continue to inform prospective climbers of the religious significance of the site (*Bear Lodge Multiple Use Association v Babbitt*, 2 F.Supp. 2d 1448 (1998) (US)).

As Winslow cogently argues, however, the reasoning here is not consistently applied across government policy, or between different religious communities (Winslow, 1996). In particular, a number of National Historic Parks have included Christian churches; while from one perspective the entire system of reservations constitute government protection of an enclave for Native American culture, including religious culture (ibid., at 1317).

Chapter 5

Conclusions

The challenges posed by the interaction of law and religion in our jurisdictions, and in international law, are essential challenges raised by an increased respect for the increasing fact of religious difference within each jurisdiction. Where all those within a jurisdiction are co-religionists, sharing membership of a common religious organisation, the interaction is comparatively simple. Does the religion teach that Sunday should be observed as a day of rest? If so, the State can ban work on that day, and on that day only. Does the religion teach that male children should be circumcised? If so the State can define that physical change as acceptable child-care, and perhaps define a failure to carry it out as child neglect. Does the religion look to sacred texts as divinely inspired? If so, the State can protect this special status by prohibiting words likely to bring it into contempt, or outrage members of the State religion. In practice, of course, even when the State portrayed its members as having a single, shared, religious identity it is unlikely that this was truly the case. From a legal perspective, however, a State can represent this relationship even against factual evidence. Heretics can be seen as deviants, rather than as members of a religious minority within the territory.

A key change is the shift from seeing a religious minority as a group of heretics, deviants and traitors, to a group which is, perhaps grudgingly, entitled to some recognition. When a State acknowledges that citizens can be members of different religious groups then, even if membership of some of these groups leads to a lower level of civic participation, the principle of religious difference within the jurisdiction has been accepted. Within the English jurisdiction in particular, recognition was initially grudging, taking a form perhaps best understood as toleration – toleration of error, and withholding of sanctions that could be imposed against such error. Over time, however, this toleration has begun to develop into an increasing discomfort with the State exercising an authority to determine religious truth and so to decide that a minority religious group is in error. Toleration moves towards respect.

As a legal system engages with a plurality of religious beliefs, practices, communities, and organisations, the range of issues which need to be dealt with increase. What if one community sees Saturday as the day of rest? The State will need to consider whether members should be allowed to insist on this day of rest against the commercial requirements of an employer; whether members should be allowed to work on Sunday, perhaps when members of other communities are required to refrain from commercial activities on that day. What if one community sees circumcision of infant males as a sinful act? The State will need to consider whether to allow them to refrain from this conduct, and also how to resolve disputes between parents where one regards the circumcision as religiously mandated, and the other regards it as religiously prohibited.

This text has explored some of the key issues of complexity raised by the interaction of State legal power, and religious plurality. We began by considering working definitions of both 'law' and 'religion', and the importance of each to the other. We then moved to consider the increasingly significant provisions of international law. Although in many cases these legal norms do not constitute law in the same sense as national law, primarily due to issues of enforcement, they are immensely influential on how States develop and apply their national law. Of more direct significance, however, are the overarching constitutional guarantees to be found in the written constitutions of many States, and the unwritten constitutions of an idiosyncratic minority. These overarching guarantees provide important practical rules to regulate the relationship between law and religion. They also contribute substantially to broader debates concerning the proper treatment of this relationship. 'Human rights talk', in the particular form of 'religious rights talk' can have an impact far beyond constitutional litigation.

While laws are made in the general, they are applied in the particular, and the remainder of our discussion considered particular areas of interaction. These areas were divided into two categories – the interaction of the State with the individual, and the interaction of the State with the religious organisation and community. Although a variety of jurisdictions were considered in this discussion, we can see clear similarities of approach as democratic States seek to balance the competing concerns of differently placed citizens, and the State more generally. The similarities also lead to States looking to solutions developed elsewhere in forming their own response. We can see this in the cross-citation of authorities by English, United States, and South African Courts faced with religious use of cannabis; and the increasing influence of Russian-style registration regimes. Combined with the influence of international law, we may be able to look forward to a period of relative homogenisation of religious rights, at least within our jurisdictions. The differences of legal context, and broader society, remain very considerable, however, as a consideration of the discussion of constitutional guarantees indicates.

Further Reading

International Guarantees of Religious Interests

General

Dickson B., 1995, 'The United Nations and freedom of religion', *International and Comparative Law Quarterly*, 44, 327.

Evans M.D., 2000, 'The United Nations and freedom of religion: The work of the Human Rights Committee' in Ahdar R.J. (ed.), *Law and religion*, Aldershot: Ashgate.

Janis M.W. and Evans C. (eds.), 1999, *Religion and international law*, The Hague: Martinus Nijhoff Publishers.

Witte J. and van der Vyver J.D. (eds), 1996, *Religious human rights in global perspective*, London: Martinus Nijhoff Publishers.

Universal Declaration of Human Rights

Scheinin M., 1992, 'Article 18', in Eide A. (ed.), *The universal declaration of human rights: a commentary*, Oslo: Scandinavian Press.

International Covenant on Civil and Political Rights

Cumper P., 1995, 'Freedom of thought, conscience and religion', in Harris D. and Joseph S., *The international covenant on civil and political rights and United Kingdom law*, Oxford: Clarendon Press.

1981 Declaration

Davis D.H., 2002, 'The evolution of religious freedom as a universal human right: examining the role of the 1981 United Nations declaration on the elimination of all forms of intolerance and of discrimination based on religion or belief', *Brigham Young University Law Review* 217.

Sullivan D.J., 1988, 'Advancing the freedom of religion or belief through the UN declaration on the elimination of religious intolerance and discrimination', *American Journal of International Law* 82, 487.

European Convention on Human Rights

Dunne K.A., 1999, 'Addressing religious intolerance in Europe: The limited application of Article 9 of the European Convention of Human Rights and fundamental freedoms', *California Western International Law Journal* 30, 117.

Edge P.W., 1998 'The European Court of Human Rights and religious rights', *International and Comparative Law Quarterly* 47, 680.

Evans C., 2001, *Freedom of religion under the European Convention on Human Rights*, Oxford: Oxford University Press.

Evans M.D., 1997, *Religious liberty and international law in Europe*, Cambridge: Cambridge University Press.

Gunn T.J., 1996, 'Adjudicating rights of conscience under the European Convention on Human Rights', in Van Vyver J.D. and Witte J., *Religious human rights in global perspectives: legal perspectives*, New York: Kluwer Law International.

Introductions to Particular Jurisdictions

United Kingdom

Bradney A., 1993, *Religions, rights and laws*, Leicester: Leicester University Press.

Edge P.W., 2001, *Legal responses to religious difference*, New York: Kluwer Law International.

United States

Feldman S.M., 2003, 'Religious minorities and the First Amendment: The history, the doctrine, and the future', University of Pennsylvania: *Journal of Constitutional Law* 6, 222.

Guinn D.E., 2002, *Faith on trial: Communities of faith, the First Amendment, and the theory of deep diversity*, Oxford: Lexington Books.

Strongs J.K., 2002, *Law, religion and public policy: A commentary on First Amendment jurisprudence*, Lanham: Lexington Books.

Canada

Moon R., 2003, 'Liberty, neutrality, and inclusion: religious freedom under the Canadian Charter of Rights and Freedoms', *Brandeis Law Journal* 41, 563.

New Zealand

Thompson W., 1996, 'Religious practices and beliefs: a case for their accommodation in the Human Rights Act 1993', *New Zealand Law Journal*, 106.

South Africa

Freedman W., 2000, 'The right to religious liberty, the right to religious equality, and section 15(1) of the South African Constitution', *Stellenbosch Law Review* 99.

Van der Vyver J.D., 1999, 'Constitutional perspectives of Church-State relations in South Africa', *Brigham Young University Law Review* 635.

Theoretical Issues

Defining Religion

Clements B., 1989, 'Defining "religion" in the First Amendment: A functional approach', *Cornell Law Review* 74, 532.

Feofanov D.N., 1994, 'Defining religion: An immodest proposal', *Hofstra Law Review* 23, 309.

Frame R.O., 1992, 'Belief in a nonmaterial reality – a proposed First Amendment definition of religion', *University of Illinois Law Review* 819 .

Gunn T.J., 2003, 'The complexity of religion and the definition of "religion" in international law', *Harvard Human Rights Journal* 16, 89.

Significance of Law and Religion to one Another

Ahdar R.J. (ed.), 2000, *Law and religion*, Aldershot: Ashgate.

Edge P.W. and Harvey G. (eds.), 2000, *Law and religion in contemporary society: Communities, individualism and the State*, Aldershot: Ashgate.

O'Dair R. and Lewis A., 2001, *Law and religion: current legal issues 4*, Oxford: Oxford University Press.

Bibliography

Abdullah Y., 1996, 'The Holy See at United Nations Conferences: Church or State', *Columbia Law Review* 96, 1835.

Adams IV N.A., 2000, 'A human rights imperative: Extending religious liberty beyond the border', *Cornell International Law Journal* 33, 1.

Addo M.K., 1999, 'The applicability of the Human Rights Act to private corporations', in L. Betten (ed.), *The Human Rights Act: What it means*, London: Martinus Nijhoff Publishers.

Ahdar R., 1996, 'Religion as a factor in custody and access disputes', *International Journal of Law, Policy and Family* 10, 177.

Ahdar R.J., 1996, 'Religion in custody and access: The New Zealand experience', *New Zealand Universities Law Review* 17, 115.

Ahdar R.J., 2000, 'The inevitability of law and religion: An introduction', in R.J. Ahdar (ed.), *Law and religion*, Aldershot: Ashgate.

Alston P., 1992, 'The Commission on Human Rights' in P. Alston, *The United Nations and Human Rights: A critical appraisal*, Oxford: Clarendon Press.

Andries E.M., 2001, 'Post-modernism, hermeneutics, and authenticity: Interpreting legal and theological texts in the twenty-first century', in R. O'Dair and A. Lewis, *Law and religion: Current legal issues 4*, Oxford: Oxford University Press.

An-Naim A.A., 1988, 'Mahmud Muhammad Taha and the crisis in Islamic law reform: Implications for interreligious relations', *Journal of Ecumenical Studies* 25, 1.

Anon, 1987, 'Case and Comment: ex parte Sarvan Singh Seera', *Journal of Planning Law* 283.

Archer P., 1999, 'The House of Lords: Past, present and future', *Political Quarterly* 70, 396.

Arzt D.E., 1996, 'Heroes or heretics: Religious dissidents under Islamic law', *Wisconsin International Law Journal* 14(2), 349.

Barber P., 1996, 'Outrageous behaviour', *Ecclesiastical Law Journal* 584.

Barker C.R., 1999, 'Religion and charity law', *Juridical Review* 303.

Basova I.G., 2000, 'Freedom under fire: The new Russian religious law', *Temple International and Comparative Law Journal* 14, 181.

Beatty D., 1995, *Constitutional law in theory and practice*, Toronto: University of Toronto Press.

Becker D.H.E., 1999, 'Note: Free exercise of religion under the New York Constitution', *Cornell Law Review* 84, 1089.

Bennion F.A.R., 1997, *Statutory interpretation: A code*, London: Butterworths.

Berg T.C., 1997, 'Religion clause anti-theories', (1997) *Notre Dame Law Review* 72(3), 693.

Bibbings L., 1995, 'State reaction to conscientious objection' in I. Loveland, *Frontiers of criminality*, London: Sweet and Maxwell.

Boister N., 2001, 'Cannabis in the United Kingdom: Does international law leave freedom for manoeuvre?', *Criminal Law Review* 509.

Bordeaux M., 1999, 'The new Russian law on religion: A view from the regions', *De Paul Law Review* 49, 139.

Boyle K. and Sheen J. (eds.), 1997, *Freedom of religion and belief: A world report*, London: Routledge.

Bradney A. and Cownie F., 2000, *Living without law: An ethnography of Quaker decision-making, dispute avoidance and dispute resolution*, Ashgate: Dartmouth.

Bradney A., 1993, *Religions, rights and laws*, Leicester: Leicester University Press.

Bradney A., 2000, 'Religion and law in Great Britain at the end of the second Christian millennium' in P.W. Edge and G. Harvey (eds.), *Law and religion in contemporary society: Communities, individualism and the State*, Aldershot: Ashgate.

Bradney A., 2000b, 'Faced by faith' in P. Oliver et al. (eds.), *Faith in law: Essays in legal theory*, Oxford: Hart.

Bradney A., 2001, 'Politics and sociology: New research agendas for the study of law and religion', in R. O'Dair and A. Lewis, *Law and religion: Current legal issues 4*, Oxford: Oxford University Press.

Braithwaite C., 1995, *Conscientious objection to compulsions under the law*, York: The Ebor Press.

Bratza N. and O'Boyle M., 1997, 'The legacy of the Commission to the new Court under the 11th Protocol', *European Human Rights Law Review* 3, 211.

Brodin E., 1996, 'The Employment status of ministers of religion', *Industrial Law Journal* 25, 211.

Bromhead P.A., 1958, *The House of Lords and contemporary politics 1911–1957*, London: Routledge.

Bromley E.B. and Bromley K., 1999, 'John Pemsel goes to the Supreme Court of Canada in 2001: The historical context in England', *Charity Law and Practice Review* 6(2), 115.

Bromley E.B., 1993, 'Religious, reformation, remedial and renaissance philanthropy', *Charity Law and Practice Review* 2(1), 53.

Brossart J., 1999, 'Legitimate regulation of religion? European Court of Human Rights religious freedom doctrine and the Russian Federation Law "On Freedom of Conscience and Religious Organisations"', *Boston College International and Comparative Law Review* 22(2), 297.

Brown F., 1994, 'Influencing the House of Lords: The role of the Lords Spiritual 1979–1987', *Political Studies* 42, 105.

Brown M.R., 1983, 'Religion: The psychedelic perspective: The freedom of religion defense', *American Indian Law Review* 11, 125.

Browne M., 1998, 'Should Germany stop worrying and love the octopus? Freedom of religion and the Church of Scientology in Germany and the United States', *Indiana International and Comparative Law Review* 9, 155.

Brownstein A.E., 1990, 'Harmonising the earthly and heavenly spheres: The fragmentation and synthesis of religion, equality and speech in the Constitution', *Ohio State Law Journal* 51, 89.

Bryce, 1918, *On the reform of the Second Chamber*, London: HMSO.

Burton M.A., 1997, 'Nally v Grace Community Church: Is there a future for clergy malpractice claims?', *Santa Clara Law Review* 37, 467.

Buruk L.M., 1986, 'Clergy malpractice: Making clergy accountable to a lower power', *Peppardine Law Review* 14, 137.

Buseton R., 2000, 'The Human Rights Act and private law', *Law Quarterly Review* 116, 48.

Butler A.S., 2000, 'Interface between the Human Rights Act 1998 and other enactments: Pointers from New Zealand', *European Human Rights Law Review* 3, 250.

Carlton Group, 1997, *The guide to the House of Lords*, Pinner: Carlton Group.

Carmella A.C., 1997, 'Religion as public resource', *Seton Hall Law Review* 27, 1225.

Carter S.L., 1987, 'Evolutionism, creationism and treating religion as a hobby', *Duke Law Journal* 979.

Carter S.L., 1993, 'Comment: The resurrection of religious freedom', *Harvard Law Review* 107(1), 118.

Charity Commission, 1999, 'Application for registration as a charity by the Church of Scientology (England and Wales)', 17/11/99.

Charlesworth H., 1999, 'The challenges of human rights law for religious traditions' in M.W. Janis and C. Evans (eds.), *Religion and international law*, The Hague: Martinus Nijhoff Publishers.

Church of England, 1999, *The role of Bishops in the Second Chamber*, London: Archbishops Council.

Clapham A., 1993, *Human Rights in the Private Sphere*, Oxford: Clarendon Press.

Clarke D.S. and Ansay T., 1992, *Introduction to the law of the United States*, Boston: Kluwer Law and Taxation Publishers.

Clements B., 1989, 'Defining 'religion' in the First Amendment: A functional approach', *Cornell Law Review* 74, 533.

Collins R.B., 2003, 'Sacred sites and religious freedom on government land', *Journal of Constitutional Law* 4, 241.

Conkle D.O., 1988, 'Toward a general theory of the establishment clause', *Northwestern University Law Review* 82, 1113.

Conkle D.O., 2000, 'The path of American religious liberty: From the original theology to formal neutrality and an uncertain future', *Indiana Law Journal* 75, 1.

Cooke of Thornden, 1997, 'Mechanisms for entrenchment and protection of a Bill of Rights: The New Zealand experience', *European Human Rights Law Review* 5, 490.

Cornwell A.J., 1994, 'Sacrificial rites become constitutional rights on the altar of Babalu Aya', *University of Arkansas at Little Rock Law Journal* 16, 623.

Cortner R.C., 1981, *The Supreme Court and the Second Bill of Rights*, Madison: University of Wisconsin Press.

Cranmer F., 2001, 'Church-State relations in the UK: A Westminster view', *Ecclesiastical Law Journal* 6, 111.

Creighton S. and King V., 1996, *Prisoners and the law*, London: Butterworths.

Cumper P., 1995, 'Freedom of thought, conscience and belief' in D. Harris and S. Joseph (eds.), *The International Convenant on civil and political rights and United Kingdom law*, Oxford: Clarendon Press.

Cumper P., 2000a, 'The protection of religious rights under section 13 of the Human Rights Act 1998', *Public Law* 254.

Cumper P., 2000b, 'Religious organizations and the Human Rights Act 1998', in P.W. Edge and G. Harvey (eds.), *Law and religion in contemporary society: Communities, individualism and the State,* Aldershot: Ashgate.

DATF, 1999, *Making a modern senate*, Essex, Democratic Audit.

Davidson S., 1997, *The Inter-American Rights system*, Aldershot: Dartmouth.

de Codes R.M.M., 1998, 'The contemporary form of registering religious entities in Spain', *Brigham Young University Law Review* 369.

Dinstein Y., 1992, 'Freedom of religion and the protection of religious minorities' in Y. Dinstein and M. Tabory (ed.), *The protection of minorities and human rights*, The Hague: Martinus Nijhoff Publishers.

Dobe K.S. and Chhokar S.S., 2000, 'Muslims, ethnicity and the law', *International Journal of Discrimination and the Law* 4, 369.

Drewry G. and Brock J., 1971, 'Prelates in parliament', *Parliamentary Affairs* 24, 222.

Drinan R.F. and Huffman J.I., 1993, 'The Religious Freedom Restoration Act: A legislative history', *Journal of Law and Religion* 10, 531.

Du Plessis J.R. and Kok L., 1989, *An elementary introduction to the study of South African law*, Cape Town: Juta and Co.

Ducharme H.M., 2001, 'The image of God and the moral identity of persons: An evaluation of the holistic theology of persons', in R. O'Dair and A. Lewis, *Law and religion: Current legal issues 4*, Oxford: Oxford University Press.

Dunne K.A., 1999, 'Addressing religious intolerance in Europe: The limited application of Article 9 of the European Convention of Human Rights and fundamental freedoms', *California Western International Law Journal* 30, 117.

Durkheim E., 1915, *The religious life*, translated by J.W. Swain, London: Allen and Unwin.

Edge P. and Loughrey J., 2001, 'Religious charities and the juridification of the Charity Commission', *Legal Studies* 21(1), 36.

Edge P., 2000, 'The employment of religious adherents by religious organisations', in P.W. Edge and G. Harvey (eds.), *Law and religion in contemporary society: Communities, individualism, and the State*, London: Ashgate.

Edge P., 2001, 'Religious remnants in the composition of the United Kingdom Parliament', in R. O'Dair and A. Lewis, *Law and religion: Current legal issues 4*, Oxford: Oxford University Press.

Edge P.W. and Pearce C.C.A., 2003, *Religious representation in a democratic legislature: A case study of the Lord Bishop of Sodor and Man in the Manx Tynwald*, Oxford: Centre for Legal Research and Policy Studies.

Edge P.W. and Pearce C.C.A., 2004, 'Official religious representation in a democratic legislature: Lessons from the Manx Tynwald', *Journal of Church and State*, 46(3), 1.

Edge P.W., 1995, 'Charitable status for the advancement of religion: An abolitionist's view' (1995), 3 *Charity Law and Practice Review* 29 .

Edge P.W., 1995b, 'The Missionary's position after *Kokkinakis* v *Greece*', *Web Journal of Current Legal Issues* 2.

Edge P.W., 1996, 'Current problems in Article 9 of the European Convention on Human Rights', *Juridical Review* 42.

Edge P.W., 1997, *Manx Public Law*, Preston: Isle of Man Law Society.

Edge P.W., 1998, 'Reorienting the establishment debate: From the illusory norm to equality of respect', *Anglo-American Law Review* 265.

Edge P.W., 1999, 'Religious organisations and the prevention of terrorism legislation: A comment in response to the consultation paper', *Journal of Civil Liberties* 4(2), 194.

Edge P.W., 2000, 'Voluntariness and religious rights under the European Convention on Human Rights',*Web Journal of Current Legal Issues* 3.

Edge P.W., 2001, *Legal responses to religious difference*, Dordrecht: Kluwer Law International.

Edge P.W., 2002, 'The construction of sacred places in English law', *Journal of Environmental Law* 14(2), 161.

Efaw A.C.S., 1996, 'Free exercise and the uniformed employee: A comparative look at religious freedom in the armed forces of the United States and Great Britain', *Comparative Labour Law Journal* 17, 648.

Eisgruber C.L. and Sager L.G., 2000, 'Religious liberty and the moral structure of constitutional rights', *Legal Theory* 6, 253.

Engle R., 1997, 'The persistence of neutrality: The failure of the religious accomodation provision to redeem Title VII', *Texas Law Review* 76, 317.

Epstein S.B., 1996, 'Rethinking the constitutionality of ceremonial deism', *Columbia Law Review* 96, 2083.

Evans C., 1999, 'Religious freedom in European human rights law: The search for a guiding conception', in M.W. Janis and C. Evans (eds.), *Religion and international law*, The Hague: Martinus Nijhoff Publishers.

Evans C., 2001, *Freedom of religion under the European Convention on Human Rights*, Oxford: Oxford University Press.

Evans M.D., 1997, *Religious liberty and international law in Europe*, Cambridge: Cambridge University Press.

Evans M.D., 2000, 'The United Nations and freedom of religion: The work of the Human Rights Committee', in R.J. Ahdar, *Law and religion*, Aldershot: Ashgate.

Farnsworth, E.A., 1996, *An introduction to the legal system of the United States*, New York: Oceana Publications.

Feldman A., 2000, 'Othering knowledge and unknowing law: Oppositional narratives in the struggle for American Indian religious freedom', *Social and Legal Studies* 9(4), 557.

Fellman D., 1978, 'The nationalization of American Civil liberties', in H.J. Abraham et al. (eds.), *Essays on the constitution of the United States*, London: National University Press.

Feofanov D.N., 1994, 'Defining religion: An immodest proposal', *Hofstra Law Review* 23, 309.

Ferrari S. and Bradney A. (eds.), 2000, *Islam and European Legal Systems*, Aldershot, Ashgate.

Flowers R.B., 1993, 'Government accommodation of religious-based conscientious objection', *Seton Hall Law Review* 24, 695.

Frame R.O., 1992, 'Belief in a nonmaterial reality – A proposed First Amendment definition of religion', *University of Illinois Law Review* 819.

Free Presbyterian Church of Scotland, 1998, *Resolution of the Free Presbyterian Church of Scotland Synod*, 19 May.

Freedman W., 2000, 'The right to religious liberty, the right to religious equality and section 15(1) of the South African Constitution', *Stellenbosch Law Review* 1, 99.

Freeman G.C. III, 1983, 'The misguided search for the constitutional definition of religion', *Georgetown Law Journal* 71, 1519.

Freeman M., 2001, 'Is the Jewish *get* any business of the State?', in R. O'Dair and A. Lewis, *Law and religion: Current legal issues 4*, Oxford: Oxford University Press.

French R.R., 1999, 'From Yoder to Yoda: Models of traditional, modern and postmodern religion in US constitutional law', *Arizona Law Review* 41, 49.

Funston C.E., 1983, 'Made out of whole cloth? A constitutional analysis of the clergy malpractice concept', *California Western Law Review* 19, 507.

Gall G.L., 1995, *The Canadian legal system*, Scarborough: Thomson Canada.

Garry P., 1992, 'Churches and the courts: The First Amendment protection from clergy lawsuits', *Journal of Law and Religion* 9, 179.

Garvey J.H., 1986 'Free exercise and the values of religious liberty', *Connecticut Law Review* 18, 779.

Gay O., 2001, 'The House of Commons (removal of Clergy Disqualification) Bill', House of Commons Research Paper 01/11.

George R.P., 1998, 'Protecting religious liberty in the next millenium: Should we amend the religion clauses of the Constitution?', *Loyola of Los Angeles Law Review* 32, 27.

Ghandhi P.R., 1998, *The Human Rights Committee and the right of individual communication*, Aldershot: Dartmouth.

Goodrich P., 1997, 'A Bishop in the House of Lords' *Law and Justice* 63.

Greenawalt K., 1998, 'Should the religion clauses of the Constitution be amended?', *Loyola of Los Angeles Law Review* 32, 9.

Gunn T.J., 1996, 'Adjudicating rights of conscience under the European Convention on Human Rights', in J.D. van Vyver and J. Witte (eds.), *Religious Human Rights in global perspectives: legal perspectives*, Dordrecht: Kluwer.

Hahlo H.R. and Kahn E., 1968, *The South African legal system and its background*, Cape Town: Juta and Co.

Hall C.G., 1996, 'Aggiornamento: Reflections upon the contemporary legal concept of religion', *Cambrian Law Review* 27, 7.

Hamilton C., 1995, *Family law and religion*, London: Sweet and Maxwell.

Hammer L.M., 2001, *The International Human Right to freedom of conscience: Some suggestions for its development and application*, Aldershot: Ashgate.

Hanks P., 1996, *Constitutional law in Australia*, Sydney: Butterworths.

Hannah G., 1954, *Christian by degrees*, London: Augustine Publishing Co.

Hardie, 1999, 'Declarations of incompatibility and the fast-track legislative procedure', *Statute Law Review* 20(3), 210.

Harris D. and Joseph S., 1995, *The International Covenant on civil and political rights and United Kingdom law*, Oxford: Clarendon Press.

Harris D.J., O'Boyle M. and C. Warbrick, 1995, *Law of the European Convention on Human Rights*, London: Butterworths.

Hay D. and Nye R., 1998, *The spirit of the child*, London: Fount.

Heim J.C., 1990, 'The demise of the confessional state and the rise of the idea of a legitimate minority', in J.W. Chapman and A. Wertheimer (eds.), *Majorities and minorities*, New York: New York University Press.

Henkin L., 1989, 'International law: Politics, values and functions', *Collected Courses of Hague Academy of International Law* 216 (IV), 13.

Hervier-Leger D., 1994, 'Religion, memory and Catholic identity: Young people in France and the "New Evangelism of Europe"', in J. Fulton and P. Gee (eds.), *Religion in contemporary Europe*, Lewiston: Edwin Mellen Press.

Hilbert J.S., 1987, 'God in a cage: Religion, intent and criminal law', *Buffalo Law Review* 36, 701.

Hill M., 1995, *Ecclesiastical law*, London: Butterworths.

Hill M., 2001, 'Judicial approaches to religious disputes', in R. O'Dair and A. Lewis, *Law and religion: Current legal issues 4*, Oxford: Oxford University Press.

Hodder-Williams R., 1988, 'The Constitution (1787) and modern American government', in V. Bogdanor (ed.), *Constitutions in democratic politics*, Aldershot: Gower Publishing.

Hofmann M.W., 1998 'The protection of religious minorities in Islam', *Encounters* 4(2), 137.

Hogan G.W., 1987, 'Law and religion: Church State relations in Ireland from Independence to the present day', *American Journal of Comparative Law* 35, 47.

Home Affairs Committee, 1997, *Third Report: Freemasonry and the Judiciary (HCP 192 1997)*, London: HMSO.

Hornborg A., 1994, 'Environmentalist, ethnicity and sacred places: Reflections on modernity, discourse and power', *Canadian Review of Sociology and Anthropology* 31(3), 524.

Horwitz P., 1996, 'The sources and limits of freedom of religion in a liberal democracy: section 2(a) and beyond', *Toronto Law Review* 54, 1.

Howarth D.R., 1986, 'Employment Law', *Cambridge Law Journal* 405.

Human Rights Committee, 1993, *General Comment 22, Article 18* (Forty-eight session, 1993). Compilation of General Comments and General Recommendations Adopted by Human Rights Treaty Bodies, U.N. Doc. HRI\GEN\1\Rev.1 at 35 (1994).

Hunt M., 1998, 'The 'horizontal effect' of the Human Rights Act', *Public Law* 423.

Iadicola P., 1998, 'Criminology's contributions to the study of religious crime', in A. Shupe, *Wolves within the fold: Religious leadership and abuses of power*, London: Rutgers University Press.

Jamar S.D., 1996, 'Accommodating religion at work: A principled approach to title VII and religious freedom', *New York Law School Law Review* 40, 719.

Jenkins P., 1998, 'Creating a culture of clergy deviance', in A. Shupe, *Wolves within the fold: Religious leadership and abuses of power*, London: Rutgers University Press.

Johnson P.E., 1984, 'Concepts and compromise in First Amendment religious doctrine', *California Law Review* 27, 817.

Jones G., 1969, *History of the Law of Charity 1532–1827*, Cambridge: Cambridge University Press.

Juss S.S., 1995, 'The Constitution and Sikhs in Britain', *Brigham Young University Law Review* 2, 481.

Kearns P., 2000, 'Obscene and blasphemous libel: Misunderstanding art', *Criminal Law Review* 652.

Knott K., 1988, 'Other major religious traditions', in T. Thomas, *The British: Their religious beliefs and practices 1800–1986*, London: Routledge.

Kobler J., 1974, *Ardent spirits: The rise and fall of prohibition*, London: Michael Joseph.

Krebs T., 1998, 'Church structures that facilitate pedophilia among Roman Catholic clergy', in A. Shupe, *Wolves within the fold: Religious leadership and abuses of power*, London: Rutgers University Press.

Lane B.C., 2001, 'Giving voice to place: Three models for understanding American sacred space', *Religion and Culture: A Journal of Interpretation* 11(1), 53.

Laski H.J., 1925, *The problem of a Second Chamber*, London: Fabian Society.

Last K.V., 2002, 'The privileged position of the Church of England in the control of works to historic buildings: The provenance of the ecclesiastical exemption from listed building control', *Common Law World Review* 31(3), 205.

Latham J., 1952, 'Interpretation of the Constitution' in R. Else-Mitchell (ed.), *Essays on the Australian Constitution*, Sydney: Law Books of Australasia Pty Ltd.

Lavender N., 1997, 'The problem of the margin of appreciation', *European Human Rights Law Review* 4, 380.

Laycock D., 1996, 'Continuity and change in the threat to religious liberty: The Reformation era and the late twentieth century', *Minnesota Law Review* 80, 1047.

Leeder L., 1997, *Ecclesiastical Law Handbook*, London, Sweet and Maxwell.

Lehman J.K., 1990, 'Clergy malpractice: A constitutional approach', *Supreme Court Law Review* 41, 459.

Lekhel A., 1999, 'Leveling the playing field for religious "liberty" in Russia: A critical analysis of the 1997 Law "On Freedom of Conscience and Religious Associations"', *Vanderbilt Journal of Transnational Law* 32, 167.

Lester, 1999, 'Interpreting statutes under the Human Rights Act', *Statute Law Review* 21(3), 218.

Linge G., 2000, 'Ensuring the full freedom of religion on public lands: Devils tower and the protection of Indian sacred sites', *Environmental Affairs* 27, 307.

Lipson J., 2000, 'On balance: Religious liberty and third-party harms', *Minnesota Law Review* 84, 589.

Livingstone S., 1997, 'Article 14 and the prevention of discrimination in the European Convention on Human Rights', *European Human Rights Law Review* 1, 25.

Longley A., 1993, 'Religion as charity: some reflections', *Charity Law and Practice Review* 1, 87.

Loveland I., 2001, 'Religious drug use as a human right?', *New Law Journal* 41.

Lumb R.D. and Ryan K.W., 1977, *The Constitution of Australia annotated*, Sydney: Butterworths.

Lupu I.C., 1987, 'Free exercise exemption and religious institutions: The case of employment discrimination', *Boston University Law Review* 67(3), 391.

Macklem T., 2000, 'Faith as a secular value', *McGill Law Journal* 45, 1.

Macklem T., 2000, 'Reason and religion', in P. Oliver et al. (eds.), *Faith in law: Essays in legal theory*, Oxford: Hart.

Malcolm D., 1996, 'Religion, tolerance and the law', *Australian Law Journal* 70, 976.

Maltz E., 1988-9, 'The nature of precedent', *NC Law Review* 66, 367.

Manfredi C.P., 1993, *Canada and the paradox of liberal constitutionalism: Judicial power and the Charter*, London: University of Oklahoma Press.

Manning J. and Kilpatrick A., 1998, 'Public law' in C. Baker, *Human Rights Act 1998: A Practitioner's Guide*, London: Sweet and Maxwell.

Markey M.E., 1995, 'The price of landlord's "free" exercise of religion: Tenant's right to discrimination-free housing and privacy', *Fordham Urban Law Journal* 22, 699.

Marshall G., 2003, 'The lynchpin of Parliamentary intention: Lost, stolen or strained', *Public Law* 236.

Marshall W.P., 2000, 'What is the matter with equality? An assessment of the equal treatment of religion and non-religion in First Amendment jurisprudence', *Indiana Law Journal* 75, 193.

Martinz-Torron J., 2001, 'The European Court of Human Rights and religion', in R. O'Dair and A. Lewis, *Law and religion: Current legal issues 4*, Oxford: Oxford University Press.

Mason A., 1986, 'The role of a constitutional court in a federation: A comparison of the Australian and the United States experience', *Federal Law Review* 16,1.

Mazumdar S. and Mazumdar S., 1999, '"Women's significant spaces": Religion, space and community', *Journal of Environmental Psychology* 19, 159.

McConnell M.W., 1990, 'The origins and historical understanding of free exercise of religion', *Harvard Law Review* 103, 1409.

McConnell M.W., 2000, 'Neutrality, separation and accommodation: Tensions in American First Amendment doctrine', in R.J. Ahdar (ed.), *Law and religion*, Aldershot: Ashgate.

McConnell M.W., 2000, 'Why is religious liberty the "first freedom"?', *Cardozo Law Review* 21, 1243.

McEldowney J.F., 1994, *Public Law*, London: Sweet and Maxwell.

McGoldrick D., 1991, *The Human Rights Committee*, Oxford: Clarendon Press.

McKay D., 1993, *American politics and society*, Oxford: Blackwell Press.

McLean G.R., 1996, 'Freedom of religion and state neutrality: A philosophical problem', *South African Law Journal* 175.

Medhurst K., 1999, 'The Church of England: A progress report', *Parliamentary Affairs* 52, 275.

Miner C.J., 1998, 'Losing my religion: Austria's new religion law in light of international and European standards of religious freedom', *Brigham Young University Law Review* 607.

Moon G., 2000, 'The draft discrimination protocol to the European Convention on Human Rights: A progress report', (2000) *European Human Rights Law Review* 1, 49.

Moosa N., 1998, 'The interim and final constitutions and Muslim personal law: Implications for South African Muslim women', *Stellenbosch Law Review* 9,196.

Morris G.S., 2001, 'Fundamental rights: Exclusion by agreement', *Industrial Law Journal* 30(1), 49.

Mower A.G., 1991, *Regional human rights: A comparative study of the West European and Inter-American systems*, New York: Greenward Press.

Mulik P., 1998, 'State and churches in the Slovak Republic', *European Journal for Church and State Research* 5, 183.

Mullholland R.D., 1995, *Introduction to the New Zealand legal system*, Wellington: Butterworths.

Mumford S.E., 1998, 'The judicial resolution of disputes involving children and religion', *International and Comparative Law Quarterly* 47, 117.

Muramoto O., 1998a, 'Bioethics of the refusal of blood by Jehovah's Witnesses: Part 1. Should bioethical deliberations consider dissident's views', *Journal of Medical Ethics* 24, 223.

Muramoto, O., 1998b, 'Bioethics of the refusal of blood by Jehovah's Witnesses: Part 2. A novel approach based on rational non-interventional paternalism', *Journal of Medical Ethics* 24, 295.

Murphy J.D. and Rueter R., 1981, *Stare decisis in Commonwealth Appellate courts*, Toronto: Butterworths.

Murray R. and Evans M.D., 2001, *Documents of the African Commission on Human and People's Rights*, Oxford: Hart.

Murray R., 2000, *The African Commission on Human and People's Rights and international law*, Oxford: Hart.

National Council for Civil Liberties, 1997, *Bringing Rights Home: Response to Labour's plans to incorporate the European Convention on Human Rights into UK Law*, London: NCL.

New South Wales Anti-Discrimination Board, 1984, *Discrimination and Religious Conviction*, Sydney: New South Wales Anti-Discrimination Board.

Newark F.H., 1946, 'Public benefit and religious trusts', *Law Quarterly Review* 62, 234.

Newman A., 1997, 'The office of Chief Rabbi: A very English institution', in N. Aston (ed.), *Religious change in Europe, 1650-1914*, London: Clarendon Press.

Opsahl T., 1992, 'The Human Rights Committee', in P. Alston, *The United Nations and Human Rights: A critical appraisal*, Oxford: Clarendon Press.

Park C.C., 1994, *Sacred worlds: An introduction to geography and religion*, London: Routledge.

Partington M., 2000, *An introduction to the English legal system*, Oxford: Oxford University Press.

Pattenden R., 1999, 'The exclusion of the clergy from criminal trial juries: An historical perspective', *Ecclesiastical law Journal* 5, 151.

Petchey P., 2003, 'Ministers of religion and employment rights: An examination of the issues', *Ecclesiastical Law Journal* 7(33), 157.

Picarda H., 1983, 'New religions as charities', *New Law Journal* 131, 436.

Picarda H., 1993, 'Religious observances and the element of public benefit', *Charity Law and Practice Review* 2(1), 155.

Potz R., 1998, 'Church and State in Austria 1997', *European Journal for Church and State Research* 5, 109.

Poulter S., 1998, *Ethnicity, law and human rights: The English experience*, Oxford: Clarendon Press.

Quint F. and Spring T., 1999, 'Religion, charity law and human rights', *Charity Law and Practice Review* 5(3), 153.

Reid S., 2000, 'Witch wars: Factors contributing to conflict in Canadian neopagan communities', *Pomegranate* 11, 10.

Reymond B., 1995, 'Architectural patterns of the relationship between states and churches', in R. Traer (ed.), *Religion and Human Rights in Europe*, Oxford: IARF.

Richards D.A.J., 1999, 'Sexual preference as a suspect (religious) classification: An alternative perspective on the unconstitutional principles and anti-discrimination laws', *University of Detroit Mercy Law Review* 76, 189.

Richardson E.C., 1985, 'Applying historic preservation ordinances to church property: Protecting the past and preserving the constitution', *North Carolina Law Review* 63, 404.

Richardson J.T., 1995, 'Minority religions ('cults') and the law: Comparisons of the United States, Europe and Australia', *University of Queensland Law Journal* 18, 183.

Ricks V.D., 1993a, 'To God God's, To Caesar Caesar's, and to both the defining of religion', *Creighton Law Review* 23, 1053.

Riis O., 1999, 'Modes of religious pluralism under conditions of globalisation', *MOST Journal of Multicultural Societies* 1(1).

Robertson A.H. and Merills J.G., 1993, *Human rights in Europe: A study of the European Convention on Human Rights*, Manchester: Manchester University Press.

Rojek C., 1995, *Decentring leisure*, London: SAGE Publications Ltd.

Runnymede Trust, 1997, *Islamophobia: A challenge for us all*, London, Runnymede Trust.

Russell M. and Hazell R., 2000, *Comments on the Wakeham Report*, London: Constitution Unit.

Rutherford J., 1989, 'Equality as the primary constitutional value: The case for applying employment discrimination laws to religion', *Cornell Law Review* 81, 1049.

Santangelo F.X., 1995, 'A proposal for the equal protection of non-indians practising Native American religions: Can the Religious Freedom Restoration Act finally remove the existing deference without a difference?', *St. John's Law Review* 69, 255.

Sapir G., 1999, 'Religion and state – A fresh theoretical start', *Notre Dame Law Review* 75, 579.

Scheinin M., 1992, 'Article 18', in A. Eide (ed.), *The Universal Declaration of Human Rights: A commentary*, Oslo: Scandinavian Press.

Scheinin M., 1999, 'Article 18' in G. Alfredsson and A. Eide, *The Universal Declaration of Human Rights*, The Hague: Martinus Nijhoff Publishers.

Schneider C.E., 'Religion and child custody', *University of Michigan Journal of Law Reform* 25, 879.

Shaw M.N., 1997, *International Law*, Cambridge: Grotius.

Sheen J., 1995, *The Secular Commonwealth, Constitutional Government, Law and Religion*, PhD Thesis: University of Queensland.

Sheffer M.S., 1998, 'God versus Caesar: Free exercise, the Religious Freedom Restoration Act, and conscience', *Oklahoma City University Law Review* 23, 929.

Shell D., 2004, 'The future of the second chamber', *Parliamentary Affairs* 57(4), 852.

Shupe A. and Bromley D.G., 1994, *Anti-cult movements in cross-cultural perspective*, London: Garland Publishing.

Shupe A., 1998a, 'The dynamics of clergy malfeasance', in A. Shupe, *Wolves within the fold: Religious leadership and abuses of power*, London: Rutgers University Press.

Shupe A., 1998b, 'Future study of clergy malfeasance', in A. Shupe, *Wolves within the fold: Religious leadership and abuses of power*, London: Rutgers University Press.

Sisk G.C., 1998, 'Stating the obvious: Protecting religion for religion's sake', *Drake Law Review* 47, 45.

Smith C., 2002, 'Episcopal seats and proposals for reform of the House of Lords', *Kings College Law Journal* 13, 109.

Spickard J.V., 1999, 'Human rights, religious conflict and globalisation. Ultimate values in a new world order', *MOST Journal on Multicultural Societies* 1(1).

Stahnke T., 1999, 'Proselytism and the freedom to change religion in international human rights law', *Brigham Young University Law Review* 251.

Stark R., 1999, 'Atheism, faith, and the social scientific study of religion', *Journal of Contemporary Religion* 14(1), 41.

Starmer K., 1999, *European human rights law: The Human Rights Act 1998 and the European Convention on Human Rights*, London: Legal Action Group, 1999.

Stavros S., 1997, 'Freedom of religion and claims for exemption from generally applicable, neutral laws: Lessons from across the pond?', *European Human Rights Law Review* 6, 607.

Stegeby E.K., 1999, 'An analysis of the impending disestablishment of the Church of Sweden', *Brigham Young University Law Review* 703.

Stein S.J., 2000, 'Religion/religions in the United States: Changing perspectives and prospects', *Indiana Law Journal* 75, 37.

Steiner H.J. and Alston P., 1996, *International Human Rights in context: Law, politics, morals*, Oxford: Clarendon Press.

Sullivan D.J., 1988, 'Advancing the freedom of religion or belief through the UN Declaration on the Elimination of Religious Intolerance and Discrimination', *American Journal of International Law* 82, 487.

Swinton K., 1996, 'Freedom of religion', in G.A. Beaudoin and E. Mendes (eds.), *The Canadian Charter of Rights and Freedoms*, Ontario: Carswell.

Tabor J.D. and Gallagher E.V., 1995, *Why Waco? Cults and the battle for religious freedom in America*, London: University of California Press.

Taggart M., 1998, 'Tugging on Superman's cape: Lessons from experience with the New Zealand Bill of Rights Act 1990', *Public Law* 266.

Tahzib B.G., 1996, *Freedom of religion or belief: Ensuring effective international legal protection*, The Hague: Martinus Nijhoff Publishers.

Tan D., 1997, 'Christian reflections on universal human rights and religious values: Uneasy bedfellows?', *Singapore Law Review* 18, 216.

Taylor B.C., 1998, 'Kansas denies religion-based defense to Rastafarians on marijuana charges', *Washburn Law Journal* 38, 307.

Thomas W.S., 1981, 'Preventing non-profit profiteering: Regulating religious cult employment practices', *Arizona Law Review* 23, 1003.

Thompson W., 1996, 'Religious practices and beliefs: A case for their accommodation in the Human Rights Act 1993', *New Zealand Law Journal* 106.

Thornton M., 1990, *The Liberal promise: Anti-discrimination legislation in Australia*, Melbourne: Oxford University Press.

Thorp A., 1998, 'The Human Rights Bill: Churches and religious organisations', *House of Commons Research Paper* 98/26.

Treene E.W., 1993, 'Prayer-treatment exemptions to child abuse and neglect statutes, manslaughter prosecutions, and due process of law', *Harvard Journal on Legislation* 30, 13.

Tregilgas-Davey M., 1991, 'Ex Parte Choudhury – An opportunity missed', *Modern Law Review* 54(2), 294.

Unsworth C., 1995, 'Blasphemy, cultural divergence and legal relativism', *Modern Law Review* 58, 658.

van Bijsterveld S.C., 2000, 'Religion, international law and policy in the wider European arena: New dimensions and developments' in R.J. Ahdar (ed.), *Law and religion*, Aldershot: Ashgate.

van der Vyver J.D., 1999, 'Constitutional perspectives of Church-State relations in South Africa', *Brigham Young University Law Review* 635.

van der Vyver J.D., 2000, 'State sponsored proselytisation: A South African experience', *Emory International Law Review* 779.

van Wyck D., 1994, 'Introduction to the South African Constitution', in van Wyck D. et al. (eds.), *Rights and constitutionalism: The new South African legal order*, Cape Town: Juta and Co.

Vickers L., 2003a, 'Freedom of religion and belief: The Draft Employment Equality (Religion or Belief) Regulations 2003', *Industrial Law Journal* 32, 23.

Vickers L., 2003b, 'The Employment Equality (Religion or Belief) Regulations 2003', *Industrial Law Journal* 32, 188.

Villiers J.D., 1996, 'Clergy malpractice revisited: Liability for sexual misconduct in the counselling relationship', *Denver University Law Review* 74, 1.

Wade W., 2000, 'Horizons of horizontality', *Law Quarterly Review* 116, 217.

Weare V., 1966, 'The Lords Spiritual', *Church Quarterly Review* 167, 208.

Weiss J., 1964, 'Privilege, posture and protection: Religion in the law', *Yale Law Journal* 73, 593.

Weller P., 1999, *Submission to the Royal Commission on the Reform of the House of Lords* (unpublished, 29 April 1999),

Wilson B., 1991, 'The flowering and deflowering of Protestantism', in P. Gee and J. Fulton (eds.), *Religion and power: Decline and growth*, London: BSA.

Winetrobe B.K. and Gay O., 1999, *The House of Lords Bill: Options for Stage Two*, House of Commons Library Research Report 99/6.

Winslow A.P., 1996, 'Sacred standards: Honoring the establishment clause in protecting Native American sites', *Arizona Law Review* 38, 1291.

Woolman S.E., 1986, 'Capitis Deminutio', *Law Quarterly Review* 102, 356.

Young M., 1998, 'External monitoring of domestic religious liberties', *Brigham Young University Law Review* 504.

Zimmerman R. and Visser D. (eds.), 1996a, 'South African law as a mixed legal system', in R. Zimmerman and D. Visser (eds.), *Southern Cross: Civil law and Common Law in South Africa*, Oxford: Clarendon Press.

Zimmerman R. and Visser D. (eds.), 1996b, *Southern Cross: Civil law and Common Law in South Africa*, Oxford: Clarendon Press.

Zines L., 1977, 'The growth of Australian nationhood and its effect on the powers of the Commonwealth' in L. Zines (ed.), *Commentaries on the Australian Constitution*, Butterworths: Sydney.

Index

g indicates glossary definition

Index entries:

Christian Gospel Church Inc. v San Francisco 128
Church of England
  and Church of Ireland 17, 23–4
  see also clergy, employment, UK; Lords Spiritual
Church of the Lukumi Babalu Aye, Inc. v City of Hileah 72, 80–81
The Church of the New Faith v The Commissioner pf Payroll Tax 31
CJ, JJ and EJ v Poland 55
clergy
  employment, UK 16–17, 111–18
  misconduct claims, US 118–22
Coker v Diocese of Southwark 112–13, 116, 117
Conkle D.O. 7
conscientious objection
  to military service, ECHR 87–9
  to tax, US 89
Constitution 12–15
  religious organisations involvement in 96–102
corporal punishment 61, 62
counselling and pastoral care 121–2
Criminal Justice Act, UK 81
Crow v Gullett 130
Cumper P. 28–9, 66, 67

Darby and Sweden 96
Dausch v Ryske 121
Davies v Presbyterian Church of Wales 114
Davis v Beason 5, 69
Declaration on Elimination of All Forms of Discrimination 49–50
Denning, Lord 29–30, 126–7
DiCarlo v Commissioner 89
Druids 58
Dudgeon v United Kingdom 52, 63
Durkheim E. 33

Edge P. 37, 63, 80, 111
  and Loughrey J. 111
  and Pearce C.C.A. 98
Education Act, UK 28
education of children 61–2
Edward Books and Art Ltd v R 3, 72, 73
employment
  clergy, UK 16–17, 111–18

Rogers v Booth 21–2, 23, 113, 115
Employment Division v Smith 71, 72, 82–3, 85, 86, 90
English charity law 9
English common law 25
English Court of Appeal 10–11, 21–2
English Highway Code 26–7
ethnic communities/racial groups 7–8, 32, 41–2, 49
  see also named groups
European Court of Human Rights (ECHR) 8
  conscientious objection to military service 87–9
  improper proselytising 90–93
  and regional human rights 50–62, 63–4
  religious drug use 83–5, 84–5
  religious interests 41–3, 52–3
Evans C. 29, 50, 81, 88
Everson v Board of Education 70, 97
ex parte Sarvan Singh Seera 128

Farnsworth E.A. 26
Finland, legal cases 88, 101–2
Florida Department of Health v Florida Nursing Home 21
Frame R.O. 33
France 56, 58–9
Free Church of Scotland 66
freedom of religion 32–3, 64–77

Gall G.L. 18, 23
Garry P. 118, 119
generally applicable domestic guarantees 64–77
generally applicable domestic prohibitions, disobeying 80–86
Germany, legal cases 41, 52, 88
Gillette v United States 88
Gilmour v Coates 111
Glimmerveen and Hagenbeek v The Netherlands 60
Re Grady 82
Grandrath v Federal Republic of Germany 88
Greece 8, 27, 41, 43, 53, 54, 57, 59, 89, 91–3, 101, 106

H v United Kingdom 53